I0815894

CarTech®
TRW
CRAGAR

DRAG RACING'S REBELS

HOW THE AHRA CHANGED QUARTER-MILE COMPETITION

DOUG BOYCE

CarTech®

CarTech®, Inc.
6118 Main Street
North Branch, MN 55056
Phone: 651-277-1200 or 800-551-4754
Fax: 651-277-1203
www.cartechbooks.com

Edit by Bob Wilson
Layout by Connie DeFlorin

ISBN 978-1-61325-766-1
Item No. CT691

Library of Congress Cataloging-in-Publication Data Available

Written, edited, and designed in the U.S.A.
Printed in China
10 9 8 7 6 5 4 3 2 1

All photos are courtesy of author Doug Boyce unless otherwise noted.

PUBLISHER'S NOTE: In reporting history, the images required to tell the tale will vary greatly in quality, especially by modern photographic standards. While some images in this volume are not up to those digital standards, we have included them, as we feel they are an important element in telling the story.

DISTRIBUTION BY:

Europe
PGUK
63 Hatton Garden
London EC1N 8LE, England
Phone: 020 7061 1980 • Fax: 020 7242 3725
www.pguk.co.uk

Australia
Renniks Publications Ltd.
3/37-39 Green Street
Banksmeadow, NSW 2109, Australia
Phone: 2 9695 7055 • Fax: 2 9695 7355
www.renniks.com

Canada
Login Canada
300 Saulteaux Crescent
Winnipeg, MB, R3J 3T2 Canada
Phone: 800 665 1148 • Fax: 800 665 0103
www.lb.ca

Contents

TOM McEWEN
The Mongoose
Hot Wheels
MATTEL
Plymouth
Coca-Cola
GOODYEAR
CRAGAR
Wynn's Duster II
B&M
The Mongoose

Dedication

This book is dedicated to those who worked to make the American Hot Rod Association (AHRA) the success that it was. Although some of these people are mentioned within this book, there are others who can't be overlooked. We recognize the people here for the support and enthusiasm that they brought to the sport during the sanctioning body's 30 years of existence: Jon Lundberg, Judy DeLuca, Roma House Moffitt, Jim Kelly, Marlene and Don Wormsley, Kerry and Betty Clark, Vance Brady, Morris Calkin, Pete Talmadge, Georgia Miller, Don Elliott, Phil Elliott, Blaine Laux, Jim Tice Jr., Keith Perry, Bret Kepner, and (last but not least) the racers and fans.

Acknowledgments

Many thanks to Bob Alberty Jr., Gary L. Anderson, Cale Aronson, C.J. Baker, Mel Bashore, John Bergener, Ron Berges, Grant Bittner, John Bloom, Forrest Bond, Tom Bonner, Tim Bouldin, Bob Bowe, Darren Boyce, Ron Braun, Dallas Brown, Rich Carlson, Tom Chase, Mike Dimery, John Eichinger, George Eisenhart, Phil Elliott, Al Eshenbaugh, Don Ewald, John Foster Jr., Gene Fiores, Bob Frey, Larry Fulton, Don Garlits, Steve Gibbs, Don Gillispie, Jim Hall, James Handy, Charles Harmon, Rick Hellman, Doug Herzog, Paul Hutchins, Steve Jacobson, Stephen Justice, Jim Kelso, Bret Kepner, Richard Kluk, Scott Kruger, Bill Mitchell, Michael Moore, Jimm Murray, Tim Newmeyer, Richard Parks, Allan Patterson, Michael Pottie, Don Prieto, Don Prudhomme, Jim Rodgers, Sally Ruble, Rick Ruiz, Rod Saint, Bill Scharing, Tommy Shaw, Vern Scholz, Ken Sitko, Bob Smith, Ed Smith, Bob Snyder, Mike Sopko Sr., Don Spencer, Larry Spitali, Richard Thomas III, Ruth Tice, Don Toia, Teri Abbott Vanderhoof, Jay Wahrmund, Dave Wallace Jr., John Wiebe, Dan Williams, Todd Wingerter, Don Wormsley, and Al Young.

Publications used to draw additional information include *Petersen*, *Lopez*, *Magnum*, *Argus*, *Professional Services*, *Drag News*, *Drag Sport Illustrated*, *TACH*, and *Drag World*.

Further credit goes to the following websites: bangshift.com, competitionplus.com, draglist.com, dragstriplist.com, and nhra.com.

Foreword *By Don Garlits*

The AHRA has long needed a book written about its formation and demise because it played a very important role in the sport of drag racing. The entire story can never be told because the records just don't exist anymore, but Doug Boyce did a tremendous amount of research while putting this book together. I predict that future historians will use this book as reference material when writing about the history of drag racing.

One aspect of this book that I enjoyed was the tremendous amount of actual race information that you won't find anywhere else. I was so surprised to learn about the many events that I did not attend, and I was thoroughly entertained as I read about my old competitors. Then, of course, this book includes many of the stories that never got into *Drag World*, which was the AHRA's own publication.

Doug also included all the information of the behind-the-scenes negotiating during the annual AHRA dragstrip meetings, which determined the policies for the next year's events. You will be entertained too, trust me! Jim Tice was at his best during these meetings. He knew how to handle the strip operators, and he knew how to handle the professional racers. It was a good mix.

There is the story about the final days of the AHRA, when "Big" Jim Tice got sick and couldn't run the company the way it that should have been run. Ruth Tice, Jim's wife, took over, and it was all very sad.

You will be surprised to learn that the original AHRA, a Pennsylvania nonprofit corporation, was not the company that Jim Tice ran for so many years. Read on to find out who really started the AHRA, how "Big" Jim Tice got control, and what happened to the original founder and the original nonprofit corporation. It's all here in this book, which I recommend for anyone interested it the sport of drag racing. This book is in no way a put down of the National Hot Rod Association (NHRA); it is about how one man singlehandedly challenged the entire sport for dominance in drag racing's formative years.

In my opinion, the AHRA could never have been as powerful as it was at one time if the NHRA had not banned nitromethane!

— Don Garlits

Introduction

This book was written to recognize the AHRA for its many contributions to the sport of drag racing. Often maligned as a rebel association, the AHRA was created to appease the racers, and it brought us many firsts.

The AHRA was incorporated in 1956 by Walt Mentzer as an alternative to the existing NHRA, and the AHRA's influence on the sport was felt almost immediately. When the NHRA denied the use of nitromethane in 1957, the AHRA approved it. When the NHRA banned the aircraft-powered dragsters in 1961, the AHRA welcomed them. When the NHRA said no to the emerging Funny Car in 1965, the AHRA said yes. When fans and racers screamed for a heads-up Super Stock category in 1968, the AHRA delivered. While the AHRA was called a rebel association, it was actually more of an association that got things done—much to the delight of fans and racers.

Jim Tice Sr., the AHRA president in 1964, opened the floodgates when he adopted promoter Ben Christ's concept of drag racing and instituted the formula class designations. The formulas nearly doubled the number of classes and ensured a class for every combination. The more classes, the more winners, and more winners meant that there was a better chance the racers would return. Furthering the concept was the introduction in 1967 of 10 elapsed time (ET) brackets, which later morphed into the Selectra Bracket and ET Stock.

In the 1970s, the AHRA continued its push to get the budding racer off the street, introducing several classes, including those for dune buggies and vans. For the more serious racer, there was the introduction of the popular Top Comp, Pro Comp Dragster, and Pro Comp Funny Car categories.

Entering the 1970s, the AHRA was on equal ground with the NHRA, drawing enormous crowds and racer entries. It was the best of times. Sadly, those times wouldn't last. Things became tough early in the 1970s due to rain dates, a fuel crisis, the emergence of the International Hot Rod Association (IHRA), and just some poor luck. Unlike the NHRA and IHRA, the AHRA had no major sponsor to help keep it afloat when things went south.

Although it remained a popular alternative to the NHRA, the AHRA never fully made it back to the peak that it enjoyed in 1970–1971. When Jim Tice passed away in 1982, internal fighting for control of the association doomed it.

In 1984, Tice's wife sold the AHRA to Mike Grey, the president of Terminal Van Lines. Although Grey was involved in drag racing, he had no experience in running a drag-racing organization and really wasn't prepared for the quagmire that he stepped into. Disgruntled track operators who were not happy with a new owner that wasn't one of them, left the fold and formed the short-lived American Drag Racing Association (ADRA). This contributed greatly to the end of the AHRA. Grey held the final AHRA race, the World Finals, in September 1984 at Eunice, Louisiana.

Preston Davis (right), in the **Tennessee Bo-Weevil** *and Jim Nicoll hang out the laundry at Bee Line Dragway in 1971. Change was in the air, as these were the final days of the front-engine dragster. (Photo Courtesy J.R. Bloom)*

This worn photo shows action from the first NHRA Nationals. The decommissioned airstrips that dotted the country after World War II helped quench the growing demand for drag strips. (Photo Courtesy Ruth Tice)

Chapter One

Giving a Little Credit

Although drag racing predates the National Hot Rod Association (NHRA) by decades, the NHRA is often credited as being the body that organized the sport by uniting the country's numerous timing associations. Wally Parks, with support from *Hot Rod* magazine founder Robert Petersen, incorporated the NHRA in March 1951. Prior to this, Parks was an acting member of the Southern California Timing Association (SCTA).

The first NHRA drag race was in April 1953 at the Los Angeles Fairgrounds at Pomona. Prior to this, numerous associations had already held their own meets. Drags Inc., the American Timing Activities Association (ATAA), the International Timing Association (ITA), and NASCAR, all organized events prior to the NHRA.

On the weekend of September 29–October 2, 1955, the NHRA held its first national event at Great Bend, Kansas, on a decommissioned B-29 landing strip.

Walter Mentzer Jr.

Similar to Wally Parks, Philadelphia's Walter Mentzer Jr. holds a major place in the sport's history. In 1952, Mentzer was a member of the Pittsburgh Pacers Car Club. In short order, he became the club's president. By 1955, Mentzer was wearing a few hats: president of the Pacers, president of the Pennsylvania Timing Association (PTA), and a regional advisor for the NHRA.

In an interview with journalist Chris Martin, Mentzer said, "The PTA was really doing well, and I told the

As well as creating the AHRA, Walter Mentzer Jr. developed and managed several racetracks. He was also involved in the formation of NASCAR's drag racing division. (Photo Courtesy Rob Saint)

At the NHRA's first Nationals, the flathead-powered belly tank of Ray Harrelson, the **Motor Reco Special** ***(Motor Reconditioning Co. of Houston) driven by a young A. J. Foyt proved to be one of the more impressive cars on hand. (Photo Courtesy Ruth Tice)***

guys in the association that we had enough money in our treasury to form our own hot rod association if we desired to do so."

Mentzer attended the NHRA's first Nationals (as did future AHRA president Jim Tice), and he was unimpressed. Mentzer felt the focus was all wrong and that the racers needed an organization that spoke for them as opposed to one that put the strip owner and promoters first. He felt the racers deserved more of a say, and he returned to Pennsylvania with his own ideas.

In June 1956, he incorporated the American Hot Rod Association (AHRA) as a nonprofit. Unlike Wally Parks's NHRA, which was created by Parks and run as he saw fit, Mentzer wanted the racers to have a voice in how the AHRA was run.

"[After one year], every member registered with the home office in Pittsburgh would have a vote in how it was run," Mentzer said.

The AHRA was governed by its members, and like the NHRA, safety was the priority. In fact, the AHRA's first motto was "United for Safety."

Great Bend Nationals

Although the racing at the first NHRA Nationals was said to be great, the turnout was below what was anticipated. Further, weather hampered the final day of activities, and the final eliminations were booked and run in Arizona six weeks later. According to Richard Parks, son of NHRA founder Wally Parks, the rain-delayed event nearly bankrupted the NHRA.

The city of Great Bend, Kansas, and the Sunflower Rod and Custom Association, which helped bring the Nationals to Great Bend in the first place, worked hard to get the NHRA to come back in 1956. A few demands were made by the NHRA, including a newly paved racing surface, were said to have been agreed upon prior to negotiations falling apart. In the spring of 1956, the

Walter Mentzer (right) appears to be giving an award to an unknown racer after his performance with this twin-engine rail. Mentzer loved the sport of drag racing immensely, and his contribution to its advancement shouldn't be understated. (Photo Courtesy Rod Saint)

NHRA announced that its Nationals would be run in Kansas City, where it was offered a greater percentage of the earnings.

Shortly after the announcement, Nelson Pointer, the president of the National Championship Drags Inc. chapter of Great Bend, reached out to Walter Mentzer in Pittsburgh, Pennsylvania. Mentzer flew to Great Bend and signed a contract to run the AHRA's first National Championship Drags at Great Bend over Labor Day weekend in 1956. Two weeks later, Wally Parks announced that his Nationals would also be held on Labor Day weekend.

By the time the AHRA Nationals rolled around, clubs from another 18 states had joined the AHRA. Prior to the meet, a convention was held where a written constitution was unveiled. It stated that each attending member was allotted a vote in the organization, and it provided for a new election of officers each year.

At the convention, a vote was taken, and Mentzer was replaced by Nelson Pointer as president. Mentzer was elected vice president, and he held the position until 1957, when he was drafted to serve in the U.S. armed forces. J.E. "Mack" MacDonald followed Pointer as president in 1957. Mentzer went on to promote numerous tracks and assist with NASCAR's drag racing division.

AHRA Championship Drags

By all accounts, the first AHRA Nationals, which were August 31–September 3, 1956, was a success. Reports from the weekend noted that the resurfaced strip was the longest and finest drag strip in the world. Close to 200 entrants would attest to that.

Winds and blowing sand failed to hamper action, which saw San Antonio's Bobby Joe Rutledge and his injected Ardun Mercury-powered A/Modified Roadster take Top Eliminator honors. Rutledge worked for his win, having destroyed two clutches in two days. Due to the generosity of local residents, he was able to use a bay at the local Chevy dealer to make his repairs.

Top speed of the meet went to the team of Hooper and Hensley, whose Cadillac-powered Special ran an even 125 mph. Low ET of the meet went to the 300-ci Mercury-powered rail of Gary Ward, which turned an 11.10 but fell in the Top Eliminator final when the engine blew a head gasket.

Notable Middle Eliminator winner Jerry Livingston drove Tom Hanna's former *Littlest Outlaw* Fuel A/Coupe to honors. Livingston later recorded a 152.14-mph top speed at Schillings Air Strip in Kansas, becoming the AHRA's first non-dragster to break 150 mph. The chopped

Rules of the Day

Through its history, AHRA rules closely mimicked those of the NHRA, which the NHRA had lifted verbatim from the Southern California Timing Association (SCTA).

Popular categories in the early days included Dragster, Hot Roadster, Modified Roadster, Gas, Altered, Open Gas, and Competition. Also on the books were four Stock classes as well as the Open 4-Cylinder, Closed 4-Cylinder, and Sports Car classes.

The chop and channel of this B/Competition coupe is made more evident when compared to the Oldsmobile that is parked next to it. Functionality over form was the rule of the day. (Photo Courtesy Bob Baxter)

Bantam coupe relied on 352 inches of Chevy to become a member of the AHRA's 150-mph club, which was instituted in April 1956. Its first member was the team of Meyers and Davis.

The Presidency

Don Garlits's long association with the AHRA began in 1959 when he was voted president, replacing Danny Daniels, who held the position in 1958. At the time, Garlits stated that he was solidly behind the group and felt it had a great future. Having entered his first (of a few) retirement, Garlits felt that he had the time to dedicate to the group. Kansas City resident Jim Tice, an insurance adjuster, was voted vice president.

Everett Goosic was a tough competitor in the early days of the sport. Goosic won Junior Eliminator at the 1960 AHRA National Championship Drags. Pictured are (left to right) Lefty Mudersbach, Dick Goosic, Everett Goosic, and a crewmember. (Photo Courtesy J.R. Bloom)

In 1960, Tice was elected president and Lee Dorrell became vice president. In 1962, Tice's third year as president, he signed an employment contract with the organization and devoted his time to the administrative affairs as its executive director. He moved the headquarters to Kansas City, where he incorporated the AHRA as a for-profit organization (solely owned by himself) and dissolved the old AHRA.

Richard Parks, son of Wally Parks, noted that Walter Mentzer was "still using AHRA letterhead that indicated the AHRA still operated out of its main office in Pittsburgh, Pennsylvania, and a western office in Great Bend, Kansas. The old AHRA was still registered as a nonprofit corporation, but Tice's AHRA was decidedly owned by Jim."

Dallas, Texas–based Karl "Buddy" Anderson's Widdle White Wabbit *was a B/Altered terror at the turn of the decade. Record ETs in the 10.80s at over 122 mph were produced by a 265-ci Chevy that featured an Engle cam and six Holley carburetors on a Weiand manifold. Beginning in 1957, the Fiat won its class four years straight at the AHRA Nationals. (Photo Courtesy Tim and Larry Bouldin)*

What else would you call the lead of a car club called the Slobs other than the Huge Slob? *Although it has been long forgotten by many, the Studebaker showed more than a few supposed superior performance cars the way home. (Photo Courtesy Ruth Tice)*

Jim Tice: A Man of Determination

Jim Tice was the third of nine children born into a poor farming family living in Topeka, Kansas. The Tice family was everything that many depression-era families were: poor in finances but rich in faith. Tice's drive to succeed stemmed from those impoverished days. This drive followed him through life as an all-state halfback on the football field and a B-24 bomber pilot in World War II.

Tice had a football scholarship to Kansas State waiting for him after the war. However, he sustained a head injury in a B-24 crash (in which he was the only survivor) that ended any hope of a football career.

Jim Tice brought the AHRA from humble beginnings to being a sanctioning body that battled on equal ground with the NHRA, briefly. (Photo Courtesy Ruth Tice)

In the mid-1950s, Tice turned his attention to the growing sport of drag racing. He campaigned several Studebakers and was given the nickname of "Mr. Studebaker."

He led a Studebaker car club called the Slobs. While other clubs had names such as the Gear Jammers and the Dyno-Busters that maybe took things a little more seriously, the Slobs never lost sight of the fact that it was all about having fun.

In May 1962, Tice met his future wife, Ruth House. The pair met at Kansas City radio station WHB.

Ruth said, "Jim was there with Art Arfons doing an interview for a race that weekend, and I was there because my friend worked for WHB. At the time, I worked as a secretary for Mercedes Benz's local Kansas City office. That week I turned 21, and Jim had four dozen red roses delivered to my apartment."

The pair wasted little time courting and married the following month.

Ruth remembers the car club meetings that she attended with Tice.

"In the 1950s and '60s, there was the Kansas City Timing Association, which consisted of a number of car clubs," Ruth said. "At the time, they held their meetings at the Kansas City (Missouri) Police Department. Officer Lee Dorrell, a founding member, was president at the time. The first meeting I attended was in 1962, and when they did the roll call, Jim said to me, 'Stand up, you're a Slob!'

It was at that moment that Ruth wondered what in the world she had gotten herself into.

Opinions vary on just how to describe Jim Tice. He could be a hard case, and some would bad-mouth him

As president of the AHRA in 1962, Jim Tice accepted an offer from Studebaker to attend a pre-introduction showing of the Avanti. Seen here at the company's proving grounds in South Bend, Indiana, Tice reportedly received the first production Avanti. (Photo Courtesy Ruth Tice)

(while accepting his money) for the way he ran the AHRA. In contrast, others felt that Tice and the AHRA were the greatest thing to happen to drag racing.

"Jim was driven and was known to have a short fuse," said Don Wormsley, former AHRA tech director. "He'd take on anyone if he felt he was right. He was a very personable guy, among guys. He could sit down and have a beer with you but never lose track of why you were having the meeting, and he usually came out of it with what he was seeking. He was very interested in markets and the marketing of drag racing. He wanted to get AHRA tracks into as many markets as he could. He was all into promotion, [and he] developed plans for smaller tracks, generating interest in the sport, which grew the [fans] in the stands."

Don Garlits described Tice as the "Barnum and Bailey of drag racing." However he is remembered, I think that history proves the AHRA never would have survived as long as it did without a person such as Jim Tice at the helm.

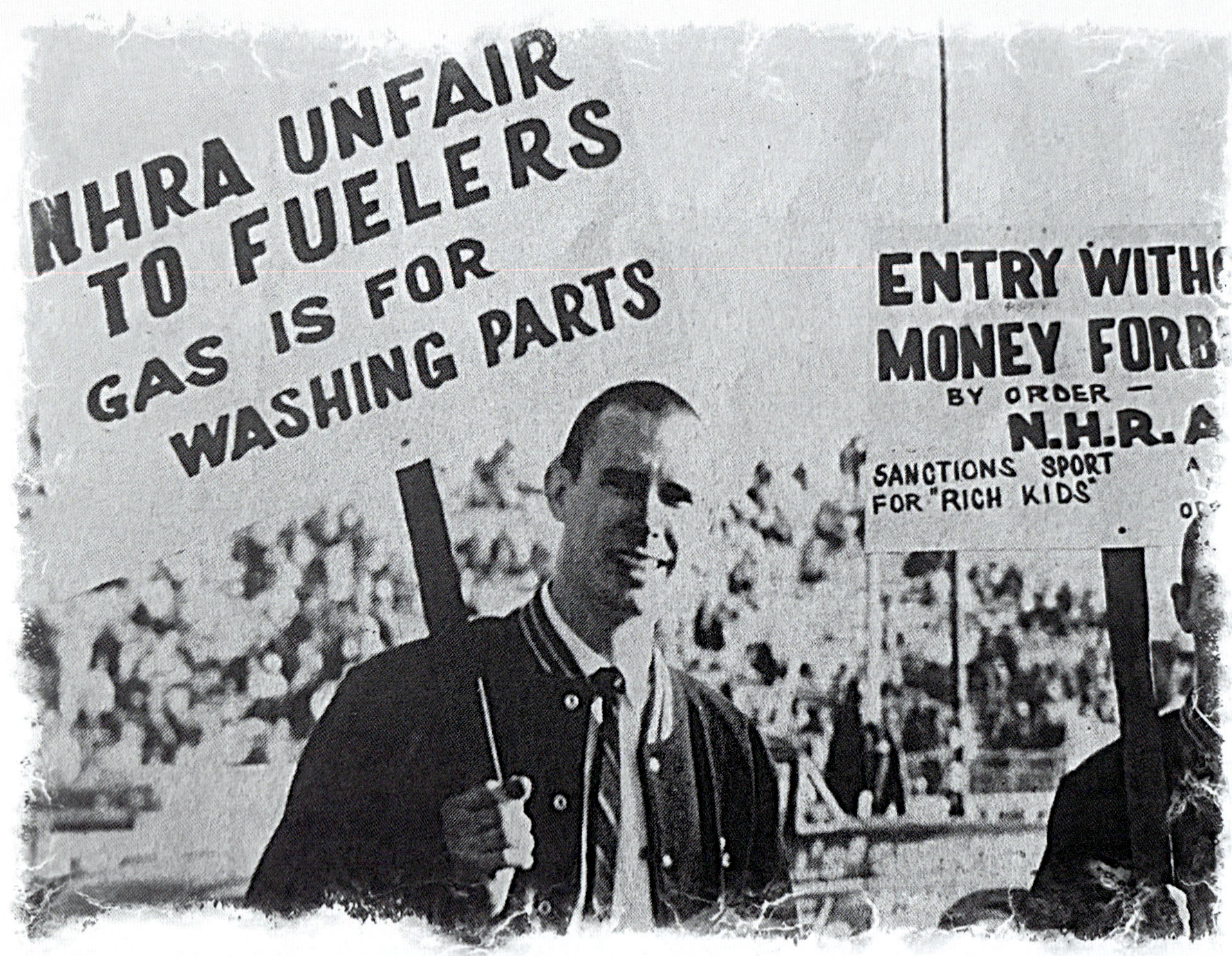

Many racers and fans were not happy with the NHRA fuel ban. The AHRA continued to run fuel cars—at a cost to the NHRA. Wally Parks later admitted that banning fuel wasn't one of his best decisions.

Chapter Two

1957-1963: Nitro Is for Racing

The NHRA really shot itself in the foot when it implemented a ban on the use of nitromethane. All it really accomplished was running the fuel racers off to other associations, including the AHRA, which had no interest in banning nitro.

The fuel ban was first activated on February 10, 1957, at Santa Ana by track manager C.J. Hart. This was brought on by Emery Cook's phenomenal record-setting 166.97-mph run at Lions Drag Strip on February 3.

"While Hart cited the lack of stopping distance at many tracks as a problem, his decision to ban nitromethane was based on an entirely different concern," said historian Bret Kepner. "Hart insisted that he was responding almost solely on the clamor from participants to curb the skyrocketing costs of drag racing."

On February 15, a meeting took place in Los Angeles, where eight other California strips agreed to join Hart's ban, which initially also included a ban on twin-engine cars and superchargers of any kind.

"The fact that Wally Parks has not yet been mentioned is no accident," Kepner continued. "While everything from Cook's 166-mph pass to the fuel ban to the meeting of the tracks took place, Wally was at the National Speed Trials in Daytona Beach, setting records in his *Hot Rod* magazine–sponsored *Suddenly* 1957 Plymouth.

"When he returned, Parks found that a monstrous number of the NHRA's western facilities issued ultimatums forcing the NHRA to accept the new rules, [otherwise] the tracks would leave the fold. Parks had no choice but to submit. The effective date for the rules revisions was moved to April 1, 1957."

While the ban on twin cars and blowers ended almost immediately, the fuel ban continued for six years.

Giving the People What They Want

For the AHRA, as well as other racing bodies, the fuel ban was nothing short of a godsend. Until the ban, the AHRA was still looking for solid footing. It had no interest in anything that was going to impede its growth or slow the speed of these cars. Over the period of the ban, the AHRA signed up many tracks and saw an explosion in membership.

Results at the time showed that the quickest fuel cars were approximately 25 mph faster and a second quicker than their gas-burning counterparts. For comparison, at the NHRA Nationals in 1957, the team of Lefty Mudersbach and Joe Dillon with their 462-ci gas-powered Oldsmobile dragster had low ET of the meet with a 10.42. Compare that to the 9.35 that Emery Cook ran at the AHRA Nationals.

Attempting to compensate for a lack of fuel, many racers who stuck by the NHRA went on to build twin-engine cars. Though this brought them closer in speed to the nitro cars, they were never able to match them, largely because they were saddled with the extra 500 to 600 pounds of weight that the extra engine added.

Emery Cook and Cliff Bedwell changed drag racing in 1957 when they went a record 166 mph. The Scott Fenn chassis housed a 354 Chrysler that ran an Isky cam and six Stromberg carburetors on a log manifold. (Photo Courtesy J.R. Bloom)

Drag racing was getting expensive. The $4 in this 1958 advertisement is equal to about $40 in 2022 (adjusted for inflation).

1957 Results

As rules dictated, Top Eliminator was made up of the four fastest cars in both Fuel Dragster and Open Gas. Emery Cook, driving the San Diego–based Cook and (Cliff) Bedwell Isky *U-Fab Special,* came out the winner at the AHRA Nationals in 1957 by defeating the Gary "Red" Greth–driven *Speed Sport Special* in the final with a 10.35 ET at 150.75 mph.

Along with the meet's low ET of 9.35, Cook and Bedwell also had the top speed at 152.54 mph. The pair had a remarkable season, and they closed it holding both ends of the Fuel Dragster record with an 8.89 ET at 168.85 mph. Producing those times was a Chrysler Hemi running a 98-percent load of nitromethane through six Stromberg carburetors.

Two of the toughest competitors, Emery Cook and Cliff Bedwell show off a sample of their winning hardware. The 1957 champs won Top Eliminator with an early Hemi mounted in a Chassis Research TE-440 chassis.

It's believed that either Cook or Greth showed Garlits how to modify the eight Strombergs on his bored-and-stroked Chrysler. Garlits's *Speed Shop Special* claimed the title of the world's fastest dragster (albeit briefly), when he ran an 8.79 ET at 176.40 mph on November 10, 1957, on the concrete track at Brooksville, Florida. This went in the books as Garlits's first national record. The 450-ci engine fed on a 95-percent load of nitro through direct drive to a set of experimental M&H slicks.

1958 Results

In 1958, Garlits won the AHRA Nationals, where he ran a best ET of 9.51 at 161.29 mph for top speed of the meet. West Coast racers questioned the recorded times and the "fast tracks back East," figuring that Garlits couldn't build a car that quick.

At the Nationals, it was the A/OG *Kansas Kustom* Oldsmobile-powered rail that was the runner-up to Garlits. In a previous round, Bob Langley and his *Scorpion* had set low ET of the meet with a 9.42 on a blend of fuel mixed by Garlits. For his Nationals win, Garlits received a $500 war bond, which he had to cash in to make it back home to Florida.

A massive railroad tank car explosion in Peoria, Illinois, on June 1 resulted in 100-percent nitromethane

Gary "Red" Greth and Lyle Fisher returned in 1959 with Speed Sport II. *A blown Hemi powered the reborn 1925 Model T, which saw so much success. (Photo Courtesy John Foster Jr.)*

The Scorpion I *was built and owned by Texas residents Bob and Ruth Langley. Powering the rail to record times and class wins was a 392 Chrysler. (Photo Courtesy Connell Miller)*

After the 1958 Nationals at Great Bend, Kansas, participants gathered at the municipal auditorium for the award presentations. Everyone who earned a trophy received one. (Photo Courtesy Ruth Tice)

becoming unobtainable to the public. According to Garlits, racers made do with reduced percentages from the manufacturers for several months until they discovered that print lithographers could still get the "good stuff." The explosion also resulted in the requirement to ship nitro only in barrels from that point forward.

Back on the good juice, Garlits shook up the world of drag racing on December 14. He drove the *Swamp Rat* to a jaw-dropping 180.00 mph at Brooksville. He backed up the record run with a 176.50 at 8.67 while defeating Langley's *Scorpion*.

1959 Results

At the 1959 Nationals at Great Bend on September 4–7, 1959, Chris "the Greek" Karamesines defeated Art Malone, who was driving Garlits's *Swamp Rat,* in the Top Fuel class final. Malone had taken the seat after Garlits was left with burns caused by a blower explosion. Karamesines's *Al's Speed Shop Special* won with an ET of 8.83. Malone had previously set the low ET and top speed of the meet with an 8.23 ET at 179.28 mph.

Driving his 90-inch-wheelbase *Chassis Research* TE-440 rail, Karamesines battled his way to the Top Eliminator final by defeating Bob Langley, twice. The first win was on a false start, and he won again on the rerun with an 8.89 ET at 170.41 mph. Elbert Threadgill's blown Oldsmobile proved to be no match for Karamesines, who took him in the next round with an 8.95 at 173.07.

Karamesines then faced and defeated Malone.

Taking the seat of the Swamp Rat is the green kid, Art Malone. Garlits vowed to never race again after receiving burns when a blower exploded at a race in Chester, North Carolina. To fit Malone, the Swamp Rat was stretched 6.5 inches.

1960 Results

In 1960, the AHRA divided Fuel Dragster into four classes. The three top classes were determined by cubic inches: 488 and over, 304 to 487, and 303 inches and under. The fourth class was for unblown flathead engines. In relation to the gas-powered dragster, gone in 1960 was the term Open Gas, which was replaced with simply Gas Dragster.

The Gas Dragsters held an eliminator program before the winners met the Fuel Dragsters in Top Eliminator. Those eligible to run for Top Eliminator in 1960 were the winning cars of the following classes: AA/FD, A/FD, B/FD, AA/GD, A/GD, A/Competition, and A/Modified Roadster.

An impressive lineup of Fuel cars is shown at the 1960 AHRA Nationals at Kansas City. Pictured (left to right) are Al Williams's Scientific Engineering car with driver Art Malone in the cockpit, Bobby Langley's Scorpion (mostly hidden), Bob Sullivan's Pandemonium III, Don Garlits's Swamp Rat II, and Chris Karamesines's Chizler. (Photo by Tim and Larry Bouldin)

Chris Karamesines, affectionately known as "the Greek," hailed from Michigan. Driving his Scotty Fenn rail, he took home the gold at the 1959 Nationals. (Photo Courtesy Bill Scharing)

Karamesines's opponent in Top Eliminator was Texan Eddie Hill. Karamesines made quick work of Hill's injected Pontiac, running away with the win by multiple car lengths while recording an 8.75 ET at 173.74 mph.

The Nationals

The 1960 Nationals moved to Kansas City, Missouri. It was felt that the race would draw larger crowds due to the city's more central location. The race featured the only Fuel Dragster to have run more than 200 mph: Chris "the Greek" Karamesines's *Chizler*. Karamesines

On April 24, 1960, at Alton Dragway, Chris Karamesines is off on his 204.54-mph run. The Greek failed to back up the time, leaving many questioning the Fosdick clocks. (Photo Courtesy Tim and Larry Bouldin)

clocked an unheard-of 204.546 mph in 8.87 seconds at Alton, Illinois, on April 24, 1960. Powering the dragster was a Don Maynard–tuned 392 running on a 90-percent load of nitro.

According to a *Rodding & Restyling* magazine article covering the Alton event, "The *Chizler* was running a wild new fuel blend developed by Scotty Fenn's Chassis Research firm in cooperation with Don Maynard and Al's Speed Shop."

It has been long speculated that this "wild new fuel blend" included hydrazine.

"Whether this potent brew can be tamed enough to gain reliability without sacrificing power remains to be seen," the *Rodding & Restyling* article stated.

Top Eliminator

Karamesines failed to repeat his 1959 win, falling to Art Malone in class eliminations. Malone, who was now teamed with Al Williams, ran low ET of 8.63. Malone was then eliminated by Garlits in the class semifinals.

Garlits had returned to driving in August and set a

Bob Sullivan's Pandemonium III _was one of the more dominant dragsters as the decade began. The 392 rode a 102-inch-wheelbase Rod Stuckey chassis. A twin-disc Schiefer clutch directed the power to an Oldsmobile rear end. The total weight was a reported 1,675 pounds. (Photo Courtesy Forrest Bond)_

This C/FD is running an injected Chevy mill and features an aluminum chassis. The class required that the engine fall between 310 and 364.9 ci. (Photo Courtesy Tim and Larry Bouldin)

new track record at US-30 Drag-O-Way in York, Pennsylvania, with an 8.39 at 191.448. At the Nationals, he earned top speed of the meet with a 183.66. When the oil pump in his Hemi failed while running against Malone, Garlits received a helping hand in making repairs from Bob Langley, Bob Sullivan, Chris Karamesines, and cam grinder Ray Giovannoni, proving camaraderie was alive and well in the world of drag racing. Within an hour, the *Swamp Rat* was good to go. It was a shame that it proved to be all for not, as Garlits's fuel pump gave out and he had to watch Sullivan's *Pandemonium III* sail past.

The Swamp Rat III-A *is seen here at the 1961 AHRA Nationals at Green Valley on Labor Day weekend. Connie Swingle reportedly drove the* Swamp Rat *to a best ET of 7.88 in 1962 in Blaney, South Carolina. (Photo Courtesy Forrest Bond)*

Other favorites fell by the wayside: Langley in his new-for-1960 *Scorpion III* could only muster a best of 9.19 and dropped out early after snapping U-joints on separate runs. Rod Stuckey in Bill Taylor's *Missouri Missile* had no luck, tossing a blower then popping a frost plug in eliminations against Sullivan. This left Sullivan as the last man standing in Top Fuel.

Sullivan then faced the winner of Gas Dragster, Bob Rodgers, whose 454-ci blown Chrysler ran a 158.45 to win class. In the lopsided final, Sullivan took the win with an 8.91 ET at 164.23 mph.

1961 Results

The AHRA's first Winter Championship Drags, the first major winter event in the West, took place at Henderson, Nevada, on January 28–29, 1961. This was three weeks prior to the NHRA's first Winternationals meet at Pomona.

Henderson had dirt pits, a return round, and lacked basic amenities. So why was Henderson chosen when there were better, less-primitive tracks? One can only assume it's because of its location close to Vegas and its crowds.

Winter Championship Drags

The number of racers who turned out for the first winter meet was thin due to the fact that many out-of-towners were put off by the lack of tow money offered. Those that did make the haul included Cagle & Rawleigh and their B/FD, Lefty Mudersbach in the A/GD twin-injected Chevy-powered *Herbert Cam Special*, Hayden Proffitt in

Garlits's AHRA Preference

Don Garlits's relationship with Jim Tice and the AHRA was built on a mutual understanding that the racer was the draw and should be treated and paid accordingly. Tice always wanted to put on the best show possible for both the fans and racers, while Garlits did his best to ensure that the racers were given their fair shake.

Garlits's relationship with NHRA president Wally Parks, on the other hand, always seemed strained. Although Garlits had a few issues with Parks's NHRA over the years, he always had respect for the man himself. Their strained relation dates back to the first Winternationals, which was held in 1960 at the Spruce Creek Drag Strip in Daytona, Florida.

The meet was a conglomeration between the NHRA and the drag racing division of NASCAR. There had been runoffs each evening of the meet, with the one racer performing the best being crowned winner for the week. The story goes that on Wednesday evening, Garlits was lined up in his brother Ed's Gas Dragster against the Chevy-powered B/FD of Lewis Carden for the final run. Carden was given a handicap lead as the lower-class car. As the flagman waved go, Garlits was off. Carden failed to go, as he felt Garlits had jumped the flag. Garlits, seeing what happened, slowed, turned around mid-track, and headed back to the starting line, figuring there was going to be a rerun. Instead, he was told to shut it off by Parks. He had been disqualified for crossing the centerline. The announcer broadcasted that Carden would single for the win. Garlits was up in arms.

"I said, 'No he's not,' and I gave the signal to Art Malone in my push car to push me," Garlits said. "Wally was leaning into my cockpit, talking to me, and the push-car started pushing me. He [Wally Parks] had to jump on the hood of the Cadillac push car, a '50 Cadillac, and lift his feet up, [otherwise] he was going to get run over. So, he had to ride on the hood for a couple hundred feet while the engine started. Cardon was already underway when I screeched across the starting line and caught him about halfway down.

"The announcer said 'Garlits wins the race, but he's disqualified for crossing the centerline.' I didn't give a s——, I won the race and that's all I wanted to hear to suit me."

Jim Tice (riding the cowl of the **Swamp Rat***) had a mutually respectful relationship with Don Garlits. You would most likely not see Wally Parks doing something like this. (Photo Courtesy Ruth Tice)*

the Bayer & Freitas twin Chevy Gas rail, Tom Waters in the Waters-Sughrue-Guinn fueler, and Tom McEwen driving the McEwen & Adams blown Oldsmobile Gas rail.

Saturday action saw Gary Cagle in the Cagle & Rawleigh B/FD drop a few jaws when he unleashed an 8.89 ET at 170.13 mph (20 mph over the existing class record and a full second less than the record). A displacement check confirmed that his Chrysler engine was under the 300-ci class requirement. Cagle later discovered he cracked a cylinder, and he lost out during Sunday's eliminations while running on seven cylinders.

In the Fuel Dragster eliminations, Bill Crossley defeated Dale Grantham with an 8.91. In other first-round action, Tom Waters eliminated the *Speed Sport Special* with an 8.97 ET at 163.24 mph. In final head-to-head action, California's Lucky Farris defeated Dale Lewis.

In the Top Fuel final, Tony Waters soloed as Ernie Hashim's rail was stuck in the staging lanes, unable to fire. Then, Farris was disqualified when he failed to report. That left Waters to solo for the class win. At this point, darkness brought an end to action, and there was no Top Eliminator final.

The Gas Dragster Eliminator final was run earlier in the day. It saw Mudersbach in the ET record-holding (8.83) *Herbert Cams Special* defeat the McEwen & Adams AA/GD.

With darkness setting in and no lights to illuminate the Henderson strip, the Top Eliminator final had to be canceled. Lefty Mudersbach (shown) was declared the Top Eliminator winner by virtue of his low ET of 8.53 seconds. (Photo Courtesy Randy Lewis Collection)

The twin blown Chevy rail of Bayer & Freitas was driven at the Winternationals by Hayden Proffitt. Proffitt fell to Lefty Mudersbach in the Gas Dragster final. (Photo Courtesy Dan and Dave Westlund/Randy Lewis Collection)

Frank Fuchs's A/FD was state of the art in the day. The Chrysler Hemi with a front-mounted GMC 6-71 blower got the job done. (Photo Courtesy Randy Lewis Collection)

Mudersbach was awarded the Top Eliminator win based on his low ET. It was an impressive feat, as he flew in the face of a field of nitromethane-powered cars. Waters and his Desoto-powered *Dragmaster* rail was runner-up, and the winnings were shared among Mudersbach, McEwen, and Fred Dobney, whose fuel-burning A/MR was the third car still in competition when the race was called.

The Henderson race was a financial loss to the city, as track operator Orel Bender poorly managed the event. He was dismissed as the track operator, and the city took over. Money from the event was unaccounted for, and the usual court battles ensued. Needless to say, the Winter Championship Drags found a new home in 1962.

The Nationals

The Nationals were held August 31–September 4, 1961, at Green Valley Raceway. It was a fairly new track located in Smithfield, Texas, and it was built in 1960 by dairy farmers Bill and Dorothy McClure. The track earned national prominence on Thanksgiving weekend 1960 when it hosted a "Race of Champions," which saw cars from all categories of the NHRA and AHRA battle

Art Chrisman's sleek **Hustler 1** *was a top car in its day. At the Nationals, Chrisman won A/FD class. He retired after 1961 to take a job with Ford's Autolite division. (Photo Courtesy Forrest Bond)*

head to head. Art Malone went home with Top Eliminator honors at the meet and set low ET with an 8.44. At the Nationals, 300 cars entered in hopes of going home a winner.

Serious Fuel Dragster action was underway on Saturday morning. Swingle ran Garlits's *Swamp Rat III* and opened up with an 8.34 ET at 180.36 mph against a reported 30- to 35-mph headwind. Malone, fresh off a $10,000 payday for being the first to round Daytona International Speedway at over 180 mph, drove his *Golden Rod* to an 8.65 ET at 176.12 mph. This was followed by runs of more than 175 mph by Sullivan and Chrisman.

Final elimination action began early Monday under favorable weather. Swingle took an easy victory over Mayhew & Dyer, whose car lost power on the line. J.L. Payne in Vance Hunt's *Chassis Research* car then defeated Malone with an 8.26 at 175.78. Sullivan then took it to Swingle—but on a false start. The two cars ran again, with Swingle pulling a half-car lead off the line. Sullivan closed the gap three-quarters down the track and surpassed Swingle for the win. It was a costly one for Sullivan, who blew the *Pandemonium*'s engine in the process.

Back in the pits, work began immediately on swapping the engine from Bob Rodgers's Gas Dragster into the *Pandemonium*. However, the pair failed to have it buttoned up within the allotted one-hour time frame. This left Chrisman and his *Hustler* to solo for A/FD honors. Chrisman had defeated J.L. Payne in the previous round.

Ed Garlits was the last man standing in Gas Dragster, so he had the pleasure of facing the AA/FD of Chet Herbert and Zane Shubert for overall Top Eliminator. Shubert had previously won class with a record 8.68 ET at 179.28 mph. Herbert's Lefty Mudersbach–built rail featured

Art Malone built his **Golden Rod** *(near lane) after giving up the seat of Garlits's* **Swamp Rat**. *The square-tube-chassis dragster was one of the more successful as the decade began. (Photo Courtesy Paul Wilson)*

twin-injected Chevys that were supplied to Herbert by Chevrolet's own Zora Arkus-Duntov. Herbert increased the bore and stroke to 4.125x4.25, which gave each engine 454 ci. Against Garlits, Shubert took the race with an 8.75 ET at 168.22 mph.

Grand prizes included a Pontiac Tempest for Shubert and a travel trailer for Garlits. It was a great year for Shubert, who had previously won the U.S. Fuel and Gas Championship at Bakersfield.

1962 Winter Championship Drags

The NHRA was showing no letup on its fuel ban, which was hurting the sanctioning body. The AHRA continued to draw racers. Although the gas burners had made headway, they still lagged (and always would) behind the fuel burners. Comparing winning times at the season-opening winter meets, Jim Nelson recorded a Top Eliminator–winning ET of 8.71 at 170.13 mph while defeating a slowing McEwen at the NHRA meet.

Where were you on March 10–11, 1962? Well, it probably wasn't at Fontana to see the second running of the AHRA Winter Championship Drags. Although it was one of the state's largest turnouts of hot cars, unusual freezing temperatures kept the number of spectators to a minimum.

The weekend belonged to chassis builder Rod Stuckey. Stuckey not only drove Lou Senter's Ansen Auto A/FD to a Top Eliminator win but also returned after the final eliminations to set the class record with an 8.51 ET at 188.66 mph, beating Bob Sullivan's old mark by 4 mph. Hot on Stuckey's heels all weekend was Mudersbach in Herbert's twin. Mudersbach cranked a best of 8.54 ET at 185.18 mph.

Top Eliminator

The first round of Top Eliminator had Gordon "the Collector" Collett and his Scotty Fenn–chassis A/GD run an 8.72 ET at 174.74 mph, defeating Lin Huiet in the Burris-Huiet A/FD by a car length. Stuckey was up next to put away Jack Reed with an 8.52 ET at 178.52 mph, which was low ET up to this point in

The AHRA welcomed cars such as Walt Arfons's Green Monster, *which the NHRA refused. The 1962* Cyclops *was powered by a Westinghouse J-46, which delivered 7,000 pounds of thrust. (Photo Courtesy John Foster Jr.)*

The NHRA fuel ban of 1957 to 1963 contributed to an increase in popularity of the unordinary. Ashland, Ohio–based Lee Pendleton's Allison-powered Spitfire, *seen here at Green Valley Raceway, was said to produce 2,700 hp. Due to its weight, the car never timed well, but it did record a best of 185 mph while running AA/D at Lions Drag Strip in 1962. (Photo Courtesy David Huff)*

Rod Stuckey, a driver and chassis-builder extraordinaire, hailed from Kansas. This Winter Championship–winning car became the dominant Greer-Black-Prudhomme car. (Photo Courtesy Stephen Justice)

In 1962, Jeep Hampshire and partner Roy Steen campaigned this twin Oldsmobile Fueler for Chet Herbert. The stroked Oldsmobile engine featured 180-degree cranks that helped the car record 180-mph-plus speeds. (Photo Courtesy J.R. Bloom)

the meet. After an all-night thrash, the Chicago-based team of Bobby Vodnik and Larry Reimer managed to get the broken A/FD back together in time to defeat the team of Fox-Adair-Holdings B/FD.

Chrisman then defeated Mudersbach with an 8.89, but he damaged his Hemi and couldn't make it back for the next round. Emery Cook advanced by defeating Lee Pendleton's Allison–powered rail.

Jim Nelson's Dodge-powered AA/GD *Dragmaster* Dart then faced Ted Cyr and Jim Ward's Scotty Fenn–chassis Lincoln, and what a battle it was. Ward's big-inch Lincoln mill tossed the blower belt and Nelson blew out the rear end. It was a slow race to the finish that saw Ward coasting through the traps first.

In a battle that no doubt had the fans on their feet, reigning Nationals champion Zane Shubert faced 1960 champion Bob Sullivan. It was Shubert out with an early lead, but mechanical ills led to him shutting off early and watching Sullivan sail past for the win. Other action included Bill Coburn tossing a blower belt and losing to Ed Pink.

The field narrowed as Cyr & Ward with their Chrysler-powered car (the team had two cars in the show) eliminated Kondaroff & Powers, who faded by a few car lengths. Stuckey and Pink were up next and ran identical 8.61 times. However, Stuckey's slight holeshot gave him the win. Cyr took the next round over Vodnik with an ET of 9 seconds flat. Cook then wasted time going skyward (as opposed to forward) and lost to Sullivan.

Cyr & Ward made a move closer to a final-round appearance by defeating Collett with an 8.84 ET at 179.64 mph. It's a shame that their Lincoln gave up the ghost in the next round against Stuckey. No worries though, they still had their Hemi car, and in the semifinals they defeated Bob Sullivan with an 8.72 ET at 179.64 mph.

This set the stage for a final-round match of Cyr

against Stuckey—and what an anticlimactic final it was. Stuckey took the win by a reported six car lengths, recording an 8.76 ET at 182.54 mph.

The 1962 Nationals

Considering that the Nationals were the same Labor Day weekend as the NHRA Nationals, participation and attendance numbers were impressive. A reported 600 entries and 40,000 spectators passed through the Green Valley Raceway gates over the weekend. Although poor weather on Friday and into Saturday did its best to hamper the event, coordinator Ben Christ received high praise for the job he did in keeping the show moving.

Top Eliminator

Dawn on Sunday morning was clear, and the competition was up with the sun to get an early start on class eliminations. Action opened with J.L. Payne in the Vance Hunt car defeating Colorado-based Marvin Schwartz with a slowing 9.24. Next, Rod Stuckey singled after his opponent shut off on the line. Don Prudhomme in the Greer-Black-Prudhomme ride then defeated Gary Bailey in the Austin & Bailey Fueler.

The year 1962 saw the emergence of Prudhomme, who joined the fuel ranks in 1960 after purchasing a car from Tommy Ivo. Against Bailey, Prudhomme's run of 8.09 at 189.06 mph had officials checking the clocks.

The Top Fuel class final was a battle between Prudhomme and Payne. Controversy ensued when Payne crossed the start line while staging. Some construed this as a jump start (leaving before the flag came up),

One of the sport's true stars was "TV" Tommy Ivo. In October 1962, here at San Gabriel, he used his Dave Zeuschel 464-ci Hemi Barnstormer *to become the first to break the 8-second barrier when he ran a 7.99 ET. (Photo Courtesy Phil Bellomy)*

In 1962, no team was as feared as Greer-Black-Prudhomme. Don Prudhomme really came into his own as a driver that year.

which meant an automatic disqualification. Reports of the event vary, but, apparently, the Greer-Black-Prudhomme team let it slide. Showing no hard feelings, Prudhomme told *Popular Hot Rodding*, "We didn't come 1,500 miles to argue; we came here to race. Give me 30 minutes to cool off my engine, and we'll race him!"

When the dust finally settled, the race took place. Payne got the jump on Prudhomme, who lost early after hanging the front wheels. Payne tripped the lights with an 8.41 ET at 182.18 mph. Years later, Prudhomme made it clear: "Vance [car owner] kicked our a—— when we were in Texas that year."

The Top Eliminator final boiled down to the two cars that won their perspective classes. Bennie Osborn, who defeated Ken Scott in the Top Gas final, was Payne's opponent. It was an anticlimactic ending to the four-day event, as Osborn broke on the line and handed the win to Payne, who recorded an 8.43 ET at 177.51 mph.

Vance Hunt had his own ideas regarding twin engines. It's too bad that Jim Tice didn't think along the same lines. (Photo Courtesy Vance Hunt)

Not So Fast

Vance Hunt recalled the weekend well, as he attempted to run a nitrous kart engine bolted to the front of his 392. Hunt felt that it was a unique way of combating the onslaught of the twin-engine cars.

AHRA rules regarding twin-engine cars stated they had to run on the same fuel, have their own shut off, and be connected to the drivetrain—nothing more.

"So, I mounted it on a plate attached to the top frame rail and used blower pulleys on the kart engine and an extra pulley on the blower to connect the systems together," Hunt said.

The combination passed tech inspection and made one strong pass.

Back in the pits, Hunt was confronted by Tice, who told him to take it off.

"I told him that it was built to match his rule book to the letter, and I intended to race it," Hunt said. "Jim's answer to me was, 'You will never make it past the first round without getting a red light.'"

So, Hunt removed the engine and went on to make 11 strong passes to win the Championship.

"The first race of 1963, Jim looked me up and handed me a new 1963 rule book," Hunt said. "He [Jim] said it was written just for me. On nearly every page it said, 'IF IT DOES NOT SAY YOU CAN DO IT > YOU CAN NOT.'"

1963 Winter Nationals

In 1963, the Winter Championship Drags found a new home and a new name. The meet moved from Fontana to a more centrally located track just north of Phoenix,

Vance Hunt's first of three Don Garlits–chassis dragsters ran a 392 in A/Fuel Dragster. As of 1962, rules stated that cars traveling more than 135 mph in the quarter-mile (120 mph in the eighth-mile) had to pack a drag chute. (Photo Courtesy Vance Hunt)

Lou Cangelose was a racer who could never be taken lightly. At the Winternationals, Dick Belfatti caught Cangelose on an off day and defeated him in the first round of eliminations. (Photo Courtesy Forrest Bond)

Rod Stuckey, driving the* Chizler *for Chris Karamesines, ran low ET of the meet but was disqualified when he failed to make the first-round call for class eliminations. Stuckey's chassis shop had three cars in the program: Karamesines's* Chizler*, Lou Cangelose's* Missouri Mule*, and Bob Sullivan's* Pandemonium IV*. (Photo Courtesy J.R. Bloom)

Arizona. Arizona Raceway was a new facility and was AHRA sanctioned through 1963. The track opened with its first race on January 6, followed by the Winternationals from February 22–24.

The initial spelling of the Winternationals was one word, the same way the NHRA had been spelling it since its first winter meet back in 1961. You just know this was a deliberate move on the part of Tice, who couldn't pass up the opportunity to get under the skin of Wally Parks and steal a little publicity. Wally took issue with the AHRA copying the spelling and went to court, where a cease-and-desist order was apparently issued. The AHRA was forced to change the spelling of its winter meet, and it went with "Winter Nationals" as two words.

A cloud hung over the 1963 Winter Nationals, as a towing accident prior to the race took the life of Don Maynard, who was one of the best wrenches in the business. Maynard, a partner and the crew chief for Chris Karamesines, was killed on the tow out to the meet when the Kenny Hirata and Phil Hobbs tow truck he was riding in was hit head-on by an errant driver while traveling through New Mexico. Both Hirata and Hobbs suffered serious injuries in the accident but recovered.

Top Eliminator

Rod Stuckey drove the *Chizler* for Chris Karamesines, and he laid down a blistering 7.81 for low ET of the meet at a phenomenal 214.78 mph! Stuckey was unable to back up his times, so the 196.06-mph run by Sullivan in his all-new Rod Stuckey–built *Pandemonium IV* that was recorded on opening day would stand as the new track record.

Moments after this photo was taken, Jim Tice was flattened by a sucker punch thrown by Al Eshenbaugh. It was a moment when emotions got the best of Eshenbaugh. Years later, he suggested he never should have done that. (Photo Courtesy J.R. Bloom)

Bob Sullivan built his first fuel car back in 1954. With his wife, Shirley, by his side, his string of Pandemonium *cars became some of the sport's most feared. (Photo Courtesy J.R. Bloom)*

Sullivan had the new car humming as he waded through the Top Eliminator field on Sunday. As rounds procceded, he dismissed the Stewart-Little-Money car in the first, then ran an 8.49 at 185.18 to eliminate Gary Bailey in the second. Other action saw the Steinegger & Eshenbaugh rail advance after putting away the *Shadow* of Dick Belfatti. Belfatti surprised many, including himself, when he defeated Lou Cangelose in the first round. Gary Cagle was another who went home earlier than expected when his A/MFR (Modified Fuel Roadster) broke. Red Greth was having a good day in his new A/MFR *Speed Sport*, advancing to the semifinals before his day came to an end.

Sullivan met Al Eshenbaugh in the A/FD final. While going through the push start, the parachute of the Steinegger & Eshenbaugh rail caught on the push truck and unraveled. Sullivan had already fired and was waved to shut off by the starting line crew. Tice jumped in and signaled for him to make the run but take it easy, even though the Steinegger & Eshenbaugh crew, push car, and rail were still on the track.

Sullivan knew he had to qualify for top in his class runoff and couldn't come up with less than a 9.25. So, he got on it and tripped the lights with a 9.06. Of course, this didn't please Eshenbaugh and crew at all. Eshenbaugh hunted down Tice, and unpleasantries were exchanged before Eshenbaugh sucker punched him, knocking Tice to his knees. Eshenbaugh was immediately banned from AHRA competition, a ban that was rescinded weeks later.

"I should have never hit him, but he never should have sent Bob down the track," Eshenbaugh said. When calm finally returned, Sullivan faced and defeated Heidt & Heidt in the Top Fuel final with an 8.21 ET at 187.21 mph.

Due to darkness, the Top Eliminator final never happened. The decision was made to split the win and the $500 bond between Top Gas winner Danny Ongais, who was driving the *Dragmaster* Dart, and Bob Sullivan. A coin toss saw the *Dragmaster* team take home the 4-foot trophy.

The Nationals

Nationals champion Art Malone kicked off the year by winning Bakersfield's Fuel and Gas Championship, where he defeated Tom McEwen in the Top Fuel final. He continued by taking honors at Fremont's fourth-annual West Coast Championship by beating Chris Karamesines. At the AHRA Nationals, he defeated Bob Langley to win Top Eliminator.

Malone took the win the hard way. He had to make a total of nine runs through the weekend: five times in the Fuel Dragster class, twice in an unusual four-car Top Fuel Eliminator, and twice in Top Eliminator, where the 4 low-ET cars in A/FD, B/FD, A/GD, and B/GD faced off.

Multitalented Bob Langley was a tool-and-die maker by trade. He fabricated his own chassis and did his own tin work. A 392 engine kept the Scorpion III *in contention. (Photo Courtesy John Bergener)*

Top Eliminator

Malone won Top Fuel class by defeating Connie Swingle with an 8.58 ET at 189.86 mph. His top ET for the weekend was 8.16 at 200.88 mph. Others breaking the magical 200-mph barrier was Stellings, Sullivan, Safford, and Swingle.

Swingle was driving for Jim Duet and set top speed and low ET of the meet at 207.36 mph with an 8.15. This led officials to double-check the recording equipment and measure the track to confirm that the times were legitimate.

The final four cars in Top Eliminator came to two. Malone defeated J.E. Kristek's B/FD with an 8.16 ET at 189.86 mph.

Tragedy Strikes

The 1963 Nationals crowd saw the untimely death of veteran racer Ted Arnold. Arnold was driving for Vance

Art Malone and the CKC dragster face off at Green Valley in the Top Eliminator final. Malone took the win after winning class. (Photo Courtesy Forrest Bond)

Pictured (left to right) are Jake Johnson, Dean Davis, Ted Arnold, Bob Taylor, and Vance Hunt. This photo was taken at Amarillo in 1963. (Photo Courtesy Vance Hunt)

Hunt, who entered the race as the defending Top Eliminator champion. Arnold started driving the Garlits-chassis car earlier in the year after J.L. Payne and Vance Hunt parted ways.

"I believe it was around 10:00 a.m. Sunday morning," Hunt said. "We were in line to make a qualifying pass. The track workers came to us and said a roadster had just ran and oiled down the track, causing a delay of 20 to 30 minutes. Ted was suited up and strapped into the race car. He chose to not get out of the car, and the time it took to clean the track was quite a bit longer than expected.

"When we did run, things went normal till about half-track, then the problem happened. My wife's brother was seated in the stands, watching with binoculars, [and] he told me Ted's head turned down forward like he had passed out. There were no guardrails about the finish line where he left the track on the right side, never lifting, full speed. He missed the catch net, crossed the road that ran alongside the strip, and flipped into the big trees of the house on the other side of the road."

Arnold was pronounced dead upon arrival at the hospital.

The NHRA Rethinks Its Stance

The NHRA fuel ban was a bust, and president Wally Parks knew it. He stated later in life that it was the biggest mistake he made. It cost the sanctioning body plenty over the six years that it sat by and watched the fuel-friendly AHRA grow. Realizing the error of his ways, Parks reintroduced nitromethane to the NHRA at the 1963 Winternationals, which ran an eight-car Fuel Dragster field, although only seven showed. Taking top honors was Don Garlits, who defeated Art Malone in the final with an ET of 8.26.

Although there was no fuel at the NHRA Nationals over Labor Day weekend (in fear no one would attend) the NHRA returned to all fuel classes beginning in 1964.

The NHRA finally welcomed back fuel. Racers were a little gun shy and didn't trust the NHRA. Although an eight-car field was promoted at the 1963 Winter Nationals, only seven spots were filled.

The evolution of Stock to Funny Car was well on its way by the time that this photo was taken in December 1965. The breathing mask on Cecil Yother helps to filter the nitromethane fumes produced by his Unlimited Fuel Plymouth Hemi. (Photo Courtesy J.R. Bloom)

Chapter Three

1961–1966: Home of the Funny Car

It may be difficult to picture, but the Funny Cars that we see today evolved from the Stock-class cars of the early 1960s. It only took a few short years to go from showroom models to fiberglass flip-up bodies, from OEM chassis to fabricated tube chassis, and from carburetors chugging gasoline to blowers and nitromethane. Although the NHRA initially had no interest in these funny-looking creations, the AHRA welcomed them with open arms.

Where It Began

During the early 1960s, heads-up match-race battles between hot stockers created legends in the sport, such as Sox & Martin, Hubert and Huston Platt, Phil Bonner, and Don Nicholson. As interest grew, the serious match racers in the South soon took on a "run what you brung" mentality, which meant that the cars were stripped of all nonessentials, such as bumpers, seats, glass, radiator supports, etc. It was all removed in the name of dropping weight and going faster.

In 1962, Detroit's Big Three manufacturers jumped in with both feet, when they discovered that racing on Sunday really did contribute to selling showroom models on Monday. Detroit quickly expanded its list of track-specific goodies mid-season to include aluminum body panels, multi-carburation, big-valve heads, and "lopey" camshafts.

The AHRA's tech manual listed July 1, 1962, as the date when all factory options were to be introduced to be considered stock. This meant that the mid-season options rushed into production specifically for big events (such as the Labor Day National Championship Drags)

"Dyno" Don Nicholson was ready to take on the world when he headed East from California in mid-1961. Nicholson was the first Stock-category competitor to go out on tour. Yes, they loved him on the East Coast, just as they did on the West Coast. (Photo Courtesy Mike Strickler)

Dick Harrell earned the nickname "Mr. Chevrolet" on the back of a string of W-motor Chevys dating back to 1958. His 1963 Impala Z11 was later sold to fellow racer Bryan Teal and eventually wrecked. (Photo Courtesy John Bergener/Bill Fronterhouse)

were not considered regular stock equipment. Thus, they would not be allowed to run in the Stock category. A special class, Experimental, was created for these cars.

At the AHRA Championship Drags, Frank Sanders took Top Stock over all comers with his A/S 409-equipped 1962 Chevy Bel-Air. He defeated the Glenn E. Thomas–sponsored A/SA Dodge driven by Al Vanderwoude.

Factory-built drag cars were all the rage in 1963. Detroit's leading manufacturers each produced lightweight, big-inch cars specifically for drag-strip use. At the season-opening Winter Nationals, Dick Harrell's 427-equipped 1963 Impala defeated the Hayden Proffitt–tuned Ritchie & Ritchie S/SA Plymouth for Top Stock.

Al Eckstrand in the Ramchargers' lightweight Dodge set low ET and top speed for the Stockers with an 11.78 ET at 120 mph. With concerns rising about trick fuels, the Stockers were required to drain their tanks and fill up with track-supplied fuel prior to eliminations. Racers were given one run to make tuning adjustments to their cars. For many, it wasn't enough.

The 2-Percent Difference

Chrysler took things a little further in 1964 when it released four 2-percent altered-wheelbase drag cars. In sanctioned drag racing, rules required these cars to run AHRA Ultra Stock (or NHRA Factory Experimental). Joining them in class were 427-equipped Chevy IIs and Chevelles that were pieced together by several independent racers.

Phil Bonner used his Ultra Stock *Georgia Peach* Falcon to win Mr. Stock Eliminator at the World Finals, defeating a red-lighting Gene Snow with an 11.45 ET at 120.32 mph.

The Dodge Chargers were exhibition cars and are considered by many to be the grandfather of today's Funny Car. Out of the gate, the cars recorded ETs in the 10s at 140 mph. Three cars were built, but the third was wrecked during its initial outing. (Photo Courtesy J.R. Bloom)

Stock's Stockers

While Stock was branching off in a "funny" direction in 1963, the roots of the Stock class remained. A minimum of allowable modifications ensured that the classes remained affordable.

Production Stock, Modified Stock/Sportsman, and Compact Stock were all reasonably affordable categories at the beginning of the decade. Each category produced owners and builders who obtained celebrity, or "pro" status (in their own right) among a growing legion of fans.

Studebaker jumped into the performance-car market with its R2 Supercharged Lark in 1963. Chuck Bradshaw's A/Compact Sedan was a Winter Nationals class winner, recording a 14.50 ET at over 96 mph. (Photo Courtesy J.R. Bloom)

Jim Rodgers can be thanked for giving us Bee Line Dragway in 1963 and Kansas City International Raceway in 1968. Rodgers was a regular participant in the sport he loved. Here, he's in action in 1963 at Bee Line Dragway with his 320-hp 1959 Impala. (Photo Courtesy J.R. Bloom)

Along with the 2-percent cars, Chrysler also commissioned Jim Nelson and Dode Martin of Dragmaster in Carlsbad, California, to build three "Supercharged Experimental Stock" Dodge Chargers. The lightweight 330 model sedans were powered by blown and injected Max Wedge engines that were bored and stroked to 480 ci. Out of the gate, drivers Jim Johnson and Jimmy Nix recorded times in the 10s at 140 mph. Many fans of the sport consider these to be the first real Funny Cars.

In 1964, Ronnie Sox and Buddy Martin were socking it to the competition with this 427-powered Comet. They would then take an offer from Chrysler in 1965. (Photo Courtesy Randy Hernandez)

Mercury Rising

The Mercury division of Ford entered the world of drag racing in 1964, and the timing couldn't have been better for racers, such as Dyno Don Nicholson and the team of Sox & Martin. With General Motors halting all racing activity in 1963, these racers were looking for factory support, and Mercury obliged.

Working with a limited racing budget, Fran Hernandez, Mercury's performance and evaluation manager, had Dearborn Steel Tubing build 11 drag race–only, 427 hi-rise–powered 1964 Comet Calientes. In such a limited number, the cars were destined to run in either the AHRA's Ultra Stock class or the NHRA's A/FX class.

Two prototypes were initially built: a station wagon that was raced by Nicholson and a hardtop that was scrapped after testing. Success with his Chevy II wagon back in 1962 showed Nicholson the advantage of running a wagon. The added rear weight and shorter wheelbase of the Comet wagon (109.5 versus the hardtop's 114 inches) helped plant the narrow 10-inch tires.

"It was a handful," Mercury's Al Turner said regarding the wagon. "It was a bit of a monster, more temperamental than the hardtop."

Chrisman's Comet

Hot on the heels of Chrysler's Chargers was Jack Chrisman and his blown and injected 1964 Comet. Chrisman ran a pinch of nitro through the 427 and had direct drive in place of the transmission. Smoky quarter-mile

Evolution from Stock to Funny Car took a jump when Jack Chrisman unveiled his Sachs & Sons–sponsored blown 427 Comet in mid-1964. The car featured direct drive and nitromethane. (Photo Courtesy Richard McInstry)

Don Nicholson stirred up some controversy with his 427-equipped Comet wagon. Even the other Mercury factory racers complained of his success. (Photo Courtesy J.R. Bloom)

runs in the 10.40s were common. It would have been a good show to see the Comet go off against a Charger, but Chrysler refused to allow its drivers to go head-to-head.

In August, Chrysler recalled the Chargers and retired them. Jimmy Nix had hoped to retain his ride and beat Chrisman to the magical 150-mph mark, which was a speed yet to be obtained by a stock-body car. Chrisman blasted through the barrier on August 23 at Aquasco, Maryland. By increasing the percent of nitro, he obtained a top speed of 154.10 mph in 10.13 seconds.

All in and Way Out

By the fall of 1964, both "Dandy" Dick Landy and Bill "Maverick" Golden further altered the wheelbase on their Dodges. Maverick bumped up the rear wheels of his 2-percent car. Landy, going hog wild, bumped the rear suspension up 8 inches and then replaced the factory torsion-bar front suspension with a Dodge truck's straight axle, moving it forward 6 inches. It was a taste of things to come, as Chrysler had big plans for 1965.

In late 1964, Chrysler handed Amblewagon of Troy, Michigan (best known for its station wagon-to-ambulance conversions), six Belvederes and five Coronets with instructions to move the front suspension forward 10 inches and the rear forward 15 inches. These cars were complete race-only packages consisting of acid-dipped bodies and fiberglass panels.

The bodies of these cars were so thin that Lee Smith, one of the lucky gents who received a Plymouth, recalled that he buckled the roof while standing on the sill of the open door. He strengthened his car with a stiff roll cage.

Initially, the cars ran carburetors and pump gas or aviation fuel through their Hemis. The transmission was either the rock-solid A-833 4-speed or the heavy-duty 727 TorqueFlite automatic.

"Dandy" Dick Landy got a jump on the field when he altered the wheelbase of his Dodge in 1964. The rear suspension was moved forward, and a lighter straight front axle replaced the factory torsion-bar suspension. (Photo Courtesy Forrest Bond)

1965: The Funny Cars Find a Home

Although the NHRA initially balked at these funny-looking cars (refusing to make a class for them), the AHRA welcomed them with open arms. In fact, the story goes that it was an AHRA announcer who, for lack of a better name, stuck these radically altered cars with the Funny Car moniker.

The cars made their debut at the season-opening Winter Nationals at Bee Line Dragway in January 1965, running Ultra Stock. Over the three-day event, a reported 65,000 fans watched a multitude of altered cars battle to make the 16-car Mr. Stock Eliminator field. When the dust had

Lee Smith was recipient of one of the acid-dipped, altered-wheelbase cars produced by Chrysler in 1965. Of the six lightweight Plymouths produced, Lee's is said to be the last one remaining. (Photo Courtesy Lou Hart)

Richard Petty chose to go drag racing in 1965 when NASCAR banned the Hemi. His Hemi Barracuda weighed approximately 2,600 pounds and ran 10.40-second ETs at Bee Line Dragway. Petty's crew consisted of Dale Inman and Maurice and Gene Petty. (Photo Courtesy J.R. Bloom)

settled, all but one of the cars was a Chrysler product.

Phil Bonner made the cut with his 427-powered Falcon. But prior to eliminations, he discovered that someone had sabotaged his efforts by pouring a handful of nuts and bolts down his engine. There was much speculation as to who the culprit may have been, but no firm suspect was tagged.

As it was, the field now consisted of the following qualifiers: Bud Faubel was number-one with a 10.84. He was followed by Sox & Martin, the Ramchargers, the Golden Commandos with two cars that were driven by Al Ekstrand and Forest Pitcock, Tommy Grove, Roger Lindamood, Dick Landy,

Two of Pennsylvania's finest, Dave Strickler and Bud Faubel, battle at the 1965 Winter Nationals. Faubel earned Mr. Stock honors. (Photo Courtesy J.R. Bloom)

The Mr. Stock final boiled down to two mighty Mopars. Al Eckstrand driving for the Golden Commandos came up short against Bud Faubel. Note the different location of the wheel-well openings. (Photo Courtesy J.R. Bloom)

Butch Leal, Bob Harrop, Dave Strickler, Baney Plymouth driven by Preston Honea, Bill Jenkins, Lee Smith, the Sites brothers, Dick Housey, and Melton & Snow.

Bud Faubel from Chambersburg, Pennsylvania, marched to the Mr. Stock final by defeating fellow Pennsylvanian Dave Strickler and then Roger Lindamood in the semifinals. Faubel's *Hemi Honker* then faced Al Ekstrand in the Golden Commandos' 2-percent car in the final round. It was a close one between the two drastically different cars with Faubel taking the win by defeating Ekstrand's 10.98 with a 10.96.

In June, at the Summer Nationals, it was Jim Thornton in the Ramchargers' Dodge that won Mr. Stock honors with a 10.14. At the World Finals, Dick Brannan's *Bronco* Mustang ran a 10.08 to defeat the Mustang of Gas Ronda.

The Need for More Speed

By the spring of 1965, fuel injection had all but replaced carburation, as both factory-built and independent match racers went looking for more power. Gasoline was replaced by alcohol and nitromethane. The initial results of these changes showed an increase in speed of up to 2.5 mph. Some racers leaned on the performance-enhancing fuel additive hydrazine. The additive was so dangerous that many motors, cars, and limbs were destroyed by its use. In October 1966, the AHRA banned it. The NHRA followed suit in 1967.

Ford Counters

Not willing to sit by and watch Chrysler dominate, Ford had Holman-Moody-Stroppe build six longnose Mustangs. The cars followed the two steel-bodied Factory Experimental Mustangs that Ford built in 1965. These new Mustangs took things further by incorporating fiberglass bodies and a 2x3 square-tube chassis. The rear suspension was shuffled forward, and more than 1 foot was added to the chassis ahead of the windshield. The final wheelbase measured out to 112 inches, which was 4 inches over stock. Positioning the front wheels was an unusual, twisted, quarter-elliptic leaf-spring front suspension.

Gas Ronda used his longnose Mustang to win Unlimited Gas at the 1966 AHRA Winter Nationals. He had a

Gas Ronda debuted his longnose Mustang at the AHRA Winter Nationals at Irwindale. The approximately 2,400-pound car managed 9.30 ETs during its first outing. It was definitely the most successful of the Holman-Moody-built Mustangs. (Photo Courtesy J.R. Bloom)

Hayden Proffitt and his single-overhead-camshaft (SOHC) Comet meant business. It took him a while to sort out the new combination, but the competition knew to never count him out. (Photo Courtesy J.R. Bloom)

phenomenal season, winning the C/FD class at the NHRA Winternationals then at the Smokers meet at Bakersfield. There, he drove the Mustang to an 8.96 ET at 155.97 mph to defeat Sox & Martin. This was the first 8-second run produced by an unblown Funny Car.

Ronda backed up his 1965 Top Stock win at the AHRA World Championship Drags by defeating Hayden Proffitt in Fuel Stock. A week later, he defeated the Chevy II of Dick Harrell in Fuel Stock at the Grand American race at Green Valley.

Mercury Out Does Them All

Lincoln-Mercury's Fran Hernandez and Al Turner had the foresight to see where the Funny Cars were headed. They took a giant leap forward when they designed and developed the tube-chassis, flip-up Comet that debuted in 1966.

Using Jack Chrisman's 25-percent-setback single overhead cam (SOHC) 1965 Comet as an evolutionary tool, Hernandez and Turner spec'd out their vision for the 1966 Comet drag car. Unlike the 1965 altered-wheelbase cars, the Comets kept the factory 116-inch wheelbase and the overall physical appearance of the production car.

Ron and Gene Logghe were given the task of building the chassis while Plastigauge of Jackson, Michigan, formed the bodies using a Mercury design plug. The initial plan was for the Comets to have complete lift-off bodies, but the shells proved to be too heavy. Ron Logghe suggested hinging the bodies at the rear, and the flip-up Funny Car was born.

Four of these Comets were built and dealt out to Jack Chrisman, Eddie Schartman, Ron Leslie, and Don Nicholson. Powering the Comets was the SOHC 427 engine. Chrisman ran a GMC blower on top of his, while the other three chose to run injection. In competition, all four Comets ran beefed-up C-6 automatic transmissions.

Jack Chrisman's Comet received a makeover for the 1965 season, including a 25-percent engine setback. The car played a serious part in the evolution of the Funny Car.

Don Nicholson's Comet won just one AHRA national event in 1966: the Grand American race at Wisconsin. However, he did compile a 95-percent match-race win record. In a September 17 match race against Eddie Schartman, Nicholson recorded Funny Car's first ever 7-second pass with a 7.96 ET at 171.75 mph. (Photo Courtesy Forrest Bond)

Chrisman's Comet differed from the rest of the batch. It ran as a roadster with a blower atop the Cammer. Direct drive transferred the power. (Photo Courtesy John Foster Jr.)

1966 Winter Nationals Debut

The Comet made its debut with Nicholson at the AHRA Winter Nationals at Irwindale in February. It didn't go quite as planned. On its first hard pass, the body blew off as the car approached the traps, leaving Nicholson exposed to the elements at approximately 150 mph. It was reported that wind pressure had pushed in the retaining latch, causing the body to come up. The mangled remains were hauled off to a desolate corner of the track and set ablaze.

With Nicholson and the Comet out of action, Dick Brannan and his *Bronco* Mustang were the pair to beat in Fuel Stock. Competition was tough, with speeds averaging in the mid-9-second range. Brannan marched to the final, where he faced and defeated Wayne "Tex" Darnaby's *Temptation* with a 9.21 at 149.50 mph. Gas Stock was won by Tasca Ford's Bill Lawton, whose 9.78 ET at 140.40 mph defeated Gas Ronda's 9.85 at 141.95 in the final.

A Class of Their Own

The AHRA rule book for 1966 shows an Unlimited Stock (U/SU) category for blown or injected cars

Phil "Daddy Warbucks" Bonner stopped the crowds with a bumper-dragging wheel-stand against opponent Dick Brannan during eliminations. As impressive as it was, it knocked Phil out of eliminations. (Photo Courtesy J.R. Bloom)

Wayne "Tex" Darnaby's 1964 Plymouth Temptation *ran low 9-second ETs and was runner-up in Fuel Stock at the Winter Nationals. Tex was an independent in the truest form; he and his wife did all of the work. (Photo Courtesy Stephen Justice)*

The Tameless Tiger of Arnie Beswick optimized everything that fans loved in the new Funny Cars. At the Winter Nationals, Beswick and the Tempest ran 9.20 ETs at 135 mph. (Photo Courtesy Stephen Justice)

Out of Deming, New Mexico, came Eddie Marcak and his 427-Wedge-equipped Flyin' Farmer *Mustang. Marcak ran injection and later swapped the setup for a blower and ran 8-second ETs. (Photo Courtesy Forrest Bond)*

and five Factory Experimental classes: Ultra Stock Injected (US/I), Ultra Stock (U/S), Super Stock (S/S), A/Stock, and B/Stock. However, with new cars and configurations debuting weekly, classes were added, and descriptions evolved to keep up. At national events alone, the AHRA offered numerous class descriptions, including Fuel Cars, Mr. Stock, Super Stock, Run What You Brung (Unlimited Stock). At the World Championship at Lions Drag Strip and the Points Finale at Green Valley, there was Fuel Stock and Gas Stock.

The eighth-mile Spring Nationals in 1966 was where the "Funny Car" category name first appeared. Funny Car was won by the Dodge of Russell Funk, which ran a 6.29 ET to defeat Shirley Shahan. At the end of June, the category name was used again at the Grand American race at Union Grove.

Unlimited Stock: Match Race Galore

Not everyone enjoyed the advantages of having factory support. Those who didn't made a small fortune match racing and qualifying at the numerous Funny Car programs that dotted the nation's tracks weekly.

Fifteen of these independents faced off in Unlimited Stock (Run What Ya Brung) at the 1966 AHRA World Championship Drags in October at Lions. The behinds of the near-capacity crowd rarely touched the seats, as spectators clamored to the fencing. They cheered on the likes of Jim Liberman, who wheeled both his own Coyle Chevrolet–sponsored Chevy II and Lew Arrington's Hemi-powered *Brutus* GTO. Others on the program included Roger Wolford in the 392-powered *Secret Weapon* Jeep, Gary Southern in the 392-powered Astra kit car dubbed *Stinger II*, Gary Dyer in Mr. Norm's recently debuted *Super Charger*, Paula Murphy's STP Mustang, Maynard Rupp's mid-engine Hemi Chevelle, and Fred Goeske driving the mid-engine *Hemi-Cuda*.

The racing was great and the results were unpredictable. The first match of the first round featured Liberman in Arrington's *Brutus* taking it to Dyer. Dyer's *Super Charger* had run a warmup at 8.43, but a liberal amount of rosin didn't help him against Liberman, who ran an 8.74 at 164 mph for low ET of the meet.

Next was the 2,100-pound Astra of Gary Southern putting away Wolford with a smoky 8.89. Rich Hammons and his still fresh *Hairy Canary* Plymouth Valiant fell to Randy Walls's *Super Nova*, which ran a 9.77.

Dale Armstrong's *Canuck* (he was Canadian) Chevy II roadster previously ran an 8.90 but fell to a red light against Dee Keaton in Sheldon Konblett's Hemi-powered *Peanuts* four-door Ford Galaxie. Konblett had built the unique Ford at home in Compton after procuring the fiberglass body from Ford Motor Company.

In other first-round action, Goeske defeated Murphy, Rupp beat Liberman and his Chevy II, and Richard Schroeder's *Bad Bossa* Nova defeated the *Bronco Buster* of Doug Nash. Nash built his 1,500-pound Ford Bronco using 0.26-inch-thick aluminum for the chassis and roll bar. The NHRA refused to accept the car, but the AHRA had no issue with it. Closing the round, Charlie Allen's Dart ran a 9.09 to sink the SOHC Mustang of Tommy Grove.

The second round opened with Liberman carrying the *Brutus'* front wheels 100 feet out of the chute and parlaying a great light into a win over Dyer. Next, beating the *Secret Weapon* proved to be no secret for the *Stinger II*, which took its second win with a 9.20 ET at 178 mph. Goeske came back to defeat Murphy once again, and Walls made it two in a row as well, defeating the *Hairy Canary* once again.

Peanuts came back to defeat the out-of-shape *Canuck*, and Schroeder gave up a weight advantage to Nash (Schroeder himself weighed 300 pounds) but managed a win for the injected Chevy. Liberman, back in *Brutus*,

The Lompoc, California–based Dart of plumber Bill Rieck ran an injected Hemi and automatic transmission. With Jim Cockrell and John Hefner helping pull wrenches, the fiberglass Quarter Bender *recorded high-8-second ETs at 160 mph. (Photo Courtesy J.R. Bloom)*

The crowds ate up Ed Pauling's mid-engine Lil Ol Whine Maker*. A back seat–mounted blown 392 engine on a full load of nitro did nothing for traction. Direct drive transmitted power to the suffering slicks. (Photo Courtesy J.R. Bloom)*

A blown Pontiac with a set of Mickey Thompson Hemi heads initially powered Lew Arrington's **Brutus***. The mill eventually gave way to a Chrysler Hemi. "Jungle" Jim Liberman shared in the driving. (Photo Courtesy James Handy)*

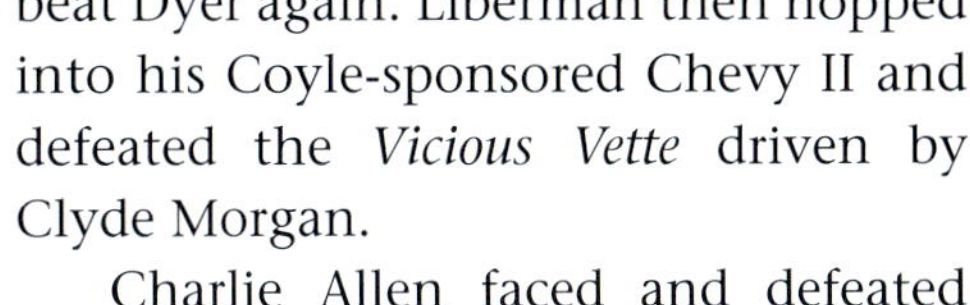

beat Dyer again. Liberman then hopped into his Coyle-sponsored Chevy II and defeated the *Vicious Vette* driven by Clyde Morgan.

Charlie Allen faced and defeated Tom Grove again. Goeske made it three straight over Murphy, Nash finally got around the *Bossa* Nova, and Grove finally took one from Allen. In the last match of the evening, overall winner Liberman used his Chevy to defeat the *Hairy Canary* with a 9.04, and in the process took out the top-end lights.

California's Richard Schroeder campaigned this gorgeous **Bad Bossa Nova** *from 1966 to 1967. A 427 propelled the deuce to 9.40 ETs. Schroeder spent a few years announcing at Lions Drag Strip from 1968 to 1970 before moving on to exhibition cars. (Photo Courtesy J.R. Bloom)*

The Changing Funny Car

From the Sportsman category in 1964 to Fuel Stock in 1966 and Unlimited Funny Car in 1967, the category evolved quickly. According to the 1967 AHRA rule book, the year started off with two Unlimited Stock classes: Unlimited Blown Ultra Stock (UB/US) and Unlimited Injected Ultra Stock (UI/US). National events that year show an Unlimited class and a Gas Funny Car class with numerous weight breaks: 2,400, 2,700, and 3,200 pounds. Remember the AHRA's unwritten motto "If we don't have a class for your combination, we'll create one."

By the close of 1967, all the competitive Funny Cars were sporting flip-up bodies, a heavy load of nitro, and a GMC 6-71 blower. This was the basis for what is seen in today's Funny Car class.

The team of Sox & Martin campaigned its Unlimited Fuel Funny Car Barracuda into 1967 before making the move to Super Stock. Here, Sox faces the Mustang of Hubert Platt at the 1967 Winter Nationals. (Photo Courtesy J.R. Bloom)

Gabby Bleeker and his 1938 Bantam evolved with the decade and was a winner from the beginning to the end. The Bantam started the 1960s with an Oldsmobile engine and ended with a Hemi. Winning Middle Eliminator at the AHRA Nationals in 1961 was just the beginning. (Photo Courtesy Lou Hart)

Chapter Four

Recapping the 1960s

The old saying "the world is your oyster," means that you can do anything and go anywhere that you desire. As the decade began, it sure seemed to hold true for Jim Tice and the AHRA.

Still in its infancy, the AHRA continued to sign up tracks and add to its national event schedule. It showed initiative throughout the decade by introducing things such as the pro-tree start, evening qualifying, the Formula classes, and heads-up Super Stock. These advancements contributed immensely to the sport as a whole and boosted participation and spectator turnout to levels that were previously only dreamt about. By the end of the decade, the AHRA challenged the NHRA as the sport's leading sanctioning body.

A Few Changes as the Decade Began

In addition to changes in the Dragster classes that were noted in Chapter 2, there were changes in 1960 in the Stock classes. Revisions stated that cars in Super Stock were now required to run only factory "assembly-line production parts," just like the lower-class Stock cars.

Introduced in 1960 were two Modified Stock classes for "cheater stocks." All cars over 300 ci were limited to a single 4-barrel carburetor. At the Nationals in September, J.L. Meador won Modified Stock and Stock Eliminator with his Ford sedan, which turned a 13.64 ET at 103.09 mph.

In 1960, the AHRA implemented a points system for its racers. The system saw the top 10 point-getters share in the prizes financed by setting aside a percentage of receipts at their season-ending American Championship Drags on Labor Day weekend. Registration fees were $5. A Top, Middle, or Little Eliminator class win was worth 10 points at a regular race and double at a sanctioned race. At the Championship Drags, points increased to 50 for each eliminator win and the overall eliminations win. The points system ran in various forms through the life of the AHRA, with points awarded at regional and national events as well as for records set.

In 1962, a Production Stock class was introduced, and Stock class rules became a little looser. Now, floor shifts, open exhaust, transmission and rear gear changes, electric fuel pumps, and distributor modifications were allowed.

In 1963, the Modified Stock category was renamed Sportsman and encompassed 11 classes. Across the board

The popularity of the Stock classes was really grabbing hold as the decade began. Additional classes and categories were introduced to meet the demand. A quick and easy classification guide was created by J.R. Bloom and used at tracks throughout the nation. (Photo Courtesy John Foster Jr.)

In 1960, San Antonio's J.E. Kristek collected points with a B/Stocker and this chopped Ford, which he ran in C/Altered. Kristek closed the 1960 season fourth in the points standing. (Photo Courtesy Tim and Larry Bouldin)

A drag racer at heart, Jim Tice loved his Studebakers. At the Nationals in 1961, he won C/Modified Stock and set the class record in the process with a 15.09 ET at 93.90 mph. (Photo Courtesy Ruth Tice)

in Stock, a maximum cubic-inch rule of 430 was implemented. Anything larger required the car to be moved to Gas.

Introduced in 1964: The Formula Classes

The AHRA adopted Ben Christ's idea that everyone who goes to the races should go home satisfied. If a racer goes home with a trophy, it is likely that he will come back again. That was the idea behind the formula designations that were developed by Christ with input from George Eisenhart. The formulas were first used at Eisenhart's Ohio Thompson Raceway in 1963.

The formula designations created additional Sportsman classes. Classes (A/S, B/S, C/S, etc.) were based upon a cubic-inch-to-weight division. The formulas broke down these classes further by dividing them based on the

JFK's Assassination

Outside of the nation's fastest-growing sport, the world changed forever on November 22, 1963, when United States President John F. Kennedy was assassinated. His death set the tone for a decade that had its share of unrest.

More assassinations followed, all while the war escalated in Vietnam. In the decade that is simply referred to as "the '60s," we mourned our losses and counted our blessings.

On a mournful late-November day, John Loper and his A/Gas Anglia soldier on. It was a trying time for the nation, but the people persevered. Loper and his Anglia pretty much dominated class action through the decade. (Photo Courtesy J.R. Bloom)

induction and camshaft. This helped ensure there was a class for everyone and every combination.

Christ and Eisenhart approached Jim Tice with the idea at the members' meeting prior to the Nationals in 1963. Eisenhart presented the idea to the members.

"It was like throwing me to the wolves," Eisenhart said. "Ben Christ knew, Jim knew, as did a few others that I was going to get my head cut off because it was a new idea that no one knew about and had no time to think about. I got quite a bit of resistance, and I remember Jim sweating about being voted back in as president.

"I told him, 'Well, we don't want to piss off these guys because you'll never get back in as president.' Ben turned to Jim and asked, 'Well, who counts the votes?' 'I do,' Jim replied. 'Well then, you should have no problem getting back in,' Ben said."

Eisenhart finished his speech, and to calm the members, Tice told them that the formula divisions were just something that they were considering. As the meeting wound down, a resolution was passed stating that there would be no more voting on the presidency.

The formula designations were implemented in time for the 1964 Winter Nationals. A typical formula class designation may read: F-2 B/S (or B/SA for automatic cars), which in 1964 meant Formula 2 (multiple carburetors, hydraulic cam) B/Stock (380 to 399 ci).

The AHRA had no means of dialing handicap starts into its timing equipment, and didn't until 1967, so each

Roy Gay's Tri-Power-equipped F-2 B/Stock 1964 GTO competed in NHRA and AHRA events through 1965. At the 1964 Winter Nationals, Gay won class with a 14.09 ET at 99.88 mph. (Photo Courtesy Forrest Bond)

From 1964 through 1966, AHRA timing equipment didn't allow for handicap starts. During that period, a handicap number determined the lead in car lengths that a participant may have. Note the professional start tree hanging above. (Photo Courtesy J.R. Bloom)

Before he became known as the man driving the **Little Red Wagon** ***wheel-stander, Bill "Maverick" Golden wheeled a number of class cars. In 1962, he won Stock at the Nationals by defeating Don Nicholson. (Photo Courtesy J.R. Bloom)***

class of car was assigned a handicap number. During final eliminations, the class winner spotted or was spotted the difference in car lengths between handicap numbers.

Stock Formulas

The formula designations for Stock class cars was written in the 1964 edition of the AHRA Rule Book. Stock cars had to run service-station-pump gasoline. No lightweight packages (aluminum or fiberglass) were permitted in Stock. The 1964 formulas are shown in the chart on the right.

Formula	Details
Formula 1	Multiple carburetion, solid lifters
Formula 2	Multiple carburetion, hydraulic lifters
Formula 3	Supercharged, fuel injection, and solid lifters
Formula 4	Supercharged, fuel injection, and hydraulic lifters
Formula 5	4-barrel carburetion, solid lifters
Formula 6	4-barrel carburation, hydraulic lifters
Formula 7	2-barrel carburation
Formula 8	Flathead V-8 and straight-8 engines
Formula 9	4- and 6-cylinder engines, 2-barrel carburation
Formula 10	4- and 6-cylinder engines, single-barrel carburation

Jerry Cookson made the short jaunt from his home in Ponca City, Oklahoma, to Smithfield, Texas, with his lightweight, Wedge-powered Plymouth to win SS/A at the 1964 World Championship Drags. Cookson had a reaction time second to none, and in the final, he ran a 12.23 ET at 114.94 mph for the win. (Photo Courtesy J.R. Bloom)

Tony Janes bought this record-holding 1957 Ford from Ron Sundell. It was powered by a Holley-equipped 312 and backed by a Ford-O-Matic with a 10.5-inch convertor. It ran a best ET of 14.26. (Photo Courtesy Tony Janes)

Cars with lightweight panels ran in the Factory Hot Rod classes of Super Stock and Ultra Stock. The wheelbase for each was a minimum of 114 inches. The minimum weight for the Ultra Stocks was set at 2,800 pounds, and the minimum weight for Super Stocks was 3,200 pounds.

Additionally, the Sportsman (SM) category ran to Stock rules but allowed for any engine in any model (as long as it was the same manufacturer) and any internal engine modifications outside of a stroke and/or roller cam. It ran with four formulas.

Formula	Details
Formula 1	Factory multiple carburetion
Formula 2	One 4-barrel carburetor
Formula 3	One 2-barrel carburetor
Formula 4	Factory supercharged, factory fuel injection

Two New Favorites

The popularity of drag racing relating to spectator turnout and racer participation was exploding in 1965. To give budding racers more options, two new categories were introduced: Hot Rod and Modified Production. They proved to be very popular over the years.

Hot Rod

The Factory Hot Rod category of 1964 became the Hot Rod category in 1965. According to the 1965 rule book, "Cars in the Hot Rod divisions must run service-station-pump gasoline. Hot Rod classes are for dual-purpose cars capable of starting under their own power and returning to the pit area after making a run. Cars in this section must also be capable of being driven on the street for sustained periods in any type of traffic conditions. Bodies, engines or drivetrains, chassis, etc. may not be altered, modified, or relocated except as noted in the Class Requirements. Push or towed starts are not allowed. Push cars are not permitted in this division. Light weight body components may be used. No Hemi V-8s, overhead-cam V-8s, or strokers are allowed in this category."

Hot Rod consisted of 26 classes and the same 4 formulas used in the Sportsman category.

Modified Production

According to the 1965 AHRA rule book, "The Modified Production division is designed for the person who desires more than a stock machine. It permits swapping of engines and more freedom to make other changes from stock. The purpose of this division is to provide

Out of the Golden State, Augie Sorichta competed in the Qualifiers II B/MP 1929 Chevy. Power came from a twin AFB Carter–induced 371-ci Chevy engine that was backed by a 4-speed transmission and a 5.13:1 Oldsmobile rear end. (Photo Courtesy J.R. Bloom)

Bee Line Dragway was named after the Arizona highway that it was near. The entrance welcomed hundreds of thousands through the gate during the span of approximately 18 years. (Photo Courtesy J.R. Bloom)

classes between Hot Rod and Gas Coupe/Sedan for what are still true street machines."

The three formulas in this category (12 classes) were classified according to the total scale weight divided by total cubic-inch displacement.

Formula	Details
Formula 1	Reserved for Hemi-head cars and overhead-cam-powered cars with multiple carburetion
Formula 2	Multiple carburetion
Formula 3	4-barrel carburetion

The Numbers Varied

The number of formulas varied over the years as categories evolved. The initial 10 Stock category formulas of 1964 encompassed 154 classes. By the time 1984 rolled around, there were four formulas in Factory Stock (the equivalent of 1964's Stock category), encompassing 136 classes.

Bee Line Dragway and the 1964 Winter Nationals

Bee Line Dragway has had a long affiliation with the AHRA. The track, which was the home of the Winter Nationals beginning in 1964, was built in 1963 in Mesa, Arizona. It was the brainchild of 20-year-old local racer Jim Rodgers.

Jim's father, Tim, a local contractor, had the means to make Jim's dream come to life. He and a group of investors leased an 80-acre parcel of land off the Bee Line Highway from the Salt River Pima Indian tribe for a 10-year period.

The Winter Nationals from February 7–9, 1964, was the track's first major event. According to *TACH* magazine, the AHRA's house paper at the time, it was the first major drag racing event televised in closed circuit by either sanctioning body. A reported 48,000 spectators attended while 600 racers looked to qualify for one of the many positions available. Ollie Riley worked the Chrondek clocks that he invented and recorded new record times for the books.

Top Eliminator

The road to the Top Eliminator final went as follows: the eight low ET cars in Fuel and Gas ran off for their respective category crown. These cars then returned to run off their respective classes. Then, the four low ET

Ron Goodsell took the seat of Bob Sullivan's Pandemonium IV *and won Top Fuel and Top Eliminator at the Winter Nationals. Goodsell was one of the better hired drivers during drag racing's golden years. (Photo Courtesy J.R. Bloom)*

Mike Snively in Scotty's Muffler *(far lane) was runner-up at the Winter Nationals. Here, he faces and defeats the Gas Dragster of Pusch & Crews. (Photo Courtesy J.R. Bloom)*

Although Art "the Dart" Malone had the low ET (8.03) at the Winter Nationals, he failed to follow up his 1963 Nationals win. The chassis of Malone's yellow bullet was built by Garlits. (Photo Courtesy J.R. Bloom)

class winners ran for overall Top Eliminator. The Top Fuel class winner was Ron Goodsell in Bob Sullivan's *Pandemonium IV*. Goodsell collected the coin by running an 8.05 in defeating the ailing *Dead-End Kids* car driven by Red Lang.

The Top Gas class final saw the Lecoist & Lore Chevy-powered rail defeat Pete Robinson. Robinson in his small-block Ford–powered rail was left sitting on the line, as he felt that Art Lecoist had fouled. He was waiting for the starter to react. It was a tough loss for the crowd favorite, but he returned for Top Eliminator.

Here, in the Mr. Stock final, Roger Caster (near lane) drives a 4-speed Plymouth that was nearly identical to the automatic-equipped car of Hayden Proffitt. Proffitt won with an 11.80 ET at 122.64 mph. (Photo Courtesy J.R. Bloom)

The Top Eliminator final four boiled down to Mike Snively in the *Scotty's Muffler* B/FD, Pete Robinson's A/GD, Pusch & Crew's B/FD, and Bob Goodsell. In the first runoff, Snively defeated Pusch & Crews with an 8.70 ET to an 8.89. The next round saw Robinson fall to Goodsell with an 8.17 to an 8.44.

In the final, Goodsell covered Snively in an oh-so-close finish. The two cars left the line together, but on the top end, the *Pandemonium* inched ahead for the win, recording an 8.26 ET at 181.08 mph to Snively's 8.38 at 181.08. For Bob Sullivan, this was a repeat win, having won the Winter Nationals in 1963, which made him the first repeat national event winner.

Low ET of the meet was shared by Goodsell and Art Malone, who each recorded an 8.03. Top speed was shared by Goodsell and Snively, who each recorded 187.10 mph.

Frank Sanders's new S/SA Plymouth was tough competition, hitting 11.80 ETs. However, it wasn't tough enough for Proffitt, who disposed of him during eliminations. (Photo Courtesy J.R. Bloom)

Stock Eliminator

The action in Top Stock did not get off to a good start. After Don Nicholson and his 427-equipped Mercury Comet station wagon laid down a blistering 11.48 on Friday, the Chrysler contingency cried foul. The wheelbase is too short, they screamed—and they were right, as the rules stated a 114-inch minimum. Mercury's head of racing tried to defend the call, stating he had a verbal agreement with Jim Tice, who said the wagon could run. Rules being rules, the word of the official stood, and Nicholson was tossed. In response, Ford representatives pulled the factory-supported cars from competition.

Wheeling Bill Casler's F-6 D/S, 348-ci-engine-equipped 1959 Chevy to Middle Stock honors was employee Wiley Cossey. The wily one's winning time was 13.74 at 100.11 mph. (Photo Courtesy J.R. Bloom)

So, outside of a few Chevys owned by Dick Harrell and Ron Campbell, it became an all-Dodge/Plymouth show, with Hayden Proffitt winning both S/SA class and Mr. Stock Eliminator in his Yeakel Plymouth. Proffitt entered the event with three cars, so how could he lose, right? Well, he did lose one to Dave Strickler, and it was the Top Stock final. Tommy Grove and his *Melrose Missile* set low ET and top speed of the meet with an 11.76 at 123.40 mph.

Other Action

Thirteen cars showed for Junior Fuel, and when all was said and done, honors went home with the team of McClain & McDowell. The team's Dragmaster *Grey Ghost* D/FD recorded a weekend-best ET of 8.99. Middle Eliminator belonged to the flathead-powered car of Dave Hasty, which recorded ETs of 9.90 all day long. He followed his Winter Nationals win by taking the top honor at the Summer Nationals. John Loper's Chevy-powered A/Gas Anglia soloed for Little Eliminator and set class marks in the process with a 10.35 ET at 134.53 mph. The Herrera family and its B/Gas Willys took Street honors with an 11.55 ET at 123.54 mph for a new track record.

The Summer Nationals

With the popularity of drag racing exploding, the AHRA expanded its schedule in 1964 by adding the Summer Nationals. This was after the Summer Championship Drags, which were held in 1963 at Aquasco in Maryland. Red Lang was one of the sport's big winners in 1963. He

Dave Hasty's F *(as in flathead) Fuel Dragster won Middle Eliminator honors over the broken straight-6 rail of Potillo & Roemer. Hasty hung it out with a 9.90 ET at 134.43 mph. (Photo Courtesy J.R. Bloom)*

Montebello, California–based John Herrera and his sons (Manuel, Richard, and Phillip) had a 1940 Willys that was a record holder and class winner through the early part of the decade. (Photo Courtesy J.R. Bloom)

With surprise, relative unknown Chuck Helper of Champaign, Illinois, found himself in Top Eliminator at the 1964 Summer Nationals. In this 1965 photo, he battles surfer Mike Sorokin. (Photo Courtesy wdifl.com)

defeated favored Bob Sullivan's *Pandemonium* in the Top Fuel Final before beating Joe Jacono to win Top Eliminator.

Jacono in his home-built rail won Top Gas by defeating John Fetty. Dick Lawrence in the Sites brothers–sponsored Plymouth took Top Stock by defeating the Ace Wilson Royal Pontiac.

The 1964 Summer Nationals were at US-30 Drag Strip in Gary, Indiana, from June 12 to14. The strip hosted the summer meet through 1966. In 1967, the AHRA shuffled its events and eliminated the summer meet when it moved the Nationals to August. The Summer Nationals name returned in 1970, but the race never found a secure home, as it bounced from Long Island, New York; West Salem, Ohio; Detroit, Michigan; San Antonio, Texas; and Kansas City, Missouri.

The 1964 Summer Nationals was marred by tragedy when Howard Wysong, driving Lee Pendleton's *Spitfire II* Allison-engine dragster, was killed when he veered off the track at approximately 170 mph.

1964 Class Winners

Winners included Pusch & Crews in their Rod Stuckey, Chevy-powered B/FD, taking Top Eliminator honors with a 9.14 ET. Top speed went to the B/FD of Gorns-Lutz-Tomazak, which recorded 195.65 mph. Top Gas was won by Hirata & Hobbs, who came from behind to defeat Dick Vest—or so everyone thought. On the track, the win light went to Vest, while in the tower, it was given to Hirata & Hobbs. Apparently, an eyewitness gave it to Vest, who himself swore he was out front but was passed between the two lines.

Junior Eliminator was taken by Gabby Bleeker, a man who was heard from plenty as the decade progressed. Bleeker and his blown Oldsmobile Bantam faced Harry Nordquist, but a false start required them to return to the starting line. Bleeker won the second go-round while Nordquist blew his engine going through the traps.

Dave Hasty proved that there was still life in the old flathead when he took Middle Eliminator with his injected F/FD. Mr. Stock Eliminator went to Len Richter in a Bob Ford–sponsored 427 Fairlane. Richter caught Jim Thornton in the Ramchargers Dodge napping on the line to take the win. Thornton returned to win Top Stock with

At the Summer Nationals in June, Pusch & Crews made up for their shortcoming at the Winter Nationals by winning Top Eliminator. The team turned to Funny Car in the coming decade. (Photo Courtesy J.R. Bloom)

Celebrating Independence Day was always a big deal for those in the AHRA. This beautiful fireworks display was captured during a break in action in 1964. (Photo Courtesy J.R. Bloom)

The weekend had its share of incidents. Val Laporte, driving Malone's number-two car, was supposed to meet Malone in the Top Eliminator runoffs, but he did serious damage when he crashed the car during the push

Bob Langley had to make 11 runs in total to win Top Fuel and Top Eliminator at the Nationals. He had the top speed of the meet at 197.36 mph.

an 11.08 ET at 128.57 mph. Running Chrysler's new Hemi, the Ramchargers Dodge recorded the weekend's top speed for Stockers with an eye-popping 132.10 mph.

1964 World Finals Recap

Bob Langley, who was a staple in Texas drag racing, showed them all the way home at the World Finals in Green Valley. He defeated J.L. Payne in class and then defeated the previous year's Nationals winner, Art Malone, in Top Eliminator. Langley and his *Scorpion V* also recorded the top speed of the meet at 197.36 mph. Against Malone, he ran a 7.84 ET at 195.22 mph to a 7.90 at 194.80.

Langley survived a parachute failure during eliminations, where he drove into the catch net on a run against Marvin Schwartz. A bent wheel and other minor damage was done to the car, but Langley repaired it with parts loaned to him by fellow competitor Al Waits. The chassis of the *Scorpion* was a unique Garlits/Connie Swingle design, which was one of four that was built specifically to allow more flex. Langley made 14 runs over the weekend, and he did not have to tear down the engine once.

Not all accidents happened on the strip. Art Malone saw some serious damage done to his number-two car when the throttle stuck on driver Val Laporte. (Photo Courtesy J.R. Bloom)

start. Laporte's throttle stuck in the open position when he tried to pull away from the push truck. The car came to a stop after it crashed into a telephone pole, which it sheared in half. Malone (in his number-one car) sat on the starting line and watched the incident unfold. It proved to be an expensive weekend for Malone, as he burnt through two engines as well.

A second incident was a freak accident, as Ronnie Swan crashed the fuel car of Jim Gillespie. In doing so, he broke his neck. It wasn't realized immediately, so it took a few hours of him wandering in a daze before he was rushed to a hospital.

Other Action

Top Gas was won by whiz kid Carl Schiefer, who drove Bob Hamilton's car like an old pro to defeat Bill Mullins in the final. In a whirlwind of activity, Schiefer and Hamilton had just completed building the 470-ci car the day before the meet. The tireless Willis Ragsdale and his Chevy-powered Street Roadster earned Little Eliminator honors, soloing in the final with an 11.60 ET. Willis had come a long way since 1958, when he first built his 1927 Model T.

Stockers Galore

Phil Bonner went back to Georgia as a happy man with Top Stock and Mr. Eliminator honors. His Ultra Stock 427-powered Falcon set the low ET (11.34) and marched through the Top Stock field to defeat a red-lighting Gene Snow in the final. Dick Harrell won Street Eliminator in his Z11 427-powered Chevelle. Rookie Bill "Mr. Bardahl" Hielscher and his *Lucky 7* G/S '57 Chevy won Middle Stock with a 14.34 ET, giving Mr. Bardahl the first national event win of his illustrious career.

Car owner Bob Hamilton along with driver Carl Schiefer spent seven days prior to the Championship Drags rebuilding the ex-Garlits team car. Their efforts paid off with a Top Gas win. (Photo Courtesy J.R. Bloom)

Willis Ragsdale did it all: built, maintained, and drove his B/Roadster. Records and class wins followed him and the Model T into the 1970s. (Photo Courtesy J.R. Bloom)

Phil Bonner and his Georgia Peach *Falcon had the reputation of being one of the toughest match-race cars. Mid-11-second ETs ensured that the success carried over into Ultra Stock at Green Valley's World Championship Drags. (Photo Courtesy J.R. Bloom)*

Grady Bryant in his Dick Harrell–prepared 1964 Impala went home with F-5 (4-barrel, solid cam) E/S class honors at the World Championships. Bryant squeezed a 14.02 ET at 98.98 mph out of the 327 engine for the win. (Photo Courtesy J.R. Bloom)

Lee Smith in the Nate Learners–sponsored Hemi Hauler 1 *won the Ultra Stock Automatic class by defeating Bill Golden. Smith and his Plymouth won the World Series at Cordova the week before. (Photo Courtesy J.R. Bloom)*

Gene Snow drew the dreaded red light in the Mr. Stock Eliminator final against Phil Bonner. L.G. Melton was Snow's partner in their successful used car business. (Photo Courtesy J.R. Bloom)

1965: Fit to Be News

Entering 1965, many things were happening within the AHRA, and the news was brought to the masses in the new AHRA tabloid *Drag World*. It was reported that the Grand American points circuit would kick off in 1965, and its first race would be in Phoenix, Arizona, from February 25 to 27.

In total, there were nine circuit meets (including the five national events) that culminated with the World Championship. Each Grand American event was a double-points meet, tying in with the World Championship at Lions Drag Strip, which was a triple-points event. The circuit was run "Pro-Amateur" for both hot cars and Stock cars. Contestants received five points for entry, five points for a class win, and five points for an eliminator win.

In the hot car section, those eligible for "Pro" status were AA/FD through B/FD, AA/GD, and A/GD. "Amateur" was comprised of Competition Eliminator on down. In Stock, Pros were considered Factory Production through Unlimited Stock. Amateurs competed in Top Stock on down and raced for merchandise only.

Legendary actor Steve McQueen looks through issue No. 1 of Drag World. *The "drag rag" was the brainchild of Mike Doherty, who sold the idea to huckster Brainard Mellinger in 1965. A year later, Gil Kohn became the second owner of the flailing paper, followed by Jim Tice, who turned it into the AHRA house organ. (Photo Courtesy Ruth Tice)*

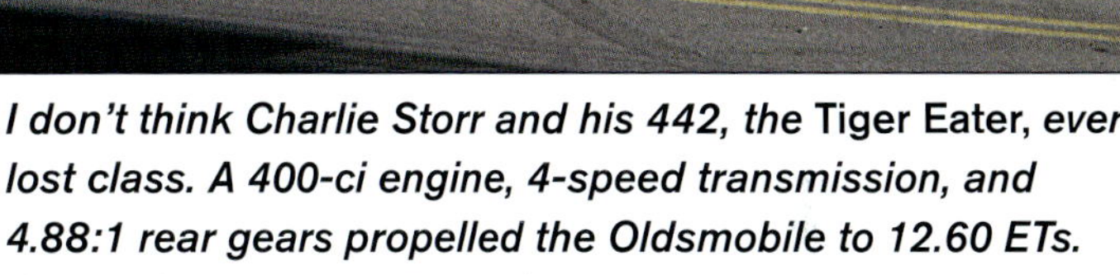

I don't think Charlie Storr and his 442, the Tiger Eater, *ever lost class. A 400-ci engine, 4-speed transmission, and 4.88:1 rear gears propelled the Oldsmobile to 12.60 ETs. (Photo Courtesy J.R. Bloom)*

Other changes in 1965 included dividing Top Eliminator. The Top Gas cars no longer had to battle the Fuelers. Beginning with the Winter Nationals, each had its own Eliminator program. The Summer Nationals had the name "Junior Fuel" dropped in favor of the title "Competition Eliminator," and later in the season, a Super Stock Eliminator was added to major events.

1965 Winter Nationals Recap

At the 1965 Winter Nationals at Bee Line Dragway, it was reported that 55,000 fans attended and 1,100 racers participated. The significance of this race was that it was AHRA's first all-200-mph Top Fuel field.

Top Fuel

This was the debut of Connie Kalitta's new Logghe-chassis car, which was powered by the equally new SOHC 427-inch Ford. NASCAR had rejected Ford's overhead-cam engine as being too exotic, which worked out well for the Ford-Mercury drag racers.

Several Cammer-equipped Top Fuel and Ultra Stock Funny Cars gave the Chrysler Hemi racer fits over the next five years. Kalitta used his Cammer to produce Bee Line Dragway's first 200-mph run of the day when he recorded a 200.48 mph. Prudhomme, in his Hemi car, blistered the track with a 203.16-mph run in 7.46 seconds to top Kalitta. Chris Karamesines and his *Chizler* grabbed low ET and a world record when he clocked a 7.42.

Eliminations were not good for Kalitta, Prudhomme, or Karamesines, as they disappeared early. At the end of the day, the last two standing were the team of Turk-Cox-Wamsley and Tom Hoover. Hoover got the jump on Dean Turk and maintained it. Turk was running with no water in his Hemi due to a cracked cylinder and managed a 7.79 ET to Hoover's 7.75. Both cars ran identical speeds of 194.38 mph. The final wasn't without its controversy because many felt that Hoover had drawn a red light but it didn't register.

Tom Hoover took home Top Eliminator honors after defeating Dean Turk in the final. Part of Hoover's booty was a new Mustang fastback. (Photo Courtesy J.R. Bloom)

At the 1965 Winter Nationals, Connie Kalitta qualified his new Cammer Logghe-chassis rail with an off-the-trailer 7.67 ET at 200.08 mph. Kalitta's weekend finished early after his Cammer threw a rod. (Photo Courtesy J.R. Bloom)

Bill Boat in the Boat Brothers B/Hot Roadster relied upon an injected Chevy and a Ford-O-Matic transmission to rack up the wins. Boat won Middle Eliminator at the Winter Nationals by defeating Don Ringer with a 10.16 ET. (Photo Courtesy J.R. Bloom)

Other Action

In other action, Gordon Collett (in a rare AHRA appearance) won Top Gas by defeating the team of Hirata & Claude. Junior Fuel went to John Garrett, whose D/FD defeated the A/HR of Dave Beebe with a 9.18 ET at 169.17 mph.

Middle Eliminator went to the Boat brothers, Bill and John, and their injected Chevy-powered B/HR. Little Eliminator was won by the Willys of K.S. Pittman, who defeated the previous year's winner, John Loper.

Manuel Herrera repeated his 1964 Street win when he drove the Doug's Headers–sponsored Anglia to victory

Dick Harrell in his new Retribution II *Chevy II ran against Mac Medley in the Harrell-prepped Chevelle. Both cars were 427 powered. Harrell won this one on his way to the Street final. (Photo Courtesy J.R. Bloom)*

over Dick Harrell's B/FX Chevy II. Herrera ran a 10.96 ET at 126.40 mph to Harrell's 11.08 ET at 120.00 mph.

Funny Car action was covered in Chapter 3, so here are additional door-car results. Ed Terry and his Mustang went home with Middle Stock honors, Dick Clark's Falcon took Little Stock, and Arnie "the Farmer" Beswick went back to his Illinois farm with Sportsman honors.

Arnie Beswick won the Sportsman category at the Winter Nationals with his 421-ci Tempest by running 11-teen ETs. The wheelbase was later altered, and the famous tiger stripes were added. (Photo Courtesy J.R. Bloom)

Lions Drag Strip Goes AHRA

Lions Drag Strip opened in October 1955 and hosted NHRA-sanctioned events through 1964 with Mickey Thompson as the track operator. In 1965, C.J. Hart, the gentleman recognized as having opened the nation's first drag strip at Santa Ana in 1950, was handed the reins.

In the late spring of 1965, Bernie Partridge, the NHRA's official announcer, called on behalf of the sanctioning body. He said that Wally Parks was asking Hart to shut down for the weekend of the *Hot Rod* magazine meet in June. When Hart refused to do so, Partridge hinted that if he didn't, the track would no longer host NHRA-sanctioned events. Hart was not one to push around. As soon as he got off the phone with Partridge, he called Jim Tice and took up with the AHRA.

Lions remained with the AHRA through June 1971. At that time, Steve Evans took over as track manager and returned the track to NHRA sanction. A statement released at the time noted: "It was the opinion of the Harbor Area Board of Directors that the sanction change was necessary for improvement in insurance coverage and sanctioning organization coverage."

The last race at the famed Lions Drag Strip was in December 1972.

Tom Sturm was a firm believer in the "Drive the Highways – Race at Lions" motto. His injected 427-powered Just 4 Chevy Lovers *Chevelle was a regular at the Long Beach track. (Photo Courtesy Don Prieto)*

1965 World Championship Drags Split

Feeling that it needed a national event in the hotbed of Southern California, the AHRA moved its world finals from Green Valley to Lions Drag Strip in 1965. In an unprecedented move, it divided the meet and ran it over the course of two weekends. The Stockers ran the first weekend (August 28), while the hot cars were to run the next weekend.

Mother Nature had her own ideas, and rain cut the second weekend short. This forced the elimination rounds of Top Fuel, Top Gas, Competition Eliminator, Street Eliminator, Middle Eliminator, and Little Eliminator to be run on the third weekend. The date was set for one day of racing: Saturday, September 11. This meant that all racing had to be completed by Lions Drag Strip's 10:45 p.m. curfew, and they made it under the wire with minutes to spare.

Overall, there were no complaints regarding the three weeks that it took to run the race. In fact, many considered it to be the best world final race they had ever attended. Throughout the meet, class records were set and reset a phenomenal 165 times on the resurfaced Lions strip. Many praised Tice and Hart for the smooth operation, quick flow, and hospitality shown. In what would become a regular occurrence at all AHRA major events, a press party took place. Food and beverages were on the house to all members of the press and VIPs in attendance.

Top Eliminator

In the Top Fuel finals on September 11, Southern California's Paul Sutherland in the (Jimmy) Brissette & Sutherland fueler took the crown. With the caliber of cars in attendance, it was no easy feat. Sutherland defeated John Martin in the first round. In the second round, Sutherland defeated Zane Shubert after the Shubert Chevy failed to fire. In the third, Bob Brooks in his Reath-sponsored car was next to fall before Sutherland used an 8.01 ET to drop John Mitchell in the Gall & Trotter rail.

Out of northern California came Paul Sutherland, who confirmed his worth as a driver at the World Championship Drags. A proven chassis builder as well, he moved south to go to work for the famed Woody Gilmore. (Photo Courtesy J.R. Bloom)

The caliber of Competition Coupes, Sedans, and Modified Roadsters in the mid-1960s was astounding. This Gang Green B/Coupe was campaigned by Marty Ikkanda and was originally built for Mike Sorokin, who drove for the Top Fuel team called the Surfers. Ikkanda ran the injected Chevy-powered Fiat to record 10.60 ETs in 1965. (Photo Courtesy J.R. Bloom)

Chet Herbert and Zane Shubert's last venture together was this 402-ci (stretched 283) Chevy-powered rail in 1965.* The Chevy *regularly had its way with the Hemis and was one of the first Chevys to break 200 mph. (Photo Courtesy Forrest Bond)

The final was anticlimactic, as opponent Tom Dyer damaged his Hemi in the semifinals while defeating Kenny Safford's B&M Tork Master with a 7.96 ET at 201.78 mph and was running on seven cylinders. Dyer lost fire on the green and Sutherland soloed.

Brissette & Sutherland were really cooking through the latter half of 1965. A month after the finals, wrench man John Yeats had the old Hemi blasting the clocks at 219 mph.

Stockers to the Lanes

It was a great weekend for the Fords, as Dick Brannan and his altered-wheelbase Mustang won Mr. Stock Eliminator, overcoming the 30-foot handicap of Gas Ronda to take the win with a 10.08 ET. Ronda won Super Stock eliminator by defeating Paul Norris in a final that had to be run twice.

Bill Rieck and his *Quarter Bender* Plymouth had actually been Ronda's opponent in the final, and Rieck defeated him. There was just one problem, though: Rieck's Hemi measured 472 ci. AHRA rules stated a maximum of 430 for the Stockers. It was an apparent oversight on the part of Rieck and tech inspection, as he had listed the displacement on his entry form. Rieck was tossed, and the final was run again with Norris, whose SOHC Mustang had lost to Rieck in the semifinals. Ronda took the win with a 10.45 ET at 134.73 mph.

The Sportsman category was made up of the cars of Hot Rod and Modified Production. These cars had no cubic-inch limit but were required to run carburation and gasoline. Darrell Droke and his SOHC-powered 1965 Fairlane Thunderbolt drove through a 21-car field to earn the category win by defeating the 1937 panel truck of Les Rose with an 11.41 ET.

Middle Stock 1 honors went to the Arizona-based F-5 G/SO 1965 Falcon of Del Blades. Blades, known for his line of strong-running Chevys, jumped at the chance to run the 289-ci Falcon when Paradise Ford of Arizona offered him a deal that he couldn't refuse. Dick Clark in his own 1965 Falcon took Middle Stock 2. Little Stock belonged to the 1963 Ranchero of Harry Luge.

The Stark Hickey–sponsored Ultra Stock Cammer Mustang was driven by Dick Brannan, the coordinator of Ford drag racing. The bronco, with its wheels-up launches, sure put the fear into its competitors. (Photo Courtesy J.R. Bloom)

This is the second A/FX Mustang that Gas Ronda ran in 1965. He crashed the first one during a match at Lions Drag Strip in May when an axle broke. Ronda used this Les Ritchey–prepped Mustang to win Super Stock at the World Championship Drags in September with a 10.45 ET. (Photo Courtesy Richard Nicholson)

Ford's lone Thunderbolt built for 1965 was campaigned by Darrell Droke. The Thunderbolt was powered by a hi-rise 427 and then a SOHC 427. (Photo Courtesy J.R. Bloom)

After a runner-up finish in Little Stock at the Winter Nationals, Harry Luge hauled his 1963 Ranchero to the World Championship Drags and won it all with a 13.65 ET. Luge ran F-6 with a 2-barrel or F-7 with a 4-barrel on top of the punched-out 260. (Photo Courtesy J.R. Bloom)

Fred Lear smiles after earning Top Gas honors at the Lions World Championship Drags in 1965. Lear defeated Mike Snively, who drew a red light in the Beacon Automotive rail. (Photo Courtesy J.R. Bloom)

Other Action

In Top Gas, Mike Snively in the Beacon Auto Parts dragster ran a record low ET of 8.20. He fought his way to the final round, where he faced underdog Fred Lear. It should have been an easy win for Snively, but it wasn't to be. Snively, running on seven cylinders, tried to cut the light and drew a red. This was Lear's one and only national-event victory.

The 389-ci injected Chevy-powered A/Altered Fiat of Mondello & Matsubara took the Middle Eliminator over the Montrelli-Galli-Modin (MGM) Willys pickup driven by Gene Ciambella. The Willys suffered a blown slick at half-track, allowing the Fiat to take the win with a 9.88 ET at 148.02 mph.

A healthy small-block and a B&M Hydro got it done for Al Hamberis and Mike Mitchell. Mitchell drove the 1933 Willys until moving into Funny Car in 1969 and becoming the "World's Fastest Hippie." (Photo Courtesy Forrest Bond)

In the Street Eliminator final, the A/Gas Anglia of Herrera & Sons defeated Grier & Barber. Little Eliminator went to Mike Mitchell in the 364-ci Chevy-powered Hamberis & Mitchell C/GS Willys. Mitchell defeated a red-lighting Johnny Loper. Competition Eliminator, open to Coupes and Roadsters, went to Howard Marjama in his B/Modified Roadster.

1966 Winter Nationals: Not Smooth Sailing

By early 1966, the AHRA sanctioned the only two tracks in Arizona and every track in Kansas. It had California covered, which must have eaten at Wally Parks. When Irwindale Raceway opened in October 1965, it was under AHRA sanction.

Jim Tice just couldn't resist moving his Winter Nationals from Bee Line Dragway to Irwindale, which was 10 miles down the road from Pomona, home of the NHRA Winternationals. The race was set for February 11–13 (a week before the NHRA Winternationals). Although Parks and Tice had a decent relationship with little animosity, the location and date of the race no doubt bumped up Parks's blood pressure a notch.

The NHRA Winternationals and the AHRA Winter Nationals being within a week of one another did confuse things. The NHRA went to the extent of placing an

Tickled Pink

When musicians Jan & Dean sang that "the Drag City races are the fastest in the nation," they were singing about Mickey Thompson's AHRA-sanctioned track in Fontana. Drag City, as it would be named, joined the AHRA fold in 1962 and hosted that season's Winter Championship Drags. The track became a regular stop for the nation's fastest fuel cars.

On November 8 and 9, 1965, 52 of the finest racers were welcomed to the first Mickey Thompson 200-mph invitational race. It's amazing how quick the sport was moving (pun intended). Just a year before, the number of cars capable of running 200 mph could be counted on one hand.

During the two-day event, Connie Swingle in Ed Pink's *Old Master* took the final-round win on Saturday against a red-lighting Don Garlits with a 7.80 ET at 207.84 mph. On Sunday, Mike Sorokin of the Surfers took honors over 1965 points-champion Paul Sutherland with a 7.67 ET to collect the $2,500 payout.

During the Mickey Thompson 200-mph invitational race in 1965, Connie Swingle (in Ed Pink's* Old Master*) defeated Don Garlits. (Photo Courtesy Forrest Bond)

Howard Marjama left the cold winter of Minneapolis, Minnesota, behind to come west and win Comp at the 1966 Winter Nationals. His B/Modified Roadster ran a 9.14 ET at 170.77 mph to defeat Ken Hotard. (Photo Courtesy Stephen Justice)

advertisement in the trade papers, stating that there was only one Winternationals, in spite of the imitators.

A Turn for the Worse

Friday's Top Fuel qualifying session took a tragic turn when Allen "Lefty" Mudersbach died while attempting to qualify the dragster of Dick Goss. As he approached the Irwindale finish line at approximately 180 mph, the dragster blew its left slick after running over an errant screwdriver. Trying to bring the car under control, Mudersbach popped the chute, but it tore lose. The car rolled numerous times as it headed off the right side of the track and over an embankment, where it came to rest. Mudersbach was pronounced dead on arrival at Santa Teresita Hospital in Duarte.

Lefty Mudersbach, shown in this photo from 1960, left his mark on the sport. Mudersbach was racing back in the 1940s, before the sport became organized. He's remembered as a driver, chassis builder, and speed-shop owner. (Photo Courtesy J.R. Bloom)

Mudersbach's list of accomplishments was long. In 1957, he was the NHRA national champion while campaigning an Oldsmobile-powered A/GD. The same year, he ran Gas Dragsters's first sub-10-second ET. In 1959, he teamed with Chet Herbert. The pair ran a twin Chevy Gas Dragster, setting a record of 195 mph at 8.53 seconds. In 1961, Mudersbach and Herbert won Bakersfield before going their separate ways in 1963.

Wanting for More

Compounding the tragedy of Friday was the fact that the race just didn't go very well. Track conditions, prep, and the chaos of a first-time national event (that should have surprised no one) really put the damper on the race. This was an ongoing issue with the AHRA, according to Steve Gibb, who himself was a part of the AHRA organization before joining the NHRA.

"The AHRA events were always a little rougher around the edges than the NHRA," Gibb said. "They didn't have the team or manpower, so events didn't always go off as smoothly."

It was a rare occurrence when the Greek, Chris Karamesines, was on the outside looking in. He failed to qualify his **Chizler** *at the Winter Nationals. (Photo Courtesy Stephen Justice)*

Top Fuel

Poor track conditions didn't help the Top Fuel and Top Gas cars at all, as they struggled all weekend to find traction. The bite was so bad that teams that would otherwise have been shoo-ins, failed to make the 32-car field. For example, both the Ramchargers and Chris Karamesines were alternates, failing to make the field.

"Sneaky" Pete Robinson qualified his SOHC Ford-powered Fueler number-one with a low ET of the meet: 7.58 at 184.42 mph. However, his weekend came to an end early when his Ford failed to fire in the second round against Frank Hedge's *A&W Root Beer Special*. Hedge and his driver Bob Downey were handed a win in the third when Prudhomme broke on the line. Their own weekend came to an end in the semifinals, when they fell to eventual-winner Bob Hightower.

Frank "Rootbeer" Hedge was a tough competitor around the Southern California tracks. Hedge received A&W support by way of his dad, who was the chief executive officer (CEO) with the company. (Photo Courtesy Stephen Justice)

Bob Hightower drove Dale Smart's Vandal *through a 32-car Top Fuel field to reach the final. He soloed for the win when opponent John Mulligan crashed while warming up. (Photo Courtesy Stephen Justice)*

In the other semifinal bout, Tom McEwen faced the John Mulligan–driven car of Adams & Wayre. It wasn't much of a race, as both cars broke on the run. Approximately 300 feet out, McEwen's throttle broke, leaving him coasting toward the finish line. Mulligan got crossed up coming off the line and then blew the engine when he got back on the throttle. With both cars coasting, it was Mulligan who crossed the finish line first with an 11.73 ET.

The final featured Mulligan and Hightower. There was a slight problem, though. Mulligan had no engine. Jimmy Nix stepped in and lent the engine out of his sidelined car to Mulligan. The thrash was on, and 45 minutes later, they were ready to go.

However, Mulligan wanted to warm the car up, so he went down the return road. Mulligan made a short blip on the throttle, which inadvertently ended his day. The car flipped, and the damage done couldn't be fixed at the track. Hightower soloed in the two-week-old Dale Smart car for the pair's one and only national event victory.

Other Action

Unlike the Top Fuel and Top Gas cars, the Funny Cars on down to the low-end Stockers found the traction to be ideal. In Stock, Ford led the way with Les Ritchey's Performance Associates' Mustang turning a 10.44 ET to win Super Stock Eliminator over the Mustang of Tommy Grove.

Dick Brannan won Unlimited Stock with his nitro-burning, injected *Bronco* Mustang with a 9.21 ET at 149.50 mph. Mr. Stock Eliminator was won by Darrell Droke and his 1965 Thunderbolt Fairlane, which defeated a red-lighting Shirley Shahan with a 10.64 ET at a slowing 109.81 mph.

Bill Lawton, in the Tasca Ford Mustang, won Gas Stock over Gas Ronda. Breaking Ford's sweep was the Chevelle of Geno Redd, which took Top Stock honors, and the Chevy II of "Big" Mike Burkhart, which earned

Tasca Ford's Mystery 9 *was the first longnose Mustang built by Holman-Moody. It was constructed using a body in white, as opposed to the remainder of Mustangs, which used fiberglass bodies. The* Mystery 9 *eventually ran 8-second times. (Photo Courtesy Michael Pottie)*

Before the Funny Cars, big Mike Burkhart was killing them with this sedate-looking Chevy II. Times in the 12.20s won Mike the Hot Rod category at the 1966 Winter Nationals. (Photo Courtesy Stephen Justice)

Hot Rod honors. In Street Eliminator, it was the team of Greer & Barber with its C/Gas Willys coming out on top.

Supercharged Gas produced great rivalries and some of the decade's most exciting quarter-mile action. Although the bleachers aren't packed on this side of the track during this battle between the Anglias of the Kohler brothers and Shores & Hess, note that not one spectator is seated. (Photo Courtesy J.R. Bloom)

So Long, Irwindale

As far as Harry Snyder (part owner of Irwindale Raceway and founder of In-N-Out Burger) was concerned, the race was a disaster. A week after the meet, the decision was made to cut ties with the AHRA. In 1967, the Winter Nationals returned to Bee Line Dragway, where it remained through 1975.

1966 Points Finale Wrap Up

The AHRA wrapped up its most successful season yet with the running of the World Points Finale. After the World Finals at Lions Drag Strip in August, action headed back to Green Valley, Texas, for the finale on Labor Day weekend. Considering that the event shared the weekend with the NHRA Nationals (the largest drag racing event of any sanctioning body), the turnout of spectators and participants surpassed expectations.

Top Fuel

The 1966 season had a diverse field of winners in Top Fuel. One notable standout was Cliff Zink, who became one of the sport's more versatile racers. His first national-event win was in April at the Grand American race in Rockford, Illinois, where he defeated Tom Hoover. A runner-up finish to Prudhomme at Union Grove in May followed.

Prudhomme himself was finding things a little tougher in 1966 after giving up the seat of Roland Leong's *Hawaiian* for the B&M Tork Master AA/FD. Prudhomme accepted an offer that he couldn't refuse from B&M's Don Spar, which gave him full rein to his own program. Prudhomme was realizing how tough it was out on his own, but he did alright by anyone's standards. Relying upon a Dave Zeuschel hemi for power, Prudhomme picked up additional wins at the United Drag Racer's Association (UDRA) Springnationals and Cordova's World Series of Drag Racing.

After winning the Spring Championship Drags in 1965, Art "the Dart" Malone returned to Pacific,

By 1966, it seemed that Art Malone had done it all, from Indy to ovals and the quarter mile. The 1966 season was a good one for Malone. (Photo Courtesy Scott Kruger)

Missouri, to win again in 1966. Malone ran eighth-mile mid-5-second times and defeated Wayne Stumpf in the final. Compare that with today's 1,000 foot times in the 3.70s. At the preceding Summer Nationals (the race was June 10–12 in Gary, Indiana, whereas the Springnationals were June 17–19), Malone lost in the final to Garlits.

At the points finale, Chris Karamesines, who had been absent from the winner's circle in recent memory but could never be counted out, took the victory over Paul Pritchett in the Pritchett and LaDue fueler with a 7.49 ET at 203.60 mph. With 75 cars showing up in hopes of making the 32-car field, the Greek's overdue win was earned.

Rudolph Chevrolet in Phoenix, Arizona, was a strong proponent of organized drag racing and sponsored numerous cars through the decade. One team that saw continuous support and success was that of John Linn and Don Comey. (Photo Courtesy J.R. Bloom)

Other Action

Eighteen-year-old Billy "the Kid" Scott, driving the Beacon Auto Parts Gas Dragster for Gene Adams and John Rasmussen, was the big winner in Top Gas at the Points Finale. Scott defeated Bill Mullins in the final with a convincing 8.18 ET to an 8.60. Scott had a great year, having previously won the season's Winter Nationals and the World Championship at Lions Drag Strip.

Don Sappington and partner Frank Sanders had a great season, winning Top Stock at the Lions Grand American season opener in 1966 and Formula Stock at Union Grove in June. S&S Headers disappeared in 1968 after being bought up by Jardine Headers. (Photo Courtesy J.R. Bloom)

The Chevy II of Don Sappington and his partner, Frank Sanders (S&S Headers) won Mr. Stock honors with mid-11 times but fell to the Plymouth of Butch Leal in the FX Gas final. Leal previously won the Grand American race at Fremont in April. Sappington and Sanders, who rarely lost with their injected 327-ci Chevy, previously won Formula Stock at Union Grove's Grand American race in June, Top Stock at Bee Line Dragway to start the year, and were runners-up at the Summer Nationals to Bill Hielscher.

Hielscher, like Sappington and Sanders, racked up the wins. He went through the 1966 season by winning class in at least one category at each national event. At the points finale, he performed the seemingly impossible by winning two categories. In the Street Eliminator final, he defeated Snyder & Lancaster, and in Top Stock, he defeated Del Blades.

Another team that saw the winner's circle more often than not was that of Don Comey and John Linn. The pair joined forces in the early 1960s and campaigned a string of Rudolph Chevrolet–sponsored Chevy Corvairs. Comey drove the team's current Corvair (an F-9 E/Stocker) to Little Stock honors at the points finale and previously took wins at the Spring Nationals and the World Championships. The 2-barrel-equipped pancake six produced mid-14s at 93 mph, keeping the guys in good standing with the Cactus Corvair Club of Phoenix.

Old Race Cars Never Die (Sort of)

Old race cars never die . . . well, sort of. The old saying holds true, as drag cars are continuously being recycled and restored. One car that saw more than one incarnation was the highly successful *Speed Sport II* of Lyle Fisher and Red Greth.

Greth retired the *Speed Sport II* in early 1963 and moved into Top Fuel before debuting his Corvair in October 1966. Hiding under the Fiberglass Trends body was the chassis and 392 Hemi of *Speed Sport II*.

Sadly, this Corvair had a short lifespan, crashing at Bee Line Dragway on its second pass. According to driver Ray Maurel, it ran over 180 mph on its first run, and although it lost its windshield, the run was smooth as silk. On its second pass, the car became airborne on the top end and was destroyed upon landing. It's said that the car's remains were carried home in 5-pound buckets.

The chassis under Red Greth's Corvair saw a lot of quarter-mile trips as the* Speed Sport II. *Under the Corvair, it made just one full pass. (Photo Courtesy J.R. Bloom)

1967: Making a Beeline Back to Bee Line Dragway

It was back to Bee Line Dragway for the 1967 Winter Nationals, where a reported 40,000 spectators turned out to welcome its return. One publication stated that racers completed close to 1,400 entry forms. Although, this number was most likely slightly exaggerated because it was probably the number released by the AHRA's own public relations department and taken at face value by the publication. Depending on the source, anywhere from 60 to 100 of those entered were Top Fuel cars. So, this was quite likely one of the finest turnouts that Bee Line Dragway had seen.

Rising star Leroy Goldstein is in the Crower & Blair Top Fueler. After a semifinal finish at the Winter Nationals, Goldstein went on to win the Spring Nationals at Odessa, defeating a red-lighting Dave Beebe in the final. (Photo Courtesy Forrest Bond)

Top Fuel

Connie Kalitta had a great weekend. He qualified his new Cammer-powered *Bounty Hunter* number-one with a 7.46 and then proceeded to move through the 32-car field. He defeated Powers & Riley in the first round and then beat Karamesines in the second round with low ET of the meet (7.44). Leroy Goldstein, driving for Crower & Blair, was the next to fall to Kalitta before Kalitta defeated the Adams-Wayre-Mulligan car in an oh-so-close semifinal with a 7.61 ET to a 7.62.

In the final, Kalitta faced Bob Downey in the *Howard Cam Special*. Downey had a great weekend going, defeating the car of

At the winter meet, the closest race of the weekend was between Connie Kalitta and John Mulligan in the Adams-Wayre rail. Connie Kalitta took the win with a 7.61 ET to a 7.62. (Photo Courtesy J.R. Bloom)

Ewell-Bell-Allison, then Ron Rivero in the *Frantic Fueler*, and a red-lighting Don Cook in the *Grecian* before facing Kalitta.

Kalitta sent Downey home when he recorded a 7.63 ET at 196.00 mph to Downey's losing 8.05 ET at 196.50 mph. This was Kalitta's first big win since Bakersfield in 1964. In 1966, Kalitta was named Detroit Dragway's Man of the Year after surviving a high-speed wreck late in the season. While recouping from his injuries, his new Logghe car was built. Kalitta did the boys at Ford Motor Company proud as he followed his 1967 AHRA Winter Nationals win by capturing Top Fuel at both the NHRA and NASCAR Winternationals.

In the Top Fuel final, Connie Kalitta took Bob Downey to the cleaners with a 7.63 ET to an 8.03. Kalitta had quick ET of the meet with a 7.46, while Leroy Goldstein held top speed at 205.46 mph. (Photo Courtesy J.R. Bloom)

Funny Car

The popularity of the Funny Car was growing by leaps and bounds, and the category soon overtook Top Fuel as the fan favorite. At the Winter Nationals, the Funny Cars were given two categories in which to compete: Unlimited and FX Fuel.

Unlimited included lightweight, blown, and injected cars, while the FX Fuel cars were reserved for injected cars weighing a minimum of 2,400 pounds. In the Unlimited Funny Car eight-car field, Dyno Don Nicholson and his *Eliminator I* Comet held the number-one qualifying spot and ran low ET with an 8.26.

In the 16-car FX Fuel field, Charlie Allen and his Dodge Dart went all the way, defeating Dave Strickler's ill-mannered Corvette, Dick Loher's Mustang, and Ted DeTar's Falcon. In the class final, Allen soloed with an 8.80 ET at 163.93 mph after his opponent, Gas Ronda, lost fire.

Nicholson finally won an AHRA event when his Comet defeated the similarly equipped Comet of Eddie Schartman. The march to the final round featured some great battles along the way. In the first, Schartman defeated the Tempest of Arnie Beswick, which was followed by wins over Roger Wolford's *Secret Weapon*

Don Sappington and Frank Sanders took a shot at Funny Car in 1967 with this 427-equipped Camaro. This early shot shows the car before the Candid Camaro name was applied. The Exhibition Engineering chassis provided a 118-inch wheelbase. (Photo Courtesy J.R. Bloom)

Charlie Allen had one of the nation's top-running Funny Cars in 1966. He began the year by winning FX Fuel at the Winter Nationals. His Hemi Dart ran 30-plus match races through the summer without a loss. (Photo Courtesy J.R. Bloom)

One of the few times that "Dyno" Don Nicholson and "Fast" Eddie Schartman came face to face was in the finals at the 1967 Winter Nationals. Nicholson prevailed. (Photo Courtesy J.R. Bloom)

Jeep. Nicholson put it to Jerry Bloom and the candy-coated Pontiac of Don Gay. In the final, Nicholson was out first and stayed there, defeating Schartman's 8.48 ET at 149.00 mph with his low ET of 8.26 and a speed of 171.75 mph.

Other Action

Top Gas was won by Jack McCleod, who soloed with an 8.34 ET at 181.44 mph after the chute on Tom Larkin's rail opened prior to staging. In Comp Eliminator, it was the *Blue Monday* rail, powered by a blown Pontiac Tempest 4-cylinder, taking it to the Carter brothers' C/GD.

The *Red Light Bandit* Corvette of Bill Bagshaw won Street Eliminator, and Hot Rod went to Joe Cunningham. In Little Eliminator, Jack Ditmar's wheel-standing 1934 Ford Altered used a handicap lead and a 10.79 ET to defeat John Loper. Although Loper and his 388-ci Chevy-powered Anglia held the A/Gas record with a 9.97 ET at 141.84 mph, his 10.36 on this run came up short.

In the newly introduced heads-up Super Stock Gas category, Gary Kimball in the Emig Automotive–sponsored big-block 1964 Chevelle defeated the Camaro of Bill Hielscher with a 11.58 ET at 120.16 mph. Top Stock belonged to the *Sweet Pea* 1964 Chevy II of Duane

Top Gas semifinal action saw Jack McLeod get out early on Sonny Diaz and stay there. McLeod, driving the McLeod-Whitamaker-Moore rail, soloed in the final round. (Photo Courtesy J.R. Bloom)

In this battle for Super Stock honors, Bill Hielscher lost early to the Chevelle of Larry and Gary Kimball. Gary took the win with a slower 11.58 ET to an 11.43. (Photo Courtesy J.R. Bloom)

Bill "Grumpy" Jenkins came to town with his potent little 327-powered Chevy II and went home with Middle Stock honors. The "F-5" on the window denotes a solid-lifter class with a displacement falling between 320 and 339 ci. The "O" is in reference to the wheelbase falling between 106 and 112.9 inches. (Photo Courtesy J.R. Bloom)

Jim Butler established himself as a tough competitor with his Rowdy Willy *Gasser before debuting this 289-powered Ranchero in 1964. The 1966 points championship–winning Ranchero was known for its wheels-up, low-11-second runs and its ability to win. Butler retired from drag racing after 1967, when a hereditary eye issue left him blind. (Photo Courtesy J.R. Bloom)*

Jacobson. Middle Stock was taken by Bill "Grumpy" Jenkins, and Little Stock went to the F/SP Corvair of Blade Swafford.

Detroit and New York Briefly Join the Fold

Ruth Tice described the AHRA growth during the mid-1960s as akin to having a tiger by the tail. Drag racing was growing exponentially, and the AHRA was sanctioning tracks left and right. In 1967, two major tracks that joined the fold were New York National Speedway and Detroit Dragway.

Both tracks were built and owned by Gil Kohn. Detroit, built in 1959 and initially sanctioned by the NHRA, held an annual AHRA Grand National event through 1970 before giving up its sanction. The track returned to the AHRA fold briefly for the 1975 and 1976 seasons.

The AHRA and NASCAR

The AHRA seemingly knew no bounds, as Jim Tice looked to expand its interests. In 1967, Tice set out to organize the nation's quarter-mile and half-mile oval tracks under the AHRA banner. The sanctioning body held interests in at least 25 oval tracks before Tice struck a hands-off deal with NASCAR's Bill France. NASCAR would stay out of drag racing if Tice would stay out of Stock Car.

New York left the AHRA fold in 1971. Between 1971 and 1975, Kohn and Ed Eaton, who managed New York, formed the United Hot Rod Association (UHRA) and sanctioned its own races.

Detroit Dragway

There's no doubt that Jim Tice considered an AHRA-sanctioned track in the backyard of Detroit's Big Three auto manufacturers as a major score. With visions of success dancing in his head, Tice's first race at Detroit was the Grand Nationals from May 21 to 23, 1967. There, Vern Anderson in the Anderson & Walton car won Top Fuel by defeating Bob Stewart in the Walton-Ross-Stewart Fueler with a 7.62. Top speed of the meet went to Chuck Kurzawa, who was driving for the Ramchargers.

Jim Tice and the AHRA were enjoying a new track in the Motor City and a fleet of new Plymouth support vehicles. Things were looking rosy for the AHRA in 1967, as it battled for sanctioning-body supremacy. (Photo Courtesy Ruth Tice)

Vern Anderson and Doug Walton from St. Paul, Minnesota, earned their only big series win at Detroit when they defeated Bob Stewart in the Top Fuel final. (Photo Courtesy Michael Pottie)

The double-dipping Ramchargers won Unlimited Funny Car when Jim Thornton drove the team's candy-striped 1967 Dart, which held low ET with an 8.47, to victory on all three days. He defeated a broken Doug Cook on the final day of events.

There were two other Funny Car classes run at the meet: A 2,400-pound fuel car class that was won by Ray Sullins, who was now driving the *Skootin' Cuda* in place of Doc Spence. The other class for 2,600-pound Gas Funny Cars was won by the Ron Brothers Mustang, which defeated Wayne Gapp in the final.

The Ramchargers Dart was wheeled by Jim Thornton. The car featured an acid-dipped body and a removable fiberglass roof. In what might possibly be a Funny Car first, the body was narrowed 6 inches. After swapping the injectors for a blower, the Dart grabbed the AHRA ET record with a 7.95. (Photo Courtesy Ken Rappaport)

Other Action

Other winners included Ron Colson in Top Gas, who drove the Nickey Chevrolet–sponsored *Stiletto* to victory over Mark Pieri. Bill Hielscher made the haul from Texas to win Street Eliminator, while Del Blades came all the way from Arizona to win Top Stock with his 283-powered *Rapier* Chevy II. Keeping some of the winning close to home was Michigan's own Neil "Pappy" Ellis, whose 427-equipped *Cheetah* took Comp honors.

The Nickey-sponsored Stiletto *of Ron Colson was a Top Gas terror. Colson had a good year going in 1967, winning both Detroit and the eighth-mile drags at St. Louis. He made the move into Top Fuel in 1968 and later into Funny Car, where he won the 1974 IHRA Funny Car championship driving the* Chi-Town Hustler. *(Photo Courtesy John Foster Jr.)*

After winning class pretty much everywhere, including the Winter Nationals, Del Blades hauled his potent Chevy II to Detroit and took home Top Stock honors. The "F-6" on the window denotes that his 283 engine has a 4-barrel carburetor and a hydraulic cam. (Photo Courtesy J.R. Bloom)

New York National Speedway

New York National Speedway was located on Long Island and hosted its first AHRA Nationals over the span of two weekends in August 1967. The Stockers ran from August 4 to 6, while the Hot Cars ran on August 11 and 12.

A wild claim reported by *Drag News* stated that a phenomenal 1,389 entries were received for the race, which it described as the Super Nationals. It was also reported that 59,000 spectators attended the meet, which was a huge number considering that the poor weather early on kept almost 40,000 of the attendees waiting until the final day.

Top Fuel

Despite setting the qualifying low ET of 7.12, Al Friedman, who drove Bruce Wheeler's *Wheeler Dealer*, never made it past the first round of eliminations. He fell to a holeshot by Larry Bucher in the Szabo-Gillespie

Larry Bucher helped put the team of Szabo & Gillespie on the map driving the* Poacher*. Drag racing advanced quickly during the 1960s, as fuel delivery, slipper clutches, and better tires greatly increased speeds. (Photo Courtesy Michael Pottie)

Poacher in the first round.

The 16-car field quickly narrowed to four cars and saw Bucher defeat the car of Pete Van Iderstine in the semifinals with a 7.57 ET. The *Brief Encounter* of Biddy Winward, driven by Walt Kinsley, had been eliminated earlier on but was now back after the Walton & Anderson car broke on a 7.00 (low ET of the meet) run. Bernie Shaker then drew a red light on a 7.20 run against Kinsley. On the money run, it was Bucher leaving first and staying there to defeat Kinsley with a 7.52 ET at 215.86 mph.

Funny Car

It was a popular category. Four Funny Car classes were contested at the Nationals: Unlimited Funny Car, which carried a 2,000-pound minimum weight rule and little else; a 2,400-pound class; a 2,700-pound class; and a 3,200-pound class.

Unlimited went to Supercharged Gas standouts Stone-Woods-Cook, who decided to cash in on the exploding popularity of Funny Car in 1967 by building a blown Mustang, dubbing it *Dark Horse 2*. It was a tough field that saw a number of outstanding battles.

First-round action had the crowd on its feet as Jim Thornton in the 200-pounds-overweight Ramchargers Dart took one from Dick Harrell. Off the line, Harrell's Camaro headed for the sky, got crossed up in the air, and came down hard. Extensive damage was done to the front half of the car, and an ensuing fire was extinguished before it destroyed the rest of the car. Thornton failed to make the second-round call after losing his second transmission of the weekend. Other first-round winners included Maynard Rupp in the Andi Granatelli STP–sponsored Cougar and Howard "Howie" Neal.

Neal and his *Stripteaser* Comet opened the semifinals with a bye. This was followed by a repeat of the previous day's eliminations that saw Cook once again defeat Rupp, who was back in contention due to a break. Cook was out front early and stayed there, beating Rupp with

Bruce Wheeler's* Wheeler Dealer *called the northeast region home but was a threat no matter where it ran. With Al Friedman at the wheel, and the more-than-capable Dick Burgess pulling the wrenches, the former Ed Pink car ran 6.80 ETs before it was retired in 1969. (Photo Courtesy Michael Pottie)

Dick Harrell's Camaro made its debut in the spring of 1967. The car featured a Don Hardy–built 2x3 chassis, a steel body, and fiberglass panels. The red flyer weighed a scant 2,300 pounds. To the left is Harrell's wrench (and sometimes driver) Charles Therwanger. (Photo Courtesy John Foster Jr.)

Roy Steffy and Maynard Rupp's SOHC-powered 1967 Cougar was reported to be the first flip-up Cougar Funny Car built. The build was bankrolled by STP with support coming from Lincoln-Mercury. The car was always competitive, but the big wins seemed elusive. (Photo Courtesy Forrest Bond)

an 8.15 ET at 174.00 mph to a losing 8.42 ET at 172.08 mph. In the final battle, Cook took it to Neal with an eye-opening 7.99 ET at 176.05 mph.

Other Funny Car Action

In the 2,400-pound FX Fuel Funny Car class it was Phil "Daddy Warbucks" Bonner taking honors. Bonner rewrote the class record when he coaxed an 8.57 ET at 165.44 mph out of his SOHC-powered Mustang. In the class final, he defeated the *Yankee Peddler* of Bill Flynn with an 8.68 ET at 163.04 mph. The 2,700-pound gas class went to Chuck McJury, who defeated the injected Plymouth of Joe Black. In the 3,200-pound class, Doc Burgess in his *Black Arrow* Plymouth ran an 11.07 ET at 126.05 mph to defeat Ken Bradley.

Phil "Daddy Warbucks" Bonner got a lot of miles out of his Holman-Moody-built longnose Mustang as well as many wins. An injected Cammer took Bonner well into the 8s. (Photo Courtesy Michael Pottie)

This car may be best remembered as the car that Grumpy Jenkins won Pomona with in 1965, but owner Doc Burgess (a veterinarian) saw his success with the Plymouth as well. This car started as a factory lightweight before being altered.

1967 World Championship

The action-packed World Finals occurred over the span of two weekends in Green Valley, Texas. The Funny Cars and Stockers ran from August 25 to 27, and the Hot Cars and Fuelers ran over Labor Day weekend. Since the NHRA Nationals were on the same weekend in Indiana,

The 1968 Nationals Incident

An AHRA national event always had various exhibition cars (wheel-standers, jet cars, and turbine cars) booked to fill the inevitable lulls that befell racing action. With an increase of these sideshows, the risk of incident increased. One of the worst incidents happened in New York during the running of the 1968 Nationals and involved the wheel-standing VW pickup driven by Dick Sembler.

Sembler's Hemi-powered *Wild Thing* made a clean pass down the track on the rear wheels, but things went awry on his return run. Reports stated that a car pulled onto the track and official Truman Nichols ran out to warn Sembler. Nichols was hit by the pickup when reportedly there was a brake failure. The truck then spun 180 degrees and went through the guardrail and fencing at full throttle in reverse, striking a number of bystanders before coming to a stop. Miraculously, no one was killed. However, three people were seriously injured, including one person whose leg had to be amputated.

Dick Sembler wowed many crowds with his wheel-standing VW before things went south in New York. (Photo Courtesy Bob Snyder)

it's not surprising that some big-name cars were missing from the program.

Top Fuel

With no Don Garlits, John Mulligan, Leroy Goldstein, or Connie Kalitta in the lineup, the Top Fuel winner was a toss-up. The Carroll brothers set low ET with a 7.25, and Vance Hunt set the top speed at 212.00 mph, but both gents failed to make rounds.

The final boiled down to relative unknown Jim Hundley in the Hundley & Boggs fueler against seasoned veteran Bob Langley in the last of his line of *Scorpion* Top Fuel cars. Langley and his T-bar chassis *Scorpion VI* came up short, as Hundley earned the team's one and only national event victory by recording a 7.32 ET to Langley's 7.90.

Funny Car

The beloved Funny Cars were divided into two categories: Unlimited and a 2,400-pound class. Eliminations were run on Saturday and Sunday for each class with payouts on both days. Big Mike Burkhart won Unlimited Funny Car by defeating Fort Worth's Bob Manion, who was driving the Sites brothers–sponsored *Bear-A-Cuda*.

The win proved to be costly for Burkhart, who broke on the run and couldn't return for the Overall Funny Car eliminations. This opened the door for Manion to take the win by

In 1967, Ralph Ridgeway's '55 Chevy spent an afternoon setting nine AHRA F-1 and F-2 class records in three Modified Production classes and two Hot Rod classes. A 301-ci engine using various inductions, carburation, and camshafts got it done.

The team of Jim Hundley and Joe Boggs made a great first impression by winning the 1967 World Finals in its first season running Top Fuel. (Photo Courtesy Michael Pottie)

Mike Burkhart and Harry Schmidt teamed up to debut this S/XS Camaro at the 1967 Winter Nationals. The 427-ci Chevy produced 8.60 ETs. (Photo Courtesy Michael Pottie)

defeating the Kansas Badman Ted DeTar. DeTar with his aging Hemi-powered Falcon put an amazing season together. Between match races and winning Super Stock at the Spring Nationals in Odessa (defeating the Chevy of Gary Kimball), DeTar maintained a winning record of higher than 90 percent during the season.

In the 2,400-pound Funny Car class, Gas Ronda was the big winner on both Saturday and Sunday. His Ed

Gas Ronda, seen here at the Hot Rod magazine meet, debuted this Mustang in the summer of 1967. With the blown Cammer, Ronda found the power was just too much for the Exhibition chassis. The Mustang hit 7.60s in 1968 before Ronda built a new car. (Photo Courtesy Michael Pottie)

Ted DeTar was ahead of the game. His Kansas Badman Ford Falcon ran a Chrysler Hemi long before it was in vogue. Bottom-9-second ETs were common by the end of 1967. (Photo Courtesy Jim Marlett)

Pink–powered SOHC Mustang put away a fouling Gene Snow on Sunday with an 8.79 ET to earn the big payout. Ronda had replaced his Hilborn injectors late in the season with a GMC 6-71 blower, which no doubt helped him win his one and only major victory of the season.

Outside of running a Cobra Jet Mustang at the 1968 NHRA Winternationals, Ronda campaigned the Funny Car through the 1968 season and went winless. He stated in an interview that the "blown Cammer was overpowering the Exhibition Engineering chassis," and he built a new car for 1969.

Other Action

In Top Gas, Bill Mullins walked off with a top speed of 191.00 mph and went on to defeat Bob Smith with an 8.31 ET. Comp went to Dan Hailey, Fred Wirz won Street, Leonard Little won Hot Rod, and Bill Hielscher was the only repeat winner, taking Super Stock.

In the Stock categories, Carl Kelly took Top Stock; the team of Johnson, Lucas, Harder & Fowler took Middle Stock; and Earl Robert's Studebaker went home with the Little Stock crown.

1968 Winter Nationals

The 1968 Winter Nationals was spread over two weeks, with the hot cars (T/F, Jr. Fuel, T/G, and Comp) running at Bee Line Dragway from January 19 to 21 and the remainder of cars running at Lions the weekend of January 26 to 28. With 92 Top Fuel cars hoping to make the 32-car field, there was no way that there was enough time to run the complete show.

Tice attested to this and said, "Last year we had over 1,300 cars in the Bee Line pits, and this proved to be too much, too big of a burden for the park. We feel this will give each and every racer his chance to race and not fight 1,300 other fellows for a spot in line. In the past when we have had split weekends (New York in 1967 and the World Points Championship at Green Valley in 1967 and again in 1968), it has worked out very well."

Bob Manion, seen here at the 1968 Winter Nationals driving the Bear-A-Cuda of Don Bigger, won the 1967 World Points Championship at Green Valley, taking overall Funny Car by defeating Ted DeTar in the final. (Photo Courtesy J.R. Bloom)

This is Kansas City International Raceway regular Willie Wagner's C/HR 1962 Chevy Bel Air. Under the bubbled hood resided a twin-4-barrel 409. His Super Rat Corvette was another well-remembered show-and-go winner. Today, Willie operates Wagner Classic Cars in Kansas City. (Photo Courtesy John Eichinger)

However, the AHRA had previously never split an event and run it at two different tracks.

Top Fuel

The qualifiers read like a "who's who" list: Don Prudhomme, Pete Robinson, Tom McEwen, the Ramchargers, "the Hawaiian," John Mulligan, and "the Greek" were just a few. This great lineup's elapsed time initially suffered because of the recently resurfaced track. However, with 92 cars and five rounds of eliminations, the traction improved.

Qualifying number-one was the *Frantic Four* driven by Ron Rivero, who recorded a 7.306 ET. Rivero won his first round but broke in the second against *Der Wienerschnitzel*.

If there was a favorite heading into eliminations it was the team of Baney, Pink, & Prudhomme, and Prudhomme didn't disappoint. He rolled through the rounds, eliminating Bob Mayer, Don Cook, Chris Karamesines, and Mike Snively in the *Hawaiian* in the fourth round with a 7.27 ET. Prudhomme made the final round by defeating Chuck Kurzawa in the *Ramchargers* car on a red light.

On the opposite side of the ladder, Pete Robinson's Ford set low ET and top speed of the meet of 7.02 at

Jim Nicoll's Der Wienerschnitzel *Top Fueler was one of a two-car team out of Southern California. The second car was initially driven by Don Cook and was later driven by Leroy Goldstein. (Photo Courtesy Don Prieto)*

Don Prudhomme kicked off a successful season by winning Top Fuel at the AHRA Winter Nationals. The Shelby Super Snake featured an Ed Pink Cammer and direct drive. The chassis was by Don Long. (Photo Courtesy J.R. Bloom)

215.30 mph in the first round while defeating the car of Herm & Kuhl. Robinson marched to the semifinals, where he was to solo, but he was unable to fire the Cammer. The promising all-Ford final failed to materialize, and Prudhomme singled for the win with a 7.25 ET at 221.12 mph.

Funny Car

Although it was only an eight-car field at Bee Line Dragway, competition by the all-star cast was fierce. First-round action opened with Clare Sanders in the *Lime Fire* Barracuda disposing of an off-pace Dick Harrell with an 8.72 ET at 176.81 mph. Next, Bob Sullivan in his topless *Pandemonium* Camaro defeated the Bob Manion–driven *Bear-A-Cuda* with an 8.47 ET at 180.00 mph.

Next, Ed Schartman defeated Ray Alley before Doug

Ed Schartman's Cougar was state of the art in 1968 with its 120-inch Logghe chassis, SOHC 427, and C-6 transmission. Arnie Behling pulled the wrenches, helping the Cougar record best of 7.50 times. Schartman rebodied the car in 1969 with a new Cougar. (Photo Courtesy Michael Pottie)

Gene Snow's weekend came to an early end when he failed to qualify in the eight-car field. He'd be back to win the eighth-mile drags at St. Louis and the World Championship at Green Valley. A Ramchargers-built Hemi and a four-disc Crowerglide clutch made 200-mph runs a regular occurrence. (Photo Courtesy J.R. Bloom)

Thorley and his Corvair closed the round by defeating Ed Pauling's mid-engine *Whine Maker*. In the next round, Sanders defeated the *Pandemonium*, and Thorley came up short against Schartman, who pushed his Cougar to an 8.48 ET at 171 mph.

This left Sanders to face Schartman for all the marbles. To the dismay of most, especially Sanders, the *Lime Fire* failed to fire. With the allotted time to make repairs expiring, Schartman headed off on his solo victory.

Lions Action

Due to unusually poor weather, all the action at Lions Drag Strip occurred Sunday, January 28. The ever-popular Fuel Funny Car category saw "Jungle" Jim Liberman win his first national event. Liberman qualified his Chevy II with an 8.52 ET, using much of his lane in a run that could only be described as hairy and scary.

His procession through the rounds came fairly easily. He defeated the red-lighting Corvair of Campbell & Moore in the first round, beat the Corvette of Marv Eldridge with a clean 7.75 ET, and then had it easy in the next round by defeating a red-lighting Jim Pickett. In the final, he ran a 7.84 ET at 181.08 mph to defeat the 1968 Dodge Dart of Gene Snow, who was in on the break rule when "Dyno" Don Nicholson was unable to make the call.

Jim Liberman began 1968 running a pair of Chevy IIs before making the switch to a pair of 1968 Novas. This 1967 Chevy II featured a Logghe chassis that would find its way under one of the Novas. A big-block Chevy and Art Carr transmission kept Liberman in the winnings. (Photo Courtesy Grant Bittner)

Heads-Up Super Stock

Heads-up Super Stock was born out of the demand of both racers and fans who desired to see a heads-up, "run whatcha brung" door-car category. The UDRA was the first to run a class legal heads-up program, doing so in 1967. The AHRA followed suit in 1968, and the NHRA did so in 1970. The AHRA crowned its first Super Stock world champion in 1969.

Super Stock first appeared at the 1968 Winter Nationals and featured just three cars: the Corvette of Bill Hielscher, the Dodge Charger of Dick Landy, and the Plymouth Road Runner of Sox & Martin. The only round of action featured Ronnie Sox taking the doors off of Heilscher's Corvette with a 10.55 ET. Landy won the toss and made a bye run. He then faced Sox in the final. It was a race lost on the line when Sox uncharacteristically drew a red light. Landy was all in and tripped the lights with a 10.51 ET at 132.45 mph.

Other Action

In the eight-car Top Gas Eliminator, the team of Schultz & Jones grabbed the number-one spot with a 7.76 ET, but it was "Mr. C," Gary Cochran, taking the

It's believed Dick Landy updated his heads-up 1968 Charger R/T late in the season with 1969 hardware, and he continued on his winning ways. Note the early six-pack scoop. (Photo Courtesy J.R. Bloom)

category win over Bill Schultz with a 7.88 ET at 189.06 mph. In Junior Fuel, Allison-Crow-McCarrell defeated Les Allen with an 8.14 ET at 185.18 mph.

Competition Eliminator was won by the A/GS Austin pickup of Ed Cluff. John Sheldon and his 1965 Chevy II took Street honors, and Little Stock went to Rex Shirley. Middle Stock went to Bob Case, and in Top Stock it was Ron Robles running a 12.05 ET to defeat the Ranchero of Dick Smith.

1968 Spring Nationals: Thunder in the Valley

As the popularity of drag racing grew, so did the AHRA. The Spring Championship Drags was a race that was added to the schedule in 1965. The race was held on an eighth-mile track located in Pacific, Missouri, in both 1965 and 1966 before moving to the quarter-mile track in Odessa, Texas, and being rechristened the Spring Nationals.

In 1968, the Spring Nationals found its home in Bristol, Tennessee, and remained there through 1970. Owners Larry Carrier, Carl Moore, and Hal Hamrick opened the spacious Bristol track in 1965 under NHRA sanction. A falling out between Carrier and Wally Parks saw Bristol make the move to AHRA sanction in 1968.

Bristol was (and remains) a beautiful racetrack built in a valley between two rolling hills. It picked up the

"Mr. C" Gary Cochran, faced and defeated Bill Schultz in the Top Gas final at the 1968 Winter Nationals with a 7.88 ET. Cochran was a proven winner, having just moved from running a successful Modified Roadster. (Photo Courtesy J.R. Bloom)

Larry Meyer and Ed Cluff from Phoenix, Arizona, campaigned this A/GS Austin. Cluff squeezed out 9.80 times to win Comp at the 1968 Winter Nationals. Life in Top Fuel would follow. (Photo Courtesy J.R. Bloom)

Isn't Jim Tice the lucky one? The AHRA enjoyed life in Thunder Valley, Bristol, Tennessee, through the 1970 season. (Photo Courtesy Ruth Tice)

nickname Thunder Valley due to the roaring echo made by the race cars as they tore down the track. For the 1968 Spring Nationals (June 7 to 9), it was reported that more than 80,000 spectators passed through the gates over the weekend.

Top Fuel

Sixteen of the nation's finest racers qualified for the Top Fuel field. Leading the way was John "the Zoo Keeper" Mulligan, who held the number-one spot with an AHRA record run of 6.85 at 226.60 mph. Other names included Creitz & Greer with driver Vic Brown, Don Cook, Chris Karamesines, and both of Jim Nicoll's *Der Wienerschnitzel*–sponsored cars (one driven by Nicoll, the other by Leroy Goldstein).

Florida's R.L. Peyton added entertainment after being disqualified because he failed to stage his

Tim Beebe and partner John Mulligan had a great season, in spite of a few incidents that robbed them of a few national event wins. They ran 6.60 times by the end of the season. (Photo Courtesy Michael Pottie)

Fueler in time. Unhappy with the decision, Peyton shut his car off on the starting line, got out and hopped into his push truck, drove up behind the dragster, and locked himself inside. Well, authorities were not putting up with that. A tow truck removed Peyton's push truck with him inside, and when he stepped out, he was arrested. Action was further delayed because track officials had to clear the track of beverage containers that were thrown by disgruntled spectators. Peyton received a lifetime ban from both the AHRA and the NHRA.

Out of northern California rolled Don Cook and his **South Wind** ***Top Fueler. Cook headed east on his first tour in 1968, where he was a semifinalist at the Spring Nationals and the winner at the Nationals in New York. (Photo Courtesy J.R. Bloom)***

Chuck Kurzawa seemed to low qualify everywhere that he and the Ramchargers ran their Dan Knapp Top Fueler. However, times as quick as 6.60s didn't always equate to wins. Leroy Goldstein took over as the driver in 1969. (Photo Courtesy Michael Pottie)

Bob Sullivan's **Pandemonium VI** *was one of the more successful topless Funny Cars. Powering the roadster was a 392 Hemi that eventually cranked 7.80 times. (Photo Courtesy John Foster Jr.)*

Back to the action, Karamesines made the semifinals, where he found himself in trouble when a loose fuel line kept him from firing against Goldstein. In the other semifinal matchup, Vic Brown drew a red light against Don Cook. Cook's run went south when he got out of shape and crossed the centerline. After a brief discussion among the teams and the track crew, it was decided that Karamesines would be reinstated.

As the two combatants pushed down the track to fire, Karamesines's car fired, but Goldstein's refused to light. *Der Wienerschitzel*'s clutch just wouldn't engage. Goldstein's day came to an end. Karamesines soloed for the win with what would be his quickest time of the weekend: a 7.02 ET at 213.76 mph.

A veteran of the early match-race days, Huston Platt remained a tough competitor through the 1960s. His **Dixie Twister** *Camaro featured a Logghe chassis and blown big-block Chevy. (Photo Courtesy Ken Rappaport)*

Funny Car

Funny Car was divided into two classes: Fuel Funny Car and Gas Funny Car. Bob Sullivan in his *Pandemonium* Camaro won Fuel Funny when opponent Charles Therwanger, driving the Camaro of Dick Harrell, broke his transmission. Therwanger set low ET for the Funnies with a 7.79, while the team of Biggers & Loo and its *Bear-A-Cuda* set top speed at 183.13 mph.

In Gas Funny, the honors went to Wayne Gapp, who drove his injected Cammer-powered *Top Cat* Cougar around a quicker and faster (9.89 ET at 139.10 mph) *Baltimore Bandit* Barracuda with a 9.91 ET at 138.24 mph.

Earl and Alan "Buckeye" Phillips's injected Gas-powered **Baltimore Bandit** *won more than it lost. Helping the Hemi along was a Winters-prepped ClutchFlite transmission and a 4.56-equipped rear that was mounted in a Logghe chassis. (Photo Courtesy Todd Wingerter)*

Other Action

Top Gas honors went to the team of Bunker & Williams, who defeated a broken C.J. Kearny. Jim Bunker had previously set the low ET for Top Gas with a 7.71. Top speed was set by the team of Pusch & Cain at 191.83 mph. The Kansas City–based team of Cox & Daniel won Jr. Fuel by defeating Don Ploch.

Wayne Morgan from Dayton, Ohio, won Comp by defeating Dave Majors's D/Altered with a 9.08 ET. Gary Blanchette hauled his 440-ci 1956 Chevy from Kankakee, Illinois, to win Street Eliminator over Walt Ferguson with an 11.67 ET.

After defeating Al Joniec's Mustang for Super Stock honors, Ronnie Sox in the Sox & Martin Hemi Barracuda mowed down the competition in Grand Stock. Sox ran 10.60s and 10.70s all weekend, saving a 10.69 ET at 129.31 mph for Dan Smoker, whose *Big Red* Plymouth ran a quicker ET in a losing cause, recording a 10.68 at 127.65 mph.

With then-husband Phil Nichols pulling the wrenches, Shay Nichols's 1967 Hemi Charger was an F/SA record holder. Shay later found herself behind the wheel of a Dick Harrell–prepped 1969 Camaro. (Photo Courtesy J.R. Bloom)

It's Mr. Bardahl to You

Bill Hielscher, the winningest driver in AHRA history, began drag racing back in 1955 behind the wheel of a 1953 Oldsmobile. He turned pro in 1966 with a 340-hp 1965 Corvette and quickly established himself as a force not to be taken lightly.

By the end of his career, 6½ years later, Hielscher (or "Mr. Bardahl"–as he had come to be known) had won 37 AHRA-series events, 9 of them in the 1966 season alone. He won 2 of those 9 at a single race when he won Top Stock and Street at Green Valley in 1966. He closed out the season as the points champion in both categories. No one in AHRA, IHRA, or NHRA competition has ever repeated the feat.

Through his career, Hielscher set or reset class records 110 times with the Corvette and a string of Camaros. By 1970, Hielscher had nine cars in his stable. His final year on the road was 1972, and, true to form, he went out on top. Using his trusty Corvette, the same car that launched his pro career, Hielscher won Super Stock Eliminator at the AHRA Grand American race in Tulsa. In his "retirement," he took over operations at Green Valley Raceway and later Amarillo Raceway.

There were few better public relations men for the sport than Bill Hielscher with his traveling van shows. Hielscher used the Camaro on the trailer to run GT-3 in 1970. (Photo Courtesy Michael Pottie)

1968 Circuit Breakers

Pee Wee Wallace's line of **Virginian** cars won more than their fair share of battles. Wallace debuted this Woody Gilmore Barracuda in 1967 and clicked off mid-9s at over 145 mph. (Photo Courtesy Forrest Bond)

Along with the AHRA major events in 1968, a few other circuits made their debut. The Grand Stock Funny Car Circuit, formerly under NASCAR rule, consisted of injected Funny Cars. There was also a Super Stock Circuit for heads-up door cars. These circuits brought in extra revenue for the tracks and car owners, as they filled in quiet weekends.

Points were issued at each circuit race, and at the end of the season, a champion was crowned. Taking the year's honor for the Funny Cars was East Coast favorite Pee Wee Wallace and his *Virginian* Barracuda. It was a banner year for Wallace, who also won the New York State Championship in May.

The Super Stock Circuit was a heads-up program consisting of five classes of door cars running pump gas and weighing as little as 2,400 pounds. The circuit kicked off in March and through the season was attended by familiar names such as Gene Rains, Hank Greenleaf, Ted DeTar, Tom Sneden, and Bill Hielscher, who won the season series.

Wrapping up results, Herb "Mr. 4-Speed" McCandless, in partner John Livingston's 1965 Plymouth, took Top Stock honors over Shay Nichols. Nichols's F-1 F/SA *Shay's Rebellion* Hemi Dodge Charger had been running little to no oil pressure all day and finally packed it in on the final run.

Part of the Sox & Martin clinic program included hosting seminars at local dealerships. It was great for fans to get up close and personal with drag racing's most famous team. (Photo Courtesy John Foster Jr.)

1968 Points Finale

Looking back on this period in drag racing's history, you quickly realize just how many of these racers grew to be true legends of the sport. Just look at the names in attendance at the 1968 Points Finale in Kansas City from October 4 to 6: Tom Hoover, Steve Carbone, Bennie Osborn, Terry Hedrick, Herb McCandless, and Bill Hielscher. Each of those names still grab our attention whenever they are mentioned.

Bill Hielscher had a grasp on the 1960s psychedelia, painting his Camaro in colors of the day before the more-subtle black and yellow paint was applied. (Photo Courtesy Gary Swearingen)

The event was hampered by weather, forcing the majority of racing to take place over a 14-hour period on Sunday. However, things went off without a hitch thanks to starter Pete Talmadge and a competent tech crew led by Don Wormsley.

Top Fuel

Northern California's Don Cook in his *South Wind Too* was having a pretty good season. His first tour east was a success that was topped with a win at the Nationals at New York. At Kansas City, he grabbed the number-one qualifying spot with a 6.95 ET at 223.88 mph. It was a shame that it didn't translate into round wins though, as he fell to Tom Hoover in the first. Hoover himself fell in the semifinals to eventual-winner Bennie Osborn. Osborn defeated Harold Wilson in the final with an easy 7.51 ET after Wilson was forced to shut off.

Osborn managed the win with his aging 392 Hemi and three-year-old Woody Gilmore chassis. By 1968, most people running Top Fuel were making the switch or had made the switch to the new 426 Hemi. Consistency being the name of the game, Osborn built his cars to be just that.

"I ran a stock-cubic-inch 392 at the time when everyone was adding a stroker, running 460 or so cubic inches, and blowing up. I couldn't afford to take the chance in blowing up because if I did, I wouldn't be running the next week," Osborn said.

It was a great period for "the Wizard," winning both AHRA and NHRA world titles and defeating McEwen in the richest match race in drag racing history, taking home $14,000 in the 1968 one-round race at Orange County International Raceway (OCIR).

Funny Car

In Fuel Funny Car, Terry Hedrick went home the happy winner after driving his *Seaton's Shaker* Corvair around Joe Black's *Green Hornet* Firebird with a 7.80 ET.

Bennie "the Wizard" Osborn had a phenomenal season in 1968. He followed his 1967 NHRA World Championship by winning the AHRA World Finals. (Photo Courtesy Michael Pottie)

Seemingly out of nowhere came Harold Wilson to take runner-up at the World Points Finale in 1968. Wilson was a TV repairman out of Kansas and had cut his teeth running Altered. (Photo Courtesy Cheryl Inkelaar)

Hedrick became the owner of Pete Seaton's Corvair in 1968 after Seaton dropped out of racing. It seems that Seaton's new wife didn't care for drag racing, and according to Hedrick, "She didn't care much for me, either."

Hedrick and Seaton had initially hooked up back in 1965 when Hedrick moved from California to Michigan. Hedrick worked a stint with Chevrolet before going to work for Jay Howell in his chassis shop. It was through Howell that Hedrick met Seaton. Seaton, son of a GM executive, loved his drag racing, but a rare blood disease kept him out of the driver's seat.

Super Stock

Heads-up Super Stock, still in its infancy exploded in popularity after 1968. At the points finale, it was Herb McCandless and his 1968 Hemi Dart taking it to Preston Honea in his similar Dart. Falling by the wayside in eliminations were Bill Hielscher, Ted DeTar, Gary Kimball, and Del Blades, among others. In the final, a race too close to call, McCandless ran a 10.79 ET at 129.12 mph to defeat Honea's 10.81 ET at 127.42 mph.

Other Action

In Top Gas, Don Cain, driving the Pusch & Cain car, ran a 7.92 ET to take honors over Dick Moritz, who was driving Ray Lundy's car. Rex Cox took Junior Fuel over Ivan Thompson, and Comp went to Ron Bolz, who defeated Hank Greenleaf's C/GS Chevy.

Ted Green, driving the Green & Snodgrass Pontiac, took Middle Stock over the 1966 Plymouth of Don Leach. Little Stock was won by the Falcon of Robert Shaw, who

Preston Honea made a name for himself on the West Coast driving Ramblers for Bill Kraft and a Dodge for Lou Baney. He returned to his home in Missouri and ended up in this highly competitive Super Stock Hemi Dart. (Photo Courtesy Gary Swearingen)

Terry Hedrick established his wrenching abilities on the West Coast while working for the Herrera brothers and Doug Thorley before moving east. He gained success as a driver when he took over Pete Seaton's Corvair. (Photo Courtesy Michael Pottie)

In 1968, Marvin Walker was crowned as the AHRA northwest champ with his 1961 Chevy Parkwood wagon. With its 170-hp 283 engine, the nine-passenger wagon was nearly unbeatable through 1971. (Photo Courtesy Marvin Walker)

defeated the 1940 Ford of Peter Koerner. Top Stock went to the 409-powered 1961 Impala of Jerry Velk, and Street honors went to Gary Belt.

1969 Winter Nationals

By 1969, the AHRA had hit its stride, and even a rain delay couldn't hamper what was reported by the newsstand magazines to be the AHRA's finest Winter Nationals showing. With the wet stuff falling, racing on the newly paved surface wasn't an option. Action didn't get underway until 5:00 p.m. Saturday.

Top Fuel

The Ramchargers' last year in Top Fuel was a formidable one. At the Winter Nationals, the team debuted a new Woody Gilmore–chassis car tuned by Phil Goulet and a new driver behind the wheel in Leroy Goldstein. Goldstein, nicknamed "the Israeli Rocket," set low ET with a 6.89 and then proceeded to drive around a 32-car field to defeat Cliff Zink in the final.

The Ramchargers followed up with a win at the AHRA Spring Nationals (defeating Prudhomme in the final) and a win at the Smokers meet at New York National Speedway. The team closed the season as the AHRA's points champion and NHRA's Division 3 points champion.

Funny Car

An all-Chevy final? With Chrysler's Hemi now dominating the category, who would have ever thought? Well, it happened. Clare Sanders in Liberman's Nova faced

As a factory-supported racer, Arlen Vanke received one of the limited Hemi Barracudas in 1968. He kicked off 1969 by winning Super Stock at the Winter Nationals. (Photo Courtesy J.R. Bloom)

The Ramchargers had a new car and driver to kick off the season. The changes paid dividends immediately with a Top Fuel win at the Winter Nationals and track-record 6.89 ET at 216.86 mph. (Photo Courtesy J.R. Bloom)

off against the Camaro of Dick Harrell. The pair waded through a significant field that included Don Schumacher, who set the class record during Thursday's qualifying with a 7.64 ET.

Danny Ongais debuted the Mickey Thompson *Mach 1*, a car that went on to dominate the season. Ongais

Debuting at the Winter Nationals was the Danny Ongais–driven Mustang of Mickey Thompson. The primered car disposed of Ray Alley here before falling to Dick Harrell. At the following Spring Nationals, Ongais took the Mustang to victory by defeating the Barracuda of Candies & Hughes. (Photo Courtesy J.R. Bloom)

Semifinal action at the Winter Nationals saw the two "Jungle Jim" Chevy Novas facing each other. Clare Sanders (in the right lane) fell victim to the boss. (Photo Courtesy J.R. Bloom)

Two of Chevy's finest racers met in the final round at the Winter Nationals at Bee Line Dragway. In agreement with Arizona Raceway, Bee Line Dragway ran only six major events beginning in 1969. Arizona Raceway, under NHRA sanction since 1964, ran each Sunday, excluding the weekends that Bee Line Dragway ran. (Photo Courtesy Michael Pottie)

made it to the third round before falling to Harrell's 7.75 ET. In the previous rounds, Harrell eliminated Gary Crane's *Travelin' Javelin* and the *Super Chief* Charger of Nelson Carter.

Meanwhile, Clare Sanders was defeated by team owner Jim Liberman in the semifinals. As Sanders was the one who qualified both cars, Liberman left it to Sanders to face down Harrell. In an oh-so-close final, Sanders won with a 7.81 ET to a just-shy 7.83.

Other Action

In Top Gas, Mark Pieri defeated Jim Bunker with low ET of the meet: 7.61. Don Enriquez in the (Gene) Adams–Enriquez Hemi Desoto rail ran a record 7.61 ET to take Jr. Fuel. Comp honors went to Ed Sigmon and his injected Chevy-powered MG.

Arlen Vanke and his Hemi Barracuda won Super Stock by toppling the Cobra Jet Mustang of Ed Terry. Don Anderson and his Ford Falcon won the Mr. Stock title, and the Chipperfield & McNichols Nova took Street over Buck Wheatley in his Jenkin Competition–prepared 1955 Chevy sedan delivery.

In Top Stock, Ronnie Sox drove the Sox & Martin Road Runner around the 1965 Mustang of Dick Hallahan with a 10.34 ET. Prior to the event, Sox was awarded the AHRA Driver of the Year award based upon his season results. He was runner-up at the year's Winter Nationals, won Grand Stock at the Spring Nationals, and took Super Stock at the Nationals in New York.

Along with Top Gas low ET, Mark Pieri also ran top speed at 202.76 mph. Pieri drove Top Fuel, Top Gas, and Top Alcohol Funny Car through his career. (Photo Courtesy J.R. Bloom)

1969 Super Stock Weight Breaks

In 1969, the AHRA implemented a points collection program for the heads-up Super Stock category. It also added the following weight requirements:

In the Top Stock final, Ronnie Sox and his Hemi Road Runner is in pursuit of Dick Hallahan's Mustang. Sox caught him.

Engine	Weight requirement
Hemi	7.8 pounds/ci
Tunnel-port Ford engines	7.0 pounds/ci
Wedge (380 ci and larger)	6.8 pounds/ci
Wedge (less than 380 ci)	6.5 pounds/ci

There was a maximum 440-ci rule and a minimum-car-weight rule of 2,500 pounds. Those who chose to run an automatic transmission were given a 100-pound allowance, while those who chose the ClutchFlite ran at the same weight as the 4-speed-equipped cars.

When the 1969 season was done, Missouri residents Larry and Gary Kimball had collected 30,000 points with their Camaro to earn the Super Stock world title. The Kimballs had been kicking around drag racing for a few years, as Gary ran a 1965 Mustang with friend John Hill while Larry teamed with Duey Adams, running a big-block-powered 1965 Chevelle. It was Hill, a wealthy Missouri farmer, who suggested that they join forces and buy Grumpy Jenkins's 1967 Camaro that had just come up for sale. The Kimballs knew a winner when they saw one and jumped at the opportunity. Hill laid out the cash for the car and a little extra for one of Jenkins's 427-ci engines. Gary took on the driving chores and went on a tear.

Rockingham: What Could Have Been

The construction of Rockingham International Raceway was a long time in the making. Bill Land and Harold Brasington first broke ground in 1964, but numerous delays pushed the grand opening to September 26, 1969, when the AHRA opened with the U.S. Open National Championship. Even that date was nearly pushed back. A week before the meet, the grounds were a mess.

"They didn't even have a return round," Don Wormsley said.

Wormsley helped save the day and worked around the clock with crews on final prep.

In 1968, the AHRA signed a contract, agreeing to hold two national events per year at the track over the next five years. Things went south when agreements within the contract were broken in 1970. Suits and countersuits followed, which dragged through the courts for the next few years.

Larry Carrier, who helped develop the Rockingham site, and Tice had a falling out over the mess. In October 1970, Carrier informed Bill Land and his investors that he was forming the International Hot Rod Association (IHRA), a sanctioning body that Carrier dreamed would run both the AHRA and the NHRA out of business.

In December 1970, Land then

The Kimball brothers and John Hill owned heads-up Super Stock during the 1969 season. Here, Gary Kimball lays to waste the Hemi Dart Red Light Bandit of Bill Bagshaw. (Photo Courtesy J.R. Bloom)

Malcolm Durham ran a multi-car team in 1970. Driving his GT-1 Camaro was Bernard Butler, who won class at Bristol but fell short here at Rockingham. (Photo Courtesy Eric Brooks/Brian K. Hankins Collection)

informed the AHRA that Rockingham would not adhere to the agreed-upon 1968 contract. In 1971, Rockingham became an IHRA-sanctioned track. In total, the AHRA held just two major events at Rockingham.

Former NHRA Super Stock world champ (1967) Ed Miller carried his success into AHRA racing as well. Miller was the recipient of a factory-supplied Hemi Barracuda in 1968. (Photo Courtesy Michael Pottie)

US Open National Championship

They like their racing in Rockingham. A reported 68,000 fans attended the September 27–28 weekend meet. Action began Friday with qualifying and the final race of the season-long Ultra Stock Circuit.

Ed Miller and his Hemi Barracuda had a slight lead in points heading into the final race with Sam Auxier Jr. and his Mustang hot on his heels. The deal was sealed when Auxier fell in the second round to the *Fever* Charger of Chick DeNinno, who Miller defeated in the final with a 10.27 ET at 135.94 mph.

Top Fuel

In Top Fuel, Leroy Goldstein and the Ramchargers appeared to be the team to beat, but the West Virginia team of Hundley & Boggs threw a wrench into that. Goldstein qualified number-one with a 6.75 ET. He singled in the first round before defeating Jim Nicoll in the second with a 6.82. In the semifinals, Goldstein defeated Bob Murray with an engine-destroying 6.75. A thrash was immediately underway to swap in a new engine before Goldstein faced Hundley & Boggs in the final.

Forming in 1967, the team of Jim King and Don Marshall won numerous national events with the 392-powered Don Long car. Their performance saw them become an AHRA paid and seeded team. A move to Funny Car came in the early 1970s. (Photo Courtesy Michael Pottie)

To reach the final, Boggs had defeated Jimmy King, who laid down in the first. In the second, he took out Jim and Allison Lee's beautiful *Great Expectations*. Then, he took a bye run in the semifinals.

In the final go, Goldstein tripped the red light. Boggs sailed on for the win with a 7.55 ET. Top speed of the meet went to Preston Davis in Ray Godman's *Tennessee Bo-Weevil*, which ran 220.44 mph in his opening-round defeat of Pete Robinson.

Funny Car

Sixteen Funny Cars and super-bite resin were the name of the game. Gene Snow won Funny Car with his

Terrors of the northeast, Jim and Allison Lee had success with Tom Raley at the wheel of their **Great Expectations II**. *Not just a pretty face, Allison was voted* **Car Craft** *crew chief of the year in 1971. (Photo Courtesy Don Prieto)*

Crower-glide-equipped *Rambunctious* Charger, turning a 7.13 ET at 213.27 mph during qualifying against Danny Ongais in the Mickey Thompson Mustang. Ongais would lose a close one to Mart Higginbotham during the following day's eliminations, running a 7.35 ET to the Chevys 7.34. This was one of Ongais's few losses of the season.

In the final, it was all Snow, who in the semifinals had beaten Fritz Callier's Chevy. Against Higginbotham

Danny Ongais went 55-3 through the season driving Mickey Thompson's blue Mustang. Thompson's Mustangs were revolutionary because they featured a narrow chassis (like T/F cars) and the first Funny Car "zoomie" headers. (Photo Courtesy James Handy)

Pat Foster drove Thompson's second Mustang with less success than the Ongais Car. Powered by an identical SOHC engine, the Mustangs varied in that this one had a longer wheelbase and frame rails that were of smaller diameter, which provided greater flex. (Photo Courtesy Don Prieto)

in the finals, Snow walked away with an easy win, blistering the still-fresh tarmac with a 7.13 ET.

Gas Funny Car

At the same event, the Gas Funny Car circuit had its final race of the season, which saw Tom Sneden in Bob Banning's Dodge Charger win the title, but not this event. The honors went to the *Baltimore Bandit* Barracuda of Alan Phillips, driven by "Skeets" Phillips to low-9-second times.

Bob Banning's sponsorship of race cars goes back to the early 1960s. The team of Reitz & Sneden enjoyed great success in a Banning-sponsored Funny Car for several years. (Photo Courtesy Todd Wingerter)

Super Stock

Twenty-five cars competed in hopes of making the 16-car field. The list of those who succeeded read like a who's who of Super Stock royalty: Ronnie Sox, Don Nicholson, Don Grotheer, Dave Lyall (who turned a suspect 9.66 ET at the Spring Nationals), Hubert Platt, Don Carlton, Ray Sullins, and others.

It was a Going Thing, *all right. Dave Lyall showed them all that the Boss 429 was no stone. Lyall's Boss was quicker than most and was said to hit the 9s. (Photo Courtesy Michael Mihalko)*

Nicholson, King of the Funny Cars, had tired of the fires and explosions and turned the reins of his Cougar over to Frank Oglesby late in 1968. Nicholson made a smooth transition back into door cars with the purchase of the proven Jerry Harvey Cammer–powered Mustang. At Rockingham, Nicholson found the going tough and fell to Sox's 10.14 ET in the opening round.

Eliminations closed with Sox defeating Arlene Vanke with an eye-popping 9.95 ET at 135.95 mph. This was the only 9-second pass made by a Super Stocker all weekend and went into the books as a new AHRA record. Top Stock honors went to Hubert Platt, whose automatic-equipped Ford Drag Team Mustang defeated Don Carlton, who drove the Sox & Martin Road Runner.

1970 Rockingham Recap

The AHRA held its second and final "big" race at Rockingham from April 24 to 26, 1970. Labeled as the first-annual Pro-Am Championship, the race was the third stop on the Grand American series and was attended by a reported 30,000 spectators. It was a shame that things fell apart between the track operators and the AHRA, as the race has been described as a success from all perspectives.

By 1969, Dyno Don Nicholson was through with the Funny Cars. He campaigned the ex-Jerry Harvey Mustang through part of 1969, recording 9.80 ETs. (Photo Courtesy Michael Pottie)

The Missouri-based **Spirit of Frank Faifer** *was driven by Bob Murray. The team (Faifer-Murray-Potts) showed well at Rockingham in 1970 after winning the Grand American race at Detroit in 1969. (Photo Courtesy Michael Pottie)*

Top Fuel

In the 16-car Top Fuel field, John Wiebe came out on top after defeating low-qualifier Chip Woodall (6.22 ET), who was driving for Jackie Peebles. Wiebe was defeated in the semifinals, but his opponent, Bob Murray in Frank Faifer's Missouri-based *Spirit*, destroyed the engine on the run, allowing Wiebe back in on the break rule.

John Wiebe found himself back in at Rockingham on the break rule. It was his second final-round appearance of the young season. (Photo Courtesy Michael Pottie)

Funny Car

Funny Car went to the World Champ Gene Snow, who drove his Challenger to a 7.14 ET at 168.53 mph over Jay Howell in the slowing Prock & Howell Mustang. Howell extracted sweet revenge when he defeated Snow at the following Grand-Am race in Detroit from May 23 to 26.

Jay Howell stated that the Prock & Howell Mustang was a Logghe test car. Backing the Ramchargers' Hemi initially was a TorqueFlite transmission, which later made way for a Lenco. Howell retired as the driver before the new combination was worked out. (Photo Courtesy Michael Pottie)

Heads-Up Categories

In Super Stock, Sox defeated Nicholson, who was now wheeling an SOHC Maverick, with a 9.92 ET. The Sox & Martin team had both its Barracuda and its Road Runner in attendance, which proved to be beneficial. Reports state they went through three engines over the weekend.

The GT classes 1, 2, and 3 were taken by the usual suspects: Gary Kimball, Dave Jones, and Hiner & Miller.

Akron, Ohio–based Bob Hiner and Jerry Miller all but owned GT-3 in 1970 with their 302-powered Camaro. With Miller at the wheel, the team won multiple events, recording low-11 times to win the world title. (Photo Courtesy Eric Brooks/ Brian K. Hankins Collection)

Other Action

Comp went to Bud Hahn and Chuck Turner and their injected Chevy-powered *Blue Mountain Express* C/FD. This Maryland-based team rarely lost and closed out the 1970 season as AHRA Comp champs. Street went to Richard Whitworth and Top Stock to Gary Stowe, whose Stowe Engineering F-1 C/S AMX out of Hicksville Rambler ran a record 10.96 ET.

Steve Carbone smiles after winning the AHRA World Finals in 1970 driving the Creitz & Donovan Top Fueler. Car owner Bob Creitz is left of the trophy. (Photo Courtesy Ruth Tice)

Grand American Points Finale: Closing Out the 1960s

The 1969 AHRA points finale was in Tulsa from October 17 to 19. The professional category points champs for the year were Leroy Goldstein in Top Fuel; Dick Harrell, the AHRA Man of the Year, was the Funny Car champ; and Gary Kimball took home the Super Stock championship. Only Kimball was able to pull off a win at Tulsa.

Top Fuel

In Top Fuel, the weekend belonged to Steve Carbone, who was driving for Creitz & Donovan. Carbone held the number-one qualifying spot with a 6.93 ET. Holding the 16th and final position was Oklahoma's Jimmy Nix, who posted a 7.34 ET. Between were the usual suspects, including Pete Robinson, Powers & Riley, and Leroy Goldstein.

Carbone's march to the final almost ended before it began. In the first round against Skip Hunt, Carbone lost fire on his burnout. Starter Pete Talmadge was ready to send Hunt off on a single when Carbone's ride sprang to life. We'll never know how this one could have turned out, as Skip was gone before the green and drew a red light. In next rounds, Carbone mowed down Wiebe and Dave Powers before facing Leroy Goldstein in the final.

Goldstein had a fairly easy go making rounds. In the semifinals, he soloed after the clutch of his opponent, Bennie Osborn, locked. Most likely, the clutch was set

Bennie Osborn, pictured here at the 1969 NHRA Winternationals, deserves his props. He was the 1967 and 1968 NHRA World Champion and won the 1968 AHRA Points Finale all with a stock-inch 392 Hemi. (Photo Courtesy Don Prieto)

a little too tight, and when the 392 warmed up, the clutch locked up. With the crew unable to move the car, Osborn was forced to shut off, bringing an end to hopes of repeating his 1968 win.

In the final, Goldstein was the odds-on favorite, but Carbone, who first came to prominence by winning the 1968 *Hot Rod* magazine meet, took the win with a 7.02 ET. Goldstein's loss came as his 426 expired in the lights.

Dick Harrell counted on Don Hardy to build his Camaro while he himself pieced together the Chevy engine. In 1970, Harrell was the first to push a Chevy Funny Car over 200 mph. (Photo Courtesy J.R. Bloom)

Funny Car

Funny Car saw a pair of Chevys holding the top two qualifying positions. Dick Harrell landed the number-one spot with an off-the-trailer 7.39 ET at more than 191 mph. Mart Higginbotham in Mike Burkhart's Chevy Nova held the number-two spot with a distant 7.60 ET. Holding the 16th and final qualifying position was Jack Ditmar, who qualified his injected A/Fuel Altered Opel Kadett with an 8.21 ET.

Out of St. Louis came Butch Hicks with his King Cuda. *Hicks ran the car through 1969 and 1970 making rounds. Bad luck at the points finale saw him run into transmission problems. Then, he failed to fire in the first round. (Photo Courtesy Mike Pottie)*

Advancing in the first round were Dick Harrell, Fritz Callier, Curtis Wasson, John Dekker, Mart Higginbotham, Gene Snow, and Connie Kalitta. Kalitta, like a few others who were cashing in on the popularity of the Funny Car, campaigned a 429-powered Mustang alongside his Cammer-powered Top Fuel car. It was a surprise to many to see

As well as running his Cammer-powered Top Fueler, Connie Kalitta also tried his hand in Funny Car with this Logghe-chassis Mustang. For motivation, the car ran the gamut from a Boss 429 to a Cammer to a Chrysler Hemi. Major event victory eluded the Mustang. (Photo Courtesy James Handy)

Danny Ongais fall in the first round in the near-faultless Mickey Thompson Mustang.

Harrell's day came to an end when he lost a close one in round two to Kalitta with a 7.88 ET to a 7.92. John Dekker in Roger Guzman's *Assassination* Corvair fell to Mart Higginbotham's 7.72. Colorado-based Guzman competed in Funny Car through 1981, but the big event win always seemed to escape him. Dekker drove for him from 1969 through 1974.

Snow's Charger was looking good, eliminating the CKC Camaro driven by Fritz Callier with a 7.68 ET. Although Butch Hicks was the odd man out in qualifying, he found himself back in after the first round, only to bow in the semifinals to Kalitta, whose 7.99 ET was enough to beat Hicks's 8.08. Snow's luck ran out in the semifinals, as he drew a red light against Higginbotham. Revenge was sweet for Higginbotham, who had fallen to Snow at the U.S. Open Championship. In the final, Higginbotham soloed when Kalitta's Ford broke on the line.

Super Stock

Thirty-four cars showed to battle for the 16 available Super Stock slots. As previously mentioned, the season belonged to the Kimballs. At the points finale, Gary qualified number-one with a 10.17 ET and steam rolled his way through the field.

Two of the toughest combatants in Super Stock were the Camaros of Wally Booth (far lane) and the Kimball brothers (near lane). In the finale, Booth fell early, while Gary Kimball marched onward to the final. (Photo Courtesy Michael Pottie)

Kimball's final-round opponent was the Dick Harrell–prepped ZL1 Camaro of Grady Bryant. In previous rounds, Bryant had defeated Jerry Ward, Preston Honea, and John Hill in the Kimball-Hill second Camaro, which was a similarly equipped car to Gary's that was also Jenkins powered.

In the all-Camaro final, Bryant really didn't stand a chance. He'd been running a good couple tenths of a second behind Kimball all day, and that's how his day ended. Kimball easily took the win, running a 10.39 ET to Bryant's 10.69.

Other Action

Top Stock came down to a pair of Corvettes with the record-holding car of Solomon & Riley defeating Billings & Furnish. Street Eliminator went to the 1955 Chevy Gasser of the Taylor brothers, driven by Jack Taylor. Competition Eliminator belonged to Wayne Morgan, who defeated the AA/A roadster of Hines & Elliott. Junior Fuel went to Cox & Daniel, who ran low ET in class with a 7.82. Top Gas honors went to D.A. Santucci, who took the win from a red-lighting Don Cain.

D.A. Santucci hailed from Coraopolis, Pennsylvania, and had a banner year in 1969, taking Top Gas at both the AHRA Spring Nationals and the World Finals. His success carried over to the NHRA, where he won the Nationals. (Photo Courtesy Bill Truby)

Jim Basko campaigned this '55 Chevy, having purchased it from Evan Wilson, who had the trippy paint laid. The Bum Trip II ran low-11-second times at 120 mph in C/HR with a 30-over 327 and a highly modified Braswell 2-barrel carburetor. (Photo Courtesy J.R. Bloom)

Chapter Five

The 1970s: Good Times and Bad Times

Due to Tice's progressive thinking, the AHRA was battling toe to toe with the NHRA as the decade began. Seeded racers, the Grand American series, and heads-up Super Stock contributed to record fan attendance for the AHRA. As the new decade began, the AHRA boasted that approximately 5 million spectators attended 2,400 events at more than 80 sanctioned tracks. It was a great start to a decade that appeared to hold promise.

Things turned south early, though, as numerous rained-out events in 1971 put a financial strain on the sanctioning body. Additionally, the strain caused by the emergence of the International Hot Rod Association (IHRA) the same year can't be overstated. Owner Larry Carrier had deep pockets and used his money to increase purses and buy-in big name racers, which was something that Tice had been doing for a couple of years.

More rain dates in 1973 nearly bankrupted the AHRA. Its first race not hampered by rain that year didn't come until the Spring Nationals at Denver's Century 21 in June. By 1975, both the IHRA and the NHRA were hauling in big sponsor money from Winston, allowing them to dish out purses that the AHRA could only dream of matching.

Carrier did bring Winston to the AHRA in 1969 and 1970, but they offered little. According to former Dragway 42 track manager George Eisenhart, "In 1969, Winston gave us nothing but paint to coat the outbuildings in their colors. In 1970, we received $20,000 as part of the AHRA Winston deal. When Carrier left the AHRA, so did Winston."

Although the AHRA had its share of sponsor accounts, it never landed "the big one."

Grand American Series

With the new decade, the AHRA unveiled its 10-race Grand American series. This was drag racing's only season-long points series that saw a champion crowned at the end of the season based upon accumulated points. This flew in the face of the NHRA, where you only had to win one race (the world finals) to be crowned the world champion.

All groups of competitors were involved in the series: the professional categories, which consisted of AA/Fuel Dragsters, Fuel Funny Cars, and Super Stock; the three

Two of Funny Cars' toughest racers, Gene Snow and Dick Harrell, prepare for battle at the AHRA Grand American race at Detroit in May. Snow made the final, where he fell to the Prock & Howell Mustang. (Photo Courtesy Michael Pottie)

Located in Epping, New Hampshire, New England Dragway was AHRA sanctioned in 1970 when this photo of Kelly Chadwick was taken. Chadwick remained true to Chevy power up until his final Funny Car in 1974.

heads-up classes of Grand Touring; and the "Pro-Am" group, consisting of Competition Eliminator, Street Eliminator, and Top Stock Eliminator.

Points winners in Funny Car and AA/FD received $20,000 each, while the winner in Super Stock received $10,000. The overall points champ received an additional $5,000 and was declared the National Champion. The money paid to the winners was over and above the posted purse at each of the 10 events. The 10 races for the first season were held at Bee Line Dragway (bonus points event Winter Nationals), Lions, Detroit, Bristol (bonus points event Spring Nationals), Minneapolis, New York (bonus points event Summer Nationals), Fort Worth, Bristol, Rockingham, and Bee Line for the finale (bonus points event World Finals).

Further changes at the beginning of the decade saw the pro categories go from 32-car fields to 16-car fields, with the top 8 cars being paid prequalifiers chosen by an AHRA selection committee based on their past performance. Don Garlits, who served as AHRA vice president from the 1960s through 1984, stated that part of his responsibilities was participating in booking the very best of the Top Fuel dragsters each year.

"That was decided based on who was the most popular, who had the best cars with the least amount of trouble [and] didn't put oil on the track [another one of Garlits's responsibilities was track prep], and [who was] popular with the fans," Garlits said. "Win or lose, the booked [seeded] drivers went home with money. Win, and they left with the pot. Lose, and they went home with the money they had previously negotiated for. A few racers negotiated a deal that enabled them to go home with both."

As impressive as the wheelie is, it didn't help Tom McEwen, as he fell to Tommy Grove here in the second round of eliminations at the Winter Nationals. The best ET for the Ramchargers-powered Duster was 7.85. (Photo Courtesy J.R. Bloom)

1970 Winter Nationals

The first Grand American series race kicked off with the Winter Nationals from January 22 to 25. Bee Line Dragway must have been a hopping place that weekend, as increased purses saw what was reported to be more than a thousand cars entered. How accurate these numbers were, we'll never know. That goes for the spectator count as well. Different numbers could be given to the magazines for publicity's sake, and different numbers may have been given to the tax man for obvious reasons.

Top Fuel

Top Fuel action was underway on Friday and saw Fred Welchman in Charlie Proite's Wisconsin-based *Telstar* record low ET during qualifying when he ran a 6.91. Impressive as it was, he couldn't match it and was dropped in the first round by Bob Murray. Other first-round losers included Chris Karamesines, Davey Babler, and Jimmy King, who all fell to red lights. Pete Robinson hauled all the way from Atlanta only to lose in the first with blower issues.

The crowd was on its feet for the final round of Top Fuel between Garlits and Wiebe. Garlits pulled off the win with a slower time. (Photo Courtesy Michael Pottie)

Leland Kolb was a big man (6 foot, 5 inches tall) and a racer with history going back to the dry lakes. In 1970, he focused on business and had Kelly Brown drive for him. Brown, a future NHRA World Champ, made rounds but failed to pick up a series win. (Photo Courtesy Michael Pottie)

Those headed to the second round were Steve Carbone, who took the holeshot win in Larry Huff's car over Jim Nicoll with a 7.08 ET to a 7.02; Don Cook; and Don Garlits in his 2-speed *Swamp Rat XIII,* which defeated Jim Hornsberger with a crowd-pleasing 6.95 ET at 218.44 mph.

Second-round action started with Richard Tharp drawing a red light against Dave Chenevert. John Wiebe then sent Steve Carbone packing. Garlits took care of Don Cook with a 7.03 ET before Bob Murray eliminated Kelly Brown.

In the semifinal, Wiebe recorded a 6.81 ET to defeat Chenevert's 6.88. Garlits had an easy go in the other semifinal round, as Bob Murray was running with a baked engine. In the final, Wiebe laid down the low ET and top speed of the meet with a 6.74 at 227.84 mph. However, it wasn't enough, as Garlits got the jump off the line and took the win with a 6.92 ET at 220.40 mph.

Funny Car

Funny Car saw more than 50 of the nation's best racers show up. Eight were seeded cars while the rest hoped to qualify for one of the eight remaining spots. Mickey Thompson showed up with three cars: the seeded Mustang of Danny Ongais, a white Mustang driven by John Wright, and a freshly built 429-powered Maverick driven by Arnie Behling. Behling qualified the Maverick in the number-two position behind the Firebird of "Flash" Gordon Mineo, which recorded a 7.45 ET.

Gas Ronda's illustrious drag racing career came to an end on Saturday when the transmission in his Mustang exploded while approaching the traps. The ensuing fireball engulfed the car, leaving Ronda with second- and third-degree burns over much of his body. Ronda required numerous skin grafts and endured months of rehabilitation. The only good to come out of the incident was that shortly after, both the AHRA and the NHRA mandated fire repression systems for all Funny Cars.

Low ET in Funny Car went to Roy Gay, whose Keith Black-hemi-powered GTO ran a 7.23. Leroy Goldstein in

Mickey Thompson was one of the few who saw any kind of success with the Boss 429 engine. His Maverick, driven by journeyman Arnie Behling and wrenched by Allan Gillis, qualified number-two at the Winter Nationals behind the Firebird of Gordon Mineo with a 7.57 ET. (Photo Courtesy Michael Pottie)

Gas Ronda nearly lost his life at the Winter Nationals in 1970 due to a fire caused by an exploding engine. The Mustang was rebuilt, but his career was over. (Photo Courtesy James Handy)

only his second ride in the Ramchargers' Challenger ran top speed of the meet at 204.08 mph. In Sunday's eliminations, Gay fell in the first round after breaking against Gene Snow. Goldstein was gone in the second round after red lighting against Larry Reyes in the *Hawaiian*.

Die-hard Ford man Tommy Grove somehow managed to fly under everyone's radar as he tooled along. He defeated Tom McEwen and his new *Hot Wheels* Duster as well as Reyes, who drew a red light in the semifinal.

Jake Johnston, driving Harry Schmidt's *Blue Max* Mustang, was another who just kept winning. He defeated Don Schumacher in the second round, and in the semifinals, he took an easy one against Gene Snow, who shut off with an oil leak.

So, the final boiled down to two Mustangs: Johnston's powered by a Ramchargers-built Hemi and Grove with SOHC Ford power. From the start, it was Grove all the way. Through the lights, Grove took the win with a 7.54 ET at 196.65 mph to Johnston's slower (but faster) 7.67 at 198.23.

Super Stock

In a refrain that was echoed through the year, the team of Sox & Martin won Super Stock. At the Winter Nationals, the team fielded two cars: its all-new 1970 'Cuda driven by Sox and the team's 1969 Barracuda, which was driven by Don Carlton.

Sox kicked off Super Stock at the Winter Nationals with a first-round win over Don Grotheer. In the second round, he made quick work of Ed Miller and his Barracuda. In the other first-round action, Chevy hopeful Dick Arons defeated a red-lighting Don Nicholson and his hastily constructed Maverick. Arons then drew a red against Bill Bagshaw in the second round. Bagshaw had defeated Carlton in the first.

Other first-round action saw Bill Hielscher go down to the Mustang of Ed Terry. The Bardahl team was out in force with five cars running in multiple categories at the Winter Nationals. Mike Fons, who hauled his shiny red 1968 Camaro all the way from

Jake Johnston in Harry Schmidt's* Blue Max *runs against Don Prudhomme during qualifying at the Winter Nationals. Prudhomme fell in the first round of eliminations, while Johnston reached the final. (Photo Courtesy J.R. Bloom)

Sox & Martin were nearly unbeatable in 1970, compiling a reported 92-percent win record. The team captured both the AHRA and the NHRA season titles. (Photo Courtesy J.R. Bloom)

Larry and Jim Leatherman were employees of Dick Harrell and campaigned this ZL1 Camaro under his banner. This car didn't last, as it was totaled on a test run at some point in 1970. The pair built another Camaro from a body in white but saw little success. (Photo Courtesy J.R. Bloom)

Michigan (along with Arons), defeated Ray Sullins in the ZL1-powered, Fred Gibb–sponsored 1969 Camaro. Second-round action concluded with the 'Cuda of Dick Humbert defeating Ed Terry, and Mike Fons sinking Booth (a fellow Michigan boy) with a 10.50 ET.

The semifinals went pretty much as the crowd expected. Sox took it to Bagshaw with a 10.11 ET before Fons eliminated Humbert with a 10.40. Sox, up on the field all weekend by at least couple tenths of a second, dismissed Fons in the final with a 10.08 ET.

Eddie Schartman tried his hand in a heads-up Super Stock Cougar in 1970 after abandoning Funny Car. The Boss 429 rarity didn't fare well here at the 1970 Winter Nationals. (Photo Courtesy J.R. Bloom)

Ray Sullins took control of the first ZL1 Camaro in late 1969 and drove it here at the Winter Nationals. Jim Hayter used the car to win the 1971 AHRA Pro Super Stock championship. (Photo Courtesy J.R. Bloom)

Heads-Up GT Classes

The heads-up Grand Touring category initially consisted of classes GT-1 through GT-3. On paper, it looked like a great idea: a heads-up, no break-out category with minimal rules. However, it ended up being dominated by Chevy Camaros. By 1971, the category was pared down to just the GT-1 and the GT-2 classes. The 1972 season spelled the end of the category.

GT rules were pretty basic: no fiberglass panels (except for the hood), a full OEM interior, stock bumpers, and any tire that fit the stock wheel well. As far as the cars themselves, they could be no older than 1967.

Classes were based on a cubic-inch-per-pound break. In 1970, here were the details: GT-1 cars had 401 ci or greater and weighed in at a minimum 8 pounds per cubic inch, GT-2 consisted of cars with 350 to 400 ci with a minimum 9 pounds per inch, and GT-3 was 300 to 349 ci at 10 pounds per inch.

Rules initially called for a single 4-barrel and any intake manifold but no tunnel rams. This would change after 1970. Blocks could be bored 0.060 over, all head work was acceptable, and any camshaft could be used.

In Winter Nationals action, the Wheatley brothers, with Jay at the wheel of their Jenkins Competition–prepared

The Kimball brothers never failed to shine, no matter what category they competed in. Gary used this 1969 Z28 Camaro to dominate the GT-3 class in 1970. (Photo Courtesy Michael Pottie)

David Jones in Bill Hielscher's GT-2 Camaro took class at the Winter Nationals. Hielscher and company also went home with Best Appearing Crew honors. (Photo Courtesy Michael Pottie)

1968 Camaro, took GT-1 by defeating a red-lighting John Hill in one of the three Kimball brothers' cars appearing at the meet. David Jones, in one of Hielscher's colorful Camaros, took GT-2 honors over the Camaro of Denny Wyckoff with an 11.78 ET. GT-3 saw Gary Kimball lose a close one to the 1969 Camaro of Ron Durham: a 12.37 ET to a 12.38. It was one of Kimball's few losses for the season.

Other Action

In Top Stock, Tom Akin's 427-powered 1969 Chevy Kingswood wagon defeated the Biscayne of Lynn Anderson with a 13.41 ET. Akin won the AHRA Top Stock points championship in 1970 after winning the World Series in 1969. Competition Eliminator went to Bob McFarland's C/FD by defeating a red-lighting Joe Williams. In Street, it was Dale Armstrong in Dave Bowers's 396, 2-barrel-equipped B/HR Camaro that defeated Dave Atkins, who was driving Bill Hielscher's A/HR Camaro.

Big Daddy's Painful Introduction to the 1970s

Top Fuel at the Lions Grand American race started out well for Don Garlits on March 7 and 8, 1970. His *Swamp Rat XIII* ran low ET of the meet and set a new AA/FD record with a 6.57. In the final against the Richard Tharp–driven car of Creitz & Donovan, Garlits's 2-speed transmission exploded, sawing the car in half and removing a portion of his right foot in the process. The explosion sent shrapnel flying in all directions, injuring bystanders and damaging the starting system.

The Funny Car final that followed had to be run under a flag start. Danny Ongais beat Don Prudhomme. While recouping in the hospital, Garlits began designing his next *Swamp Rat*.

By the time the AHRA Spring Nationals rolled around in June (13 weeks after the incident), Garlits had recovered enough to crawl behind the wheel again. Connie Swingle was

Dale Armstrong (also known as "Double A Dale") prepped and drove his old Dana Camaro for Jim Bowers at the Winter Nationals in 1970. There he ran an 11.61 ET to defeat David Atkins in the Street Eliminator final. (Photo Courtesy J.R. Bloom)

John Loper's beautiful A/Gas Maverick debuted in 1970 and featured a 486-ci Chevy in a Ron Scrima 2x3 chassis. A B&M ClutchFlite transmission and 4.88:1 gears helped produce 9.20 ETs at 148 mph. Sadly, the Maverick only lasted a handful of runs before being destroyed in an on-track wreck. (Photo Courtesy J.R. Bloom)

Don Garlits had success with* Swamp Rat XIII*, excluding the dreadful outing at Lions Drag Strip. He installed Leonard Abbott's first 2-speed transmission before designing and installing his own transmission. (Photo Courtesy Michael Pottie)

pegged to drive, but his off-pace low-7 time just didn't cut it. Knowing the car had more to give, Garlits took the wheel and, with the day winding down, made his maiden voyage. He ran a low qualifying time of 6.80 at 224 mph. Being low qualifier, the *Swamp Rat* (with Swingle back behind the wheel) took a bye in the first round. Garlits drove in the second round and lost to John Wiebe when he tossed a rod.

Although the team of Tharp-Creitz-Donovan won Top Fuel by defeating Ed Careccia with a 6.76 ET, you can bet that any memory of that race centers on Garlits's return.

Bernie Schacker's rear-engine rail was a step ahead of the rest. Nestled in the owner-fabricated 215-inch-wheelbase chassis is a 392 engine, housing the best of parts. Gary Kupfer laid on the fancy paint. (Photo Courtesy Ken Rappaport)

Evolution of the Dragster

Racers have been toying with the rear or mid-engine design from the very beginning of the sport. Taking a more modern look at the layout, it wasn't until people, such as New York's Bernie Schacker, began to see success in 1970 with the design that others opened their eyes. Though Schacker's self-made rear-engine car had its success and has been recognized as the first into the 6s, Woody Gilmore and Pat Foster can take credit for building the first modern-day rear-engine fuel dragster to win a national event.

After watching John Mulligan's fateful front engine wreck at the 1969 NHRA Nationals, Gilmore was determined not to have it happen again. In December 1969, the pair tested its first rear-engine car. The dragster crashed during an early outing, but the two were undeterred and went to work building a second car. The new car featured a

Dwane Ong had been around drag racing for some time before debuting the rear-engine Pawnbroker. *His name would go down in history after winning Top Fuel at the 1970 AHRA Summer Nationals. (Photo Courtesy Bob Snyder)*

223-inch wheelbase, and after initial testing, it went to Dwane Ong. Ong debuted the car at Orange County in February 1970 (10 months before Garlits's first rear-engine car), where he laid down a best ET of 6.93 at 214 mph.

In August 1970, Ong became the first person to win a national event with a rear-engine car when he won the AHRA Summer Nationals at Long Island, New York. Ong defeated Fred Ahrberg's conventional dragster in the final round with a 6.82 ET at 217.39 mph to a 6.85 at 221.21.

Garlits's Big Unveiling

After months of planning and four weeks of construction, Garlits debuted his mid-engine dragster on December 27, 1970, at the Sunshine Dragstrip in St. Petersburg, Florida. The new *Swamp Rat*, number 14, was built with a 215-inch wheelbase and weighed 1,250 pounds.

By the end of the day, the car was running like it was on rails. It set a new track record with a 6.81 ET at 220.04 mph. The latest *Swamp Rat* all but spelled the end of the front-engine dragster when it won its first national event: the 1971 NHRA Winternationals.

1970 Grand American Series Final

November 13 to 15 at Bee Line Dragway saw the Grand American Championship series come to a close. So big was the event that Governor Jack Williams declared the week "American Hot Rod Association Drag Racing Week" throughout the state. It was time to crown the category champs and overall points Champion.

"Big Daddy" Don Garlits's Swamp Rat 14 *wasn't the first modern rear-engine dragster, but the success he saw with the car started a revolution. The sport would never be the same. (Photo Courtesy Michael Pottie)*

Arizona Governor Jack Williams is surrounded by (left to right) Dick Harrell, Jim Tice, Gene Snow, and John Wiebe, as he declares AHRA Week in Arizona. (Photo Courtesy J.R. Bloom)

Top Fuel

John Wiebe won his first of three AHRA world championships in 1970 (repeating in 1975–1976) on the strength of his Winter Nationals runner-up finish, a win at Rockingham, and his finish at the World Finals.

Pogue's Lifetime Ban

Roy Pogue was a man who hated to lose, as was reflected in his semifinal loss at the 1970 AHRA Grand Am race at Frontier International at Oklahoma City in May. Pogue, running Stock Eliminator, made it to the semifinals before being eliminated after breaking out (running too fast).

Pogue protested the loss to event director Don Wormsley, who listened to Pogue's rant but stuck by the accuracy of the timing equipment. Still seething, Pogue stormed back to his car, which he had parked in the staging lanes. Firing the car, he headed for the starting line and proceeded to mow down the Christmas tree at full throttle. Pogue kept going, out through the pit gate and down the freeway into the sunset. This earned Pogue a lifetime ban from the AHRA. Once word of Pogue's meltdown reached the NHRA, the sanctioning body banned the sore loser as well.

Because Pogue took out the tree in his destructive exit, a number of category finals, including Funny Car and Top Fuel, had to be run under a flag start. In Top Fuel, Jim King defeated Don Cook. In Funny Car, Gene Snow was disqualified for leaving the line before the flag was thrown, handing the win to Don Prudhomme, who turned a 7.47 ET.

Richard Tharp, seen here at New England, was one of the rare souls who was successful driving either a Fueler or a Funny Car. Driving the Fueler for Creitz & Donovan, Tharp saw series wins at Lions and Bristol. (Photo Courtesy Michael Pottie)

John Wiebe was a threat no matter where he ran. Here, he's in action at Orange County International Raceway, home of the 4th annual Professional Dragster Association (PDA) Meet in 1970. (Photo Courtesy Michael Pottie)

Heading into the World Finals, the Top Fuel title was still up for grabs, as Wiebe, Richard Tharp, and Jim King all had a chance of winning it. Each had to survive, but after the first round, Wiebe was the last man standing. In the first round, Kansas John ran a 6.86 ET at 200.88 mph to defeat the red-lighting car of Walton & Anderson. Tharp kissed his hopes of winning the championship goodbye when he drew a red light against Chip Woodall. King also lost all hope when he drew a red against Tommy Allen.

With the championship in his pocket, Wiebe lasted through the second round, defeating Garlits, who drew a red but impressed the heck out of the crowd with a gigantic wheelie. Wiebe fell in the third round to Preston Davis, who in turn fell to Tommy Allen's 6.80 ET in the final.

Funny Car

In Funny Car, Gene Snow won the championship long before the series finale, collecting the $20,000 prize money on the strength of four series wins and two runner-up finishes. This race belonged to Leroy Goldstein and the Ramchargers. In the opening round, Goldstein took care of Spring Nationals runner-up Fritz Collier with a 7.31 ET at 201.78 mph. Round-two opponent Whipple & McCulloch made a race out of it, but the 7.34 ET charge fell short of Goldstein's 7.27. In the semifinals, it was Tom Hoover and his White Bear–sponsored Dodge Challenger coming up short against Goldstein's repeat 7.27 ET.

Gene Snow, Goldstein's final round opponent, was rarin' to go, having defeated the *Assassination* Barracuda driven by John Dekker in the semifinals with a 7.16 ET and the top speed of the meet (207.84 mph). Dekker, who had been defeated by Prudhomme in the second round, found himself back in because Prudhomme broke on the run and was unable to make repairs.

The final round was well worth the price of admittance, as both cars ran nearly identical times. On the top end, though, it was Goldstein pulling it out, defeating Snow's Keith Black hemi-powered Challenger with a 7.24 ET at 204.08 mph to a losing 7.23 at 202.24. You can bet that the Ramchargers team was ecstatic. No doubt their engine-building business picked up a few new customers.

The Ramchargers returned to Funny Car in 1970 and had a great season outside of the fire at Detroit in July that destroyed the Challenger body. The team's World Finals win was preceded by a win at the Summer Nationals. (Photo Courtesy Michael Pottie)

"Mr. Chevrolet" Dick Harrell broke a few hearts when he showed up at the Winter Nationals with his Camaro. Upon lifting the body, a Ramchargers-built Hemi was revealed. (Photo Courtesy Michael Pottie)

Mike Burkhart and driver Mart Higginbotham made a formidable pairing. Although they came up short in landing series victories in 1970, you could never count the pair out. (Photo Courtesy J.R. Bloom)

From 1970 to 1971, Sox & Martin led the Chrysler brigade, but many others flew the Pentastar and could step up and defeat the Fords and Chevys. Their dominance would be curtailed in 1972. (Photo Courtesy Michael Pottie)

Super Stock

It came as no surprise that the team of Sox & Martin won the Super Stock crown. The duo collected the $10,000 prize after dominating the season by winning six series events. The icing on the cake was earning the most points (10,500) of all the pro class winners to pick up the additional $5,000. Sox & Martin, as well as Gene Snow, each won their respective NHRA World Championship titles as well.

Sox started his march to the final by defeating Butch "the California Flash" Leal and his Chevy Camaro in the first round of eliminations. Leal, aching for a Chrysler deal of his own (that would soon come), uncharacteristically missed a shift, handing Sox the easy win. Round two saw Sox eliminate teammate Herb McCandless in the near-identical team 'Cuda with a 10.07 ET. Into the

Butch Leal built his Camaro with the help of Bill Thomas Race Cars in the spring of 1970. Leal ran the Chevy into 1971, winning races at Carlsbad, Riverside, and Phoenix before Chrysler signed him up. (Photo Courtesy Michael Pottie)

semifinals, Sox faced and defeated the Plymouth Duster of "Akron" Arlen Vanke with a 10.09 ET.

In the final round, Sox's opponent was Bill Bagshaw, who was handed a semifinal round win by a red-lighting Don Nicholson. Bagshaw and his state-of-the-art Challenger had run low ET of the meet against Nicholson, turning in a 10.07, ensuring a close battle against Sox. Close it was. Sox with a slight lead off the line took the win with a slower 10.12 ET at 136.57 mph to Bagshaw's 10.11 at 138.46.

Heads-Up GT-1, GT-2 and GT-3

In GT-1, it was the Camaro of Kevin Rotty narrowly defeating the Hemi Dart of Harold Tomlinson in the final round with a 10.91 ET at 126.05 mph to the THT Dart's 10.91 at 125.87. The overall points champ was Gary Kimball.

In GT-2, David Jones took the championship in his Bill Hielscher, Mr. Bardahl–sponsored Camaro. Jones had a great year, having won five series events and being the runner-up at two more. On this final day, though, Gary Kimball stepped up and defeated Jerry Velk in the final with an 11.40 ET at 126.16 mph.

In GT-3, Bob Hiner and Jerry Miller won three series races to earn the season championship and the $2,000 that went with it. Class on this day went to Gene Dunlap, who defeated Bill Hielscher in the final. Hielscher was driving one of his Mr. Bardahl Camaros

Bill Hielscher debuted the first second-generation Camaro Pro Stocker but failed to capture the same success that he saw with his first-generation Camaros. (Photo Courtesy Robert Ochs)

Gary Kimball had his work cut out for him in winning the GT-2 world title. Kimball's 1968 Camaro was powered by a Jenkins Competition 427. (Photo Courtesy Michael Pottie)

Sox & Martin riled up the guys in GT-1. Along with their Super Stock 'Cuda, they fielded this one with both Ronnie Sox and Herb McCandless taking the wheel. Three series wins had the "little guys" screaming that the GT classes were no place for a factory team. (Photo Courtesy Bob Snyder)

The years 1970 and 1971 were a boom time for drag racing, with interest in the sport continuing to blossom. A spacious cinder-block tower went up at Bee Line during the 1970–1971 season. This construction photo was taken from the back side, facing down track. (Photo Courtesy Ruth Tice)

that was usually driven by Leon Philpot. With a field consisting of Ron Durham, Gary Kimball, and Hiner & Miller, you just know Dunlap worked for it.

Other Action

In Comp, the Pennsylvania team of Hahn & Turner won the eliminator with the injected *Blue Mountain Express* C/FD and would win the Comp points championship. In the day's final, Chuck Turner defeated the B/EGD of Larry Willard with an 8.14 ET.

Why does it seem that no AHRA event escaped without incident? The World Finals was no exception. No times were recorded in the Street or Top Stock final, as a rampant rodent reportedly chewed up the wiring on the finish beams.

In winning Street Eliminator, Steve Foster and his Camaro had an easy go of it. One opponent drew a red light and one broke out. The only real race for Foster was in the semifinals, where he outdrove his opponent. In the final, Foster singled for honors. It was David Jones driving for Bill Hielscher who won the Street eliminator series championship.

Tom Akin took the $2,000 Top Stock championship money with his 427-powered 1969 Chevy wagon. However, he had to sit by the sidelines and watch Dennis

Talk about a deceptive name. Tom Akin's 427-powered 1969 Chevy wagon ran mid-13-second times in both the 2-barrel and 4-barrel configurations. (Photo Courtesy Michael Pottie)

David Jones, in a Hielscher Camaro, took a kick at the GT-2 can and came up a winner. He dominated the season series and ran away with the points championship. (Photo Courtesy Michael Pottie)

Kucera and his Ford Falcon take the category win on this day. Kucera defeated the '57 Chevrolet of W.R. McGrew in the final round.

1971 Winter Nationals

The AHRA was riding a wave of popularity as it entered 1971. Spectator turnout at the Winter Nationals, the AHRA's second race of the season after Lions in January, was one of the best. It was the Winter Nationals, and as usual many new cars were making their debut. There was an unusual chill in the February Phoenix air, but the action on the track was hot and more than made up for it.

Top Fuel

To Jim Tice's dismay, his eight seeded cars all fell by the wayside. In round-one action, Garlits defeated Dwight Salisbury but destroyed his engine in doing so. This ended Garlits's weekend way ahead of schedule. It also made it two losses in a row for Big Daddy Garlits, who was defeated by Gary Cochran in Carl Casper's *Young American* at the opening series race at Lions in January.

Don Ewald surprised everyone, including himself, when he defeated Bill Tidwell, who was driving the seeded car of Bob Creitz. Gary Cochran eliminated another seed when he took out Marvin Schwartz. Tragedy struck in the first round when Paul Pritchett, Don

Danny Ongais had a great 1970 season driving Carl Casper's Young American *before Gary Cochran took the wheel and won the Winter Nationals in 1971. The team counted on a Keith Black hemi and Don Long chassis to get the job done. (Photo Courtesy Michael Pottie)*

In semifinal action, Don Ewald faced Gary Cochran. The race was won on the line, as Ewald had no clutch left. Cochran won the meet. (Photo Courtesy Don Ewald)

In the third round, the Greek eliminated Steve Carbone with a 6.68 ET. Karamesines held the top speed of the meet at 222.76 mph. (Photo Courtesy J.R. Bloom)

Dick Harrell was happy when his move to Chrysler power worked well. Harrell won the meet in unusual fashion. (Photo Courtesy J.R. Bloom)

Cook's opponent, lost his life when his Ace Muffler–sponsored car blew the engine and rolled numerous times after veering off the track.

Ewald dropped another two seeded cars when he defeated Jim Nicoll in the second round and Cook in the third. Ewald fell in the semifinals when his clutch gave up and he lost to Cochran's 6.79.

In the final, Cochran defeated Chris Karamesines, who got there by eliminating Bob Williams; Schwartz, who was back in on a break; and Steve Carbone. Cochran ran a 6.74 ET at 218.96 mph to defeat the Greek, who faded with a 7.29.

"When I got my check, there was no questioning that Jimmy boy [Jim Tice] was not happy about giving it to me," Don Ewald said. "Gary got the same treatment. Outside cars [non-seeded] were not supposed to take his top money."

It was an added payout that Tice didn't care to make.

Funny Car

Dick Harrell surprised many when he debuted his new Don Hardy Camaro with a Ramchargers Hemi under the flip-up body. The change proved to be positive, as Harrell's 7.54 ET held him in sixth spot in the seeded eight cars, placing him ahead of Larry Reyes and Dale Pulde.

Harrell's weekend improved, as did his times, as he marched to a final-round appearance against Gene Snow. Harrell ran a low ET of 7.26 while defeating Bob McFarlane in the second round. Snow meanwhile was dipping into the 6s and proving that his Funny Car championship in 1970 was deserving. In the third round, he dismissed Mart Higginbotham's Hemi-powered Chevy Vega with a 6.84 ET at 214.28 mph. Harrell

Second-round action at the Winter Nationals saw Gene Snow defeat teammate Jake Johnston, who was driving the new 1971 Charger. (Photo Courtesy Michael Pottie)

Warren Gunter had one of the most unique Funny Cars with the Chevy-powered **Durachrome** *Bug. Gunter wouldn't make it out of the first round after falling to Slammin' Sam Miller. (Photo Courtesy J.R. Bloom)*

Al "the Flying Dutchman" Vanderwoude swapped his 1968 Charger body for a low-slung Maverick in 1971. Running a Chrysler Hemi, Vanderwoude failed to qualify here at the Maverick's debut. (Photo Courtesy J.R. Bloom)

meanwhile took care of Sam Miller with a slowing 7.46 ET.

There was no denying that Snow had the advantage going into the final round, and it wasn't much of a final. Both cars performed their burnouts, staged together, and left together. However, about 500 feet out, both cars broke. Both coasted toward the finish line with Harrell tripping the lights first, turning a 10.64 ET. This was Harrell's second Winter Nationals win, having won the race in 1969. Snow went on to win the series points championship, accumulating an unsurmountable 9,000 points prior to the World Finals at Fremont in October.

Pro Super Stock

Sox & Martin's dominance of the category was curtailed in 1971 when the AHRA implemented new weight breaks. Effective in mid-April, the breaks saw the Hemi cars running at 7.0 pounds per cubic inch to 6.80 pounds for everyone else. In protest, Chrysler pulled its supported cars from Pro Super Stock competition.

Prior to the implementation of the new rules, Chrysler teams had won two series events. First was Vanke, after playing runner-up at three NHRA events in 1970 (the Nationals, World Finals, and Supernationals), finally winning a race. He garnered Pro Super Stock honors at the Winter Nationals by defeating the Dart of Bob Lambeck in the final with a 9.85 ET at 140.62 mph.

Second was Don Carlton giving the factory-supported teams their

At the Winter Nationals, "Akron" Arlen Vanke drew his first national event victory since taking Super Stock at Rockingham in 1969. His Hemi Duster outclassed Bob Lambeck's Dart in the Pro Super Stock final. (Photo Courtesy J.R. Bloom)

only other AHRA Pro Super Stock win of the season when he defeated Jim Hayter at West Palm Beach on April 18. Carlton was now driving the *Mopar Missile* and recorded the meet's low ET and top speed in the final with a 9.71 ET at 141.50 mph.

Wins by independent Chrysler racers came at the Spring Nationals (Bob Lambeck) and the Nationals (Carmen Rotunda). It makes you wonder if it was a wise move on Chrysler's part to boycott the AHRA races. A world title just may have slipped through its fingers.

Joe Rundle and his Rundles Speed Shop in Tempe, Arizona, sponsored a number of successful cars. His own Camaro was dominant in the Hot Rod category with both 2- and 4-barrel carburation. Rundle occasionally tried his hand in Pro Stock during 1971 and 1972 (Photo Courtesy J.R. Bloom)

Don Carlton, driving Billy Stepp's Dodge at the Winter Nationals, qualified number-one with a 9.75 ET. Stu McDade would replace Carlton behind the wheel shortly after the race, as Carlton jumped at the offer to drive the Motown Missile*. Carlton would win Pro Super Stock at the next series race at West Palm Beach. (Photo Courtesy J.R. Bloom)*

Laporte, Illinois, resident Jim Hayter and his ZL1-equipped 1969 Camaro would walk away with the world title in 1971. At the World Finals, Hayter defeated the second-generation Camaro of Joe Satmary with a 9.69 ET at 139.96 mph.

Other Action

Surprisingly, the hotly contested GT-1 class was not won by a Camaro. That honor went to Butch Leal, who drove Don Grotheer's 1971 Plymouth to the win over the Camaro of Bickie & Hothe with a 10.67 ET at 129.87 mph. GT-2 was won by a Camaro, the 1968 model driven by Gary Kimball, who put it to Gene Dunlap with an 11.48 ET at 118.42 mph.

In Top Stock it was Covina, California, resident Val Hedworth in the Hedworth & Crader 1955 Chevy wagon taking home the gold by defeating Bob Lefevre's 1962 Galaxie with a 15.41 ET. Harold Babcock's 1970 Camaro took Street honors, and in Comp Eliminator, Leroy Lehman's A/Dragster went home with all the marbles.

Big Daddy's Return

After a poor showing at the 1971 winters and the Pro-Am Championship, Don Garlits bounced back with wins at the Southern Nationals in Green Valley; the Spring Nationals at Denver; the Grand Nationals at Marion, Ohio; and the World Finals at Fremont. All this accumulated in Garlits earning his first of four in a row AHRA World Championships.

The race at Marion County International on the weekend of August 27 to 29 was well remembered. Garlits faced Steve Carbone three times and beat him three times. All thanks to the break rule, which saw the previous-round low ET loser reinstated if one of the next round winners was unable to make the call.

Many historians reported that the pair raced each other four times, confusing the side-by-side runs they made in the first round as an actual race. However, neither could lose, as they weren't racing each other. The

Ed Smith's 144-ci 1961 Falcon was a record holder in 1971 and came close to defeating Val Hedworth in Top Stock eliminations here at the Winter Nationals. Hedworth would defeat Bob Lefevre's 1962 Galaxie in the eliminator final. (Photo Courtesy J.R. Bloom)

Harold Babcock won Street Eliminator at the Winter Nationals and Spring Nationals in 1971 driving the Babcock-Chrisman-Gigot D/HR 1970 Camaro to 11.90 times. The trio ran the gamut from Gassers in the early 1960s to Pro Stock in the 1970s. (Photo Courtesy Michael Pottie)

Garlits made side-by-side runs with Carbone four times at Marion. Check out Garlits's yellow tires. For a few years, Goodyear made three colors: yellow, blue, and orange. (Photo Courtesy Todd Wingerter)

real battle between the two began in the second round, which saw Garlits beating Carbone with a 6.54 ET at 219 mph.

In the semifinals, Carbone was back in to face Garlits after Jim Nicoll failed to make the call. And once again, Garlits took the win, this time with a 6.58 ET to a 6.61. In the other semifinal race, Don Cook faced John Wiebe. Wiebe drew a red light while Garlits took the win. The final round was a repeat of the previous Nationals race at York, which Garlits won when Cook's car failed to fire. Carbone, being the low ET semifinal round loser, was on standby, ready to go in case Cook or Garlits faltered.

Well, with burnouts complete, Cook's car lost fire. Unable to fire again, Carbone warmed up to face Garlits one final time. The results

Gone Too Soon

Dick Harrell, voted the AHRA's person of the last decade, lost his life on September 12, 1971, while racing near Toronto, Canada. Running at close to 200 mph, the right front tire blew, sending Harrell's Camaro crashing into a light post.

Harrell had been an active drag racer since the 1950s. He earned the title of "Mr. Chevrolet" early in the 1960s, as he successfully campaigned a number of Chevys in both AHRA and NHRA competition. He used those Chevys to win numerous events and set many records. Harrell had great success match racing and was right there at the birth of Funny Car with his fabled 427-powered Chevelle and Chevy II.

At the time of his death, Harrell was running a multi-car team, with drivers campaigning cars in Funny Car, Pro Stock, and the GT classes. Harrell had the respect of his peers on and off the track. To his fans, there was no one better. He was approachable and gave 100 percent at all times.

His final national event victory came at the rescheduled Grand Nationals held at Marion, Ohio, in August. There he defeated the *Brand X* Mustang of Sien & Lankford in the final with a 7.03 ET at 211.66 mph. Harrell was a genuine ambassador of the sport, and at 39 years old, he was gone way too soon.

One wonders what more Dick Harrell could have accomplished if his career hadn't been cut short. Harrell earned this trophy and more after winning Funny Car at the 1971 Winter Nationals. (Photo Courtesy J.R. Bloom)

would be the same. With Cook's car sitting on the track between the two combatants, Garlits took the win with a blistering 6.46 ET while Carbone drew a red light.

Garlits reflected on the break rule and events of the day.

"They introduced the break rule to cheat me," he said. "It allowed the low ET loser from the previous round to come back if the winner couldn't make the call. Well, there was always someone who broke!"

With a grin, Garlits added, "I'd hate to have been him [Carbone], beaten by Big Daddy that many times. I would have just not come back for another one. I guess he kept thinking, 'I'll get him the next time.'"

1971 World Finals Recap

Wrapping up the season was the World Finals at Fremont on the October 1 weekend. The choice of track was a late-season decision and questionable. Fremont, located south of San Francisco, had capacity for about 10,000 spectators. Now being the World Finals, you'd think a more central location for the race would have drawn much larger crowds and a greater variety of cars. Many of the AHRA's Midwest and centrally located racers chose not to make the long haul. Beyond the eight seeded cars, the AHRA found it tough to fill the remaining eight spots in the pro categories. A quick look shows few surprises in regard to winners and season champions.

Joe Williams started the year as the runner-up at the Winter Nationals with his Chevy six-powered E/Gasser. Then, he proceeded to win four series events (Florida, Green Valley, Dragway 42, and St. Louis) to earn the World Championship. (Photo Courtesy Michael Pottie)

Top Fuel

Don Garlits used his new *Swamp Rat* to defeat Hank Johnson in the final, running a 6.42 ET to Johnson's 6.51. The season saw a variety of class winners, from Gary Cochran, Steve Carbone, Jim Nicoll, and John Wiebe.

Don Cook won the Nationals at Pennsylvania's York US-30 in August by defeating Garlits. It was Cook's first series win since the 1968 Nationals at New York, and the only series event held at the famed East Coast track. By the end of the season, Garlits held both the AHRA and the NHRA ET records and was crowned the

Don Garlits debuted his new Swamp Rat at the World Finals after selling his first rear-engine car to Carl Casper. This car paid immediate dividends by winning the World Finals. (Photo Courtesy James Handy)

J.T. Stewart built this sidewinding beauty, driven here by Dennis Wiery. The best times noted were 7.40s approaching the 200-mph mark. The car was retired after a wreck at Bee Line Dragway. (Photo Courtesy J.R. Bloom)

AHRA Top Fuel World Champion (the first of four in a row) on the strength of winning the Southern Nationals, Spring Nationals, and World Finals.

Gene Snow was at the top of his game in 1970 and 1971. His two-car Funny Car team was probably the category's most feared. (Photo Courtesy James Handy)

Funny Car

Gene Snow earned his second world title in a row on the strength of four series wins and three runner-up finishes. Snow had been gaining momentum since 1968, when he set to work with Crower in developing a four-disc clutch. Snow found that the direct drive helped him power around the competition, which most at the time was running a 2-speed transmission. Snow came up empty at the World Finals, which was won by Dale Pulde in Mickey Thompson's (now) Hemi-powered titanium-chassis Pinto.

Pro Super Stock

When Chrysler walked away from Pro Super Stock in April, the series became a show of independent racers. Few seemed to miss the factory involvement, and racers such as Joe Satmary, Royce Freeman, Bob Lambeck, and Jim Hayter stepped up. Hayter won the World Finals, running a 9.69 ET to beat Satmary's 9.76. Hayter earned the World Championship, barely beating out Satmary and Lambeck, who he continuously butted heads with throughout the season.

Pro Stock champ Jim Hayter lays one on the Motown Missile *driven by Don Carlton. Fans had their favorites but generally liked to see the independents defeat the factory-backed cars. (Photo Courtesy Michael Pottie)*

Powering Jim Eubanks's Hielscher-Bardahl-sponsored Nova to reported best of 9.50 times was a 427-ci engine. Eubanks went on to win Pro Stock at the Nationals in 1972. (Photo Courtesy Bob Snyder)

Allen Patterson and his 265-ci 1955 Chevy showed many competitors those taillights. Times in the 12.80s helped earn the World Championship. (Photo Courtesy Allen Patterson)

Kevin Rotty was a genuine threat in GT-1 before moving to Pro Stock in 1973. Here, at the 1971 Winter Nationals, he failed to make it around eventual class winner Butch Leal, who was driving Don Grotheer's Plymouth Road Runner in GT-1. (Photo Courtesy J.R. Bloom)

Other Action

The two GT classes were becoming an all-Chevy show led by the Kimball brothers. Harold Tomlinson tried to make a battle of it after trading his Hemi Dart for a Hemi Challenger. Gene Dunlap and his Camaro made a good show through the season. A new face in Scott Shafiroff appeared on the block and put the scare into the leaders. Shafiroff and his 1968 Camaro won the World Finals

Jim Johnson's Vintage 37 *was one pretty Chevy. Power came by way of a 427 that sported twin Holley 660s on a Weiand intake and was backed by a Muncie transmission and an Oldsmobile rear end. The patriotic bruiser was driven to the high 9s by Jim Powell. (Photo Courtesy J.R. Bloom)*

No Money in Mexico

Jim Tice was always looking to expand drag racing interests, so when he was presented with the idea of running an exhibition race in Mexico late in 1971, he jumped at the opportunity. The trip was arranged by Rick Lynch, the AHRA public relations director, and a Mexican contact, a gentleman whose name is lost to history.

"Jim was enthused, as he felt Mexico could be an ongoing race in the future," said AHRA tech director Don Wormsley. "Jim's thinking was that it could possibly extend our racing season by one or two events."

Tice had a fairly easy time getting big-name drivers on board, as it generated extra income for them. A group of approximately 30 people made the trip: Ruth and Jim Tice; a few AHRA staff; Bill McClure, owner of Green Valley Raceway; and racers that included Frank Bradley, Don Garlits, and Tom McEwen. Additionally, aerobatic pilot Art Scholl was booked in with his *Chipmunk*, as was the Justice brothers wheel-standing Corvair pickup.

Problems reared their heads early, as initially the Mexicans wouldn't allow nitro to be brought in for the race. They stated the cars would have to run on gasoline. The racers refused, and it was Rick Lynch who finally persuaded the Mexicans to allow the use of nitro. Tickets for the three-day event were sold in advance from booths set up around Mexico City.

The AHRA did all the advertising around the city, with Garlits, McEwen, and company making appearances. The racing took place on the straightaway of the Grand Prix track located near Magdalena, Michua. The track ran Formula One cars through 1970 before the race became unmanageable due to overflow crowds. The fans loved the drag racing, even if they were kept at a distance by armed guards, and the event was considered a success.

When it came time to divvy up the weekend's take, there was no money to be found. The situation quickly became heated. Bill McClure, who held an honorary sheriff's badge in Tarrant County, Texas, called back to the sheriff's office and explained what was going on. Their suggestion was that they head to the airport and get out of there. Rick Lynch was getting the same message from local authorities.

"All of a sudden, all those people who were so friendly and gracious to us when we arrived, disappeared," Ruth Tice said. "We took their advice and returned to Kansas City. Jim covered the checks written to the racers out of his own pocket."

In later years, Tice liked the idea of taking the AHRA international and toyed with the idea of running shows with his top guys in places such as Australia and Japan. Obviously, it never materialized, but the wheels never stopped turning.

Don Garlits and his wife, Pat, stand with Jim and Ruth Tice during a break in the action in Mexico. The smiles would fade, as they were forced to leave town empty handed. (Photo Courtesy Ruth Tice)

The Mexican Jump'N Bean of "Mexican Pete" Huerta was a staple at AHRA events for years. I wonder what the Mexicans thought of it when it first made an appearance down South in 1971. (Photo Courtesy Ruth Tice)

and was runner-up at a few more races during the season.

Don Anderson and his '57 Chevy wagon won Top Stock and came up even in the season points chase with Allan Patterson and his '55 Chevy. It was decided that the points champ would be determined by having the pair run a match race. The winner (and new world champion) was Patterson. Patterson had previously won the series event at West Palm Beach.

Pro Super Stock Relabeled Pro Stock in 1972

Pro Stock, along with the new name, came with weight breaks that allowed for the short-wheelbase (down to 94 inches) subcompacts to compete in the class. Unlike the NHRA, which only accepted these cars if they ran small-block engines, the AHRA allowed them to run big-block engines. As per the 1972 AHRA rule book, there were three Pro Stock weight breaks and a minimum weight of 2,200 pounds:

- Inline-valve engines: 6.5 pounds/ci
- Stagger-valve engines: 6.7 pounds/ci
- Hemi, OHC, and over 370-ci engines in under-100-inch-wheelbase cars: 7.0 pounds/ci

Of course, the number of weight breaks fluctuated through the decade. In 1973, the AHRA was down to two breaks, but by the close of the decade they'd be up to five. This was no comparison to the 22 breaks that the NHRA served up in 1979.

Pro Stock, which was built on big-inch bruisers, found itself making way for small-block mini cars. The Kimballs were one of the first to take advantage of the new rules.

1972 Winter Nationals

A larger-than-expected turnout of competitors saw the racing activities, which usually started on Friday, pushed back to Thursday to ensure everyone had a chance to make a qualifying pass. As reported at the time, the race was the quickest, fastest, and most-attended race to date. Some might say that the AHRA had reached its pinnacle.

Hurry up and wait was the name of the game at the 1972 Winter Nationals. Dave Hough in the famed Nanook *rests his eyes, joining the throng of other racers in the staging lanes. (Photo Courtesy J.R. Bloom)*

Top Fuel

There were record turnouts in many categories, except Top Fuel, which oddly ran a short field. Garlits, a late arrival, nailed down the number-one qualifying spot with a 6.40 ET. This was followed by 17-year-old Jeb Allen, who trailed with a 6.60 ET. Both men saw their weekend come to an abrupt end in the second round: Garlits fell to Don Cook and Allen tossed a blower on a bye run.

With guys such as Steve Carbone, Chris Karamesines, John Wiebe, and Tripp Shumake in the program, it was really anybody's show now. But prevailing was Steve Carbone and Jim Nicoll. In the semifinals, Carbone got a break when starter Pete Talmadge shut down Don Cook, who sprang an oil leak.

In the other semifinal pairing, Jim Nicoll used a holeshot to defeat John Wiebe with a 6.58 ET to a 6.50. In the final, it was Carbone taking the easy win with a 6.68 ET as Nicoll's mill came apart. This would be the last AHRA national event victory by a front-engine Top Fuel car.

John Wiebe was a late holdout with his front-engine car. It could be because he kept winning. Donovan's all-new aluminum 417 got it done. (Photo Courtesy Michael Pottie)

Jerry Ruth, the King of the Northwest, spread himself thin in 1972 by debuting this AA/FC Mustang to go along with his Top Fuel car. Here at the Winter Nationals, he was dumped by Richard Tharp in the Blue Max *in the second round. (Photo Courtesy J.R. Bloom)*

Funny Car

The class saw a full 32-car field with a number of alternates. Harry Schmidt's *Blue Max* held the number-one spot with a 6.70 ET, while Gervase O'Neil sat on the bubble with a 7.40. Eliminations ran Saturday into Sunday, and things were frantic heading into the semifinals. Gene Snow was pressing the clock to swap out the engine that he damaged in the previous round. He was still buttoning up the details as he headed up

Textile manufacturer Barry Setzer got into drag racing in 1971, eventually dipping into all three pro categories. His greatest success came with this Pat Foster–driven 1972 Vega. John Buttera built the chassis, and Ed Pink provided the power. (Photo Courtesy J.R. Bloom)

Initially powered by a Boss 429, Thompson's Pinto was running a Chrysler Hemi by mid-1971. With Dale Pulde behind the wheel, the Pinto won the 1972 AHRA Winter Nationals. (Photo Courtesy Moman Hernandez)

Dragway 42 action sees "Dyno" Don Nicholson in his new-for-1972 Pinto playing catch up to Ken Dondero in Nicholson's aging SOHC-powered Maverick. Dondero would soon be wheeling a blue Pinto for Dyno. (Photo Courtesy Todd Wingerter)

the staging lanes. Against opponent Leroy Goldstein in the Candies & Hughes Barracuda, he came up short. Goldstein hurt his engine while taking the win, and without a backup, he borrowed an engine from the Vega of Mart Higginbotham.

In the other semifinal pairing, Dale Pulde (in Mickey Thompson's Pinto, now featuring a Chrysler Hemi in place of the Ford) beat Pat Foster in Barry Setzer's state-of-the-art Vega with a way-to-close-to-call 6.71 ET to a 6.72.

Time ran out for Goldstein and crew. Unable to complete the engine swap in time, Pat Foster returned on the break rule to face Pulde, again. Again, he came up short, running a 6.85 ET to a quicker 6.68.

This is the second Maverick campaigned by the team of Wayne Gapp and Jack Roush. This one featured a tube chassis and was powered by a Boss 429. (Photo Courtesy John Foster Jr.)

Pro Stock

A new look was coming to Pro Stock in the form of subcompacts. Their low-drag and high-winding small-block engines were on the verge of replacing the big-inch Camaros, 'Cudas, and Mavericks as the racers' car of choice.

You could say that Grumpy Jenkins started the wave when he quashed the Mopars at the NHRA Winternationals with his 331-ci Vega. Don Nicholson was a month behind and debuted his Cleveland-powered Pinto in February. At the end of the season, Jenkins earned the NHRA Pro Stock World Champion title, while Nicholson won the AHRA Pro Stock title.

In 1972, Butch Leal's Ron Butler–built Duster was one of the quickest Pro Stockers in the nation. A Joe Allread–Hemi propelled the Duster to 9.50 times. (Photo Courtesy J.R. Bloom)

However, at the AHRA Winter Nationals, the "big" cars were still the rule. Nicholson and his aging SOHC-powered Maverick with its trick Doug Nash 5-speed grabbed the number-one qualifying position with a 9.60

ET. Hot on his heals was Butch Leal, whose Hemi Duster recorded a 9.62 ET.

There wasn't a Chevy in the 16-car field until Dick Landy, who was to face Nicholson in the first round, withdrew. This allowed first alternative Lynn Harrison to step in with his 1971 Camaro. By pure luck, Harrison made it through to the semifinals. Against Nicholson, he made a bye run as the Cammer Maverick lost oil pressure during its burnout ritual. Harrison then advanced against Wayne Gapp, when Gapp's Maverick broke the rear end. Harrison's day ended when his 10.03 ET came up short against Bill Bagshaw's 9.99 in the semifinals.

On the other side of the ladder, Leal was making his way through a tough field. He defeated the Wedge-powered Comet of Barrie Poole, then the Hemi Duster of Reid Whisnant with low ET of the meet of 9.57. In the semifinals, he received a bye. In the final against Bagshaw, the California Flash ran a 9.66 ET at 143 mph to a trailing 9.75 at 141.

Other Action

The two GT classes had new weight breaks for the 1972 season. GT-1 ran at a minimum 8 pounds per ci, while GT-2 cars ran a minimum 9 pounds per ci. In GT-1, Bill Abraham driving Arlen Vanke's 'Cuda dropped Ken Holthe with a 10.26 ET at 135.33 mph. In GT-2, Jerry Miller in the Hiner & Miller Camaro took it to Scott Shafiroff in a close one: 11.02 at 123.45 mph to a 11.04 at 122.00 mph.

Don Toia in his Chrysler-powered Maverick won Comp, defeating the A/Dragster of Smith & Scott. Street belonged to Joe Rundle, Super Stock went to Don Anderson, and the team of Leon Ball and Mike Team took Stock over the Renault of underdog Allen Orean.

1972 World Finals Recap

It was back to Fremont again for the World Finals in October. The race would remain at this track through 1974. Although it was a more rounded field this time around, it was still Fremont and still a losing venture.

Northern California's Dennis Baca really came into his own in 1972. The Carpet Bagger *Fueler won its first series event that season. (Photo Courtesy Bob Martin)*

The Maverick of Don Toia dominated A/GS through the early 1970s and won the Comp world title in 1972. Powering the Maverick to 9.60 times was an early 354 Chrysler Hemi and turbo transmission. (Photo Courtesy J.R. Bloom)

Top Fuel

Dennis Baca, a Northern California racer, made his money to support his drag racing by operating a floor-covering business. Carpets were his thing, and at the World Finals, he had the competition covered. Baca began the year by winning Fremont's New Year Classic in January and closed the season by winning the

Don Cook ran Top Fuel and Funny Car in the 1960s and early 1970s. Cook is seen here at Bee Line Dragway in 1972. He was runner-up at Tulsa and the Marathon Nationals at Dragway 42 the same year. (Photo Courtesy J.R. Bloom)

World Finals, where he defeated John Wiebe in the final round. Although Baca and Wiebe both had a great season, neither had a hope of catching points-leader Don Garlits, who had six series wins.

Also in pursuit of Garlits were Chris Karamesines and Jim Nicoll, who each won a pair of series events. In 1973, Nicoll was lured from Top Fuel to run Funny Car, where the payouts were larger due to the increased popularity.

Funny Car

Tommy Grove, who had been in Funny Car since the very beginning and hadn't seen a win since 1970, finally broke the spell by winning the World Finals. His aging Mustang, still making it with an SOHC Ford, defeated the Dodge Charger of Gene Snow in the final with a 6.69 ET at 213.17 mph. This was Grove's last year running the Cammer, as his well of blocks and parts was running dry.

The world Funny Car champion was Leroy Goldstein, who vacated the Ramchargers at the end of 1971 to take up with Candies & Hughes. Goldstein drove the team's number-two car to victories at the Northern Nationals at Fremont in March and the Grand Nationals at Tulsa in June.

A strong season was turned in by Dale Pulde, Tom McEwen, and Bill Leavitt, who was on everyone's radar after propelling his 392-powered Mustang to Funny Car's first 6.40 ET at Lions in December 1971. Leavitt won the 1972 Winter Classic at Fremont in January as well as series events at Palm Beach and Green Valley.

Pro Stock

"Dyno" Don Nicholson won two national events, including the World Finals, and was the runner-up at two more to win the world title. His Pinto grabbed its first national event win of the season in April at Palm Beach, where Nicholson defeated number-one qualifier Ronnie Sox. Sox and his de-stroked Hemi Duster drew a red light, handing Nicholson the easy win.

Nicholson's runner-up finishes were in August. First,

Bill Leavitt's* Quickie Too *Mustang was the first Funny Car to break the 6.50 barrier. Leavitt did the deed when he recorded a 6.48 ET at Lions on December 4, 1971. Powering the Mustang was an early Chrysler 392. (Photo Courtesy Michael Pottie)

Don Nicholson proved the worth of the 351 Cleveland when he went out and won the AHRA Pro Stock Championship. The former King of the Funny Cars had a phenomenal career in Pro Stock. (Photo Courtesy Brian Beattie)

he fell to the Sox & Martin–prepared Dodge Demon of Herb McCandless at the Gateway Nationals in St. Louis. Later that month, he was defeated by Jim Hayter at the decommissioned airstrip in Olathe, Kansas.

To lock up the world title, Nicholson defeated Gene Gate, Bob Lambeck, and Larry Huff's Challenger at the World Finals before facing Dick Landy in the final round. Landy broke, and Nicholson let it all hang out with a wide-open 9.524 ET at 143.70 mph.

Other Action

In Comp, Don Toia was runner-up to the Dick Landy Hemi-powered 1962 Corvette of Fred Teixeira, running a 9.60 ET to a 9.63. Toia was more than content, though, in winning the World Championship with his hemi Maverick.

In door-car action, Bruce Wiess took GT-1, Scott Shafiroff won GT-2, and *Hot Rod* magazine editor John Dianna won Street with his Plymouth Duster. The world title went to a deserving Joe Rundle and his

Bob Lambeck and his de-stroked Hemi Duster gave Nicholson a run for his money in 1972. Lambeck won the Northern Nationals at Fremont and was runner-up at the Grand Nationals in Tulsa as well as at the Marathon Nationals. (Photo Courtesy J.R. Bloom)

The Hot Rod *magazine project car of John Dianna proved to be a winner in AHRA and NHRA competition. The Duster was powered by a de-stroked 340. (Photo Courtesy Bob Boudreau)*

Hot Rod Camaro. Super Stock went to Van Paneaham, and Stock was won by John Farris and his well-used (previously campaigned by Tony Janes) 1952 Oldsmobile.

The National Challenge 1972–1973

Tired of the serious lack of pay dished out by the NHRA to the pro class national event winners, Don Garlits created the Professional Racers Association (PRA) in 1972. The idea came about after Garlits had an argument with NHRA president Wally Parks about the measly $3,000 that Steve Carbone received for winning the Nationals in 1971. Garlits felt he should have won closer to $25,000, and he told Parks so. Parks laughed in Garlits's face and told him it would be light-years before they paid that kind of money. Garlits told Parks that he could put a race together that paid better. Parks flat-out told him, "No, you can't." So, the challenge was issued. Garlits reached out to Jim Tice, who gave him the Tulsa track to use and fronted him $150,000 cash for payouts.

Garlits's National Challenge ran the three professional categories (Top Fuel, Funny Car, and Pro Stock) on Labor Day weekend parallel to the NHRA Nationals. With a payout of $25,000 going to each category winner plus contingencies, the race had no problem presenting

One-Tire Rule Proposal

In the early 1970s, George Eisenhart managed AHRA tracks in Ohio as well as several Stock Car tracks. His Stock Car tracks prospered under his one-tire rule. The rule meant that racers used one set of tires for an entire race. This helped to level the playing field between the professionals and the amateurs who didn't have the luxury (money) of swapping tires throughout an event. Eisenhart's idea was implemented at several tracks along with a 9.5:1 compression rule.

Eisenhart wanted to apply similar logic to drag racing due to escalating costs. His proposal would see categories limited to a specific tire size and brand of tire that they could use. Eisenhart took his idea to Jim Tice, who suggested a meeting with Wally Parks and the IHRA's Jim Carrier. Tice felt that if Eisenhart could get everyone to agree, they'd do it.

"So, we had the meeting, [and] they all listened intently," Eisenhart said. "Then, Wally Parks spoke up. He said, 'George, I have no doubt in my mind what you're saying is correct and it will work. But, if you remember a number of years ago, I banned nitro from drag racing and the guy sitting next to you shoved it right up my ass. I'll never go out on a limb again.'"

That comment abruptly brought an end to the proposed one-tire idea.

Vic Brown took the Creitz & Dill, Don Long–chassis Top Fueler to class honors at Tulsa in 1973 by defeating a red-lighting Don Garlits. The car ran high gear only, at a time when everyone seemed to be switching to 2-speeds. The former Cerny & Moody car was powered by a 417 Donovan. (Photo Courtesy J.R. Bloom)

A rare shot taken in 1972 of the Tulsa track, home of the PRA National Challenge. The track opened in 1965 and was both AHRA and NHRA sanctioned at different points. (Photo Courtesy Ruth Tice)

three fields of 32 cars. There were no sportsman categories run over the weekend. Instead, they ran the Tuesday through Thursday prior. This was right up Jim Tice's alley, as he envisioned the day when the pros and the sportsman would run as separate entities.

Top Fuel

Winners during the first year's race included Don Moody in Top Fuel, who drove the all-new Carney-Moody-Walton car to an easy victory over Dennis Baca. Baca's Hemi leaked water, leaving him spinning his wheels while Moody sailed on for the win with a 6.47 ET. Number-one qualifier Don Garlits lost in the third round to Baca.

Funny Car

Leading the way in Funny Car was Dave Beebe, who drove the *Whipple and Mr. Ed* Plymouth Satellite. Beebe laid down a 6.55 ET for the number-one qualifying spot. With the nation's best on hand, it didn't mean much. Beebe was dumped in the first round by Prudhomme.

Things got interesting when Tom McEwen was defeated by the *Blue Max* Mustang driven by Richard Tharp in the second round. McEwen was reinstated after a fire put the Mustang out of contention. He went on

"Starvin'" Marvin Schwartz, a tennis instructor on the side, had his share of success. He teamed with Garlits off and on through the 1970s. Sadly, Marvin lost his life at the 1980 Winter Nationals. (Photo Courtesy Grant Bittner)

Prudhomme debuted his Snake II *in 1971. In 1972, Prudhomme had the 'Cuda running 6.50 times. John Buttera built the chassis while a stroked Keith Black Hemi produced the power. (Photo Courtesy J.R. Bloom)*

Funny Car racing didn't get much better than seeing Richard Tharp and the Blue Max. Car owner Harry Schmidt and Tharp offered up some great racing, although here at the National Challenge, their weekend ended after a second-round fire. (Photo Courtesy Michael Pottie)

to defeat Don Schumacher's *Stardust* that was driven by Bobby Rowe. In the next round, McEwen defeated Raymond Beadle, who drove Mike Burkhart's Vega.

McEwen then faced Preston Davis in the final round. In the semifinals against Prudhomme, it proved to be Davis's lucky Day. Prudhomme dropped a rod at the line, and Davis broke not far from the starting line. Davis ended up pushing the *Tennessee Bo-Weevil* the last hundred feet to earn the win.

In the final, it was McEwen all the way, running a 6.66 ET at 219 mph to the *Bo-Weevil's* losing 6.80 at 211 mph. Prior to the semifinals, the final four racers agreed to split the winnings. Each went home with $11,000.

Pro Stock

The Chrysler contingent threatened to boycott the race, as it was unhappy with the extra 1/2 pound per cubic inch that they had to carry over Grumpy Jenkins's dominant Vega. A happy medium was found when a 2,200-pound minimum weight was instated, and the use of rosin was permitted. The weight rule forced the lightweights to add ballast. In Jenkins's case, that meant an additional 48 pounds on his Vega. It made no difference. Jenkins grabbed the number-one qualifying position with a 9.39 ET, with Dick Landy's 16-plug Hemi Challenger falling in behind with a 9.44.

Jenkins steamrolled through the masses to face Herb McCandless and his Sox & Martin–prepared Dodge in the final round. With the crowd-pleasing burnouts complete, the two cars staged. On the green, Jenkins got the jump and never looked back. It was the Vega through

After defeating a wheel-standing Herb McCandless in the finals at the NHRA Summernationals, Jenkins faced and defeated him again, here at the National Challenge. (Photo Courtesy Steve Reyes)

After dominating the 1970 and 1971 seasons, Sox & Martin had a tough time buying a win in 1972. Their Hemi 'Cuda just didn't make it against the emerging compacts. (Photo Courtesy John Foster Jr.)

the lights with a 9.46 ET at 145.00 mph to McCandless's 9.51 at 145.25.

In Summary

In a 1979 *Sports Illustrated* article, Garlits stated that the 1972 race grossed $225,000 at the gate. In the same article, Garlits said that after all was said and done, he lost $11,000 on the race. Fan turnout for the inaugural event wasn't what was expected, but Garlits, Tice, and company held hope for 1973.

The 1973 National Challenge

The year 1973 was financially painful for the AHRA, as it suffered through numerous rainouts. Leasing tracks as it did, the costs quickly added up. Hoping to make up for some of the losses, it looked to the 1973 National Challenge. With pressure from sponsors that didn't want to see the NHRA destroyed, the 1973 race was held a week prior to the NHRA U.S. Nationals, giving sponsored racers the opportunity to attend both events. Looking back, Garlits felt that moving the date was a mistake, and it should have stayed on Labor Day.

The payouts were down at the 1973 race, as the winner in each category would receive $25,000. Unlike 1972, this included contingency money. In 1973, the race had a phenomenal turnout. More than 90 Top Fuel cars, more than 90 Funny Cars, and approximately 60 Pro Stocks competed in hopes of qualifying.

Top Fuel

John Wiebe qualified number-one in the 32-car field with a 6.119 ET at 229.00 mph. At the opposite end of the spectrum was Gary Cochran with a 6.41 at 205.94. Wiebe's weekend came to a quick end, as did that of 17th-qualifier Jeb Allen when the pair tangled in the first round. Wiebe's Ed Mabry–chassis car shook bad and took a hard turn into Allen, destroying both cars. Allen received burns to his face and hands, while Wiebe suffered a broken leg and ankle after riding the guardrail.

In the category final, Don Garlits soloed, running a 6.18 ET after opponent Marvin Schwartz lost fire on a warmup burnout. Schwartz had previously defeated Vic Brown, Dave Settles, Dennis Baca, and Jack Martin. Garlits made it to the final by eliminating Dan Rightsell, Don

During the 1960s, Rich Guasco and driver Dale Emery wowed the crowds with the Pure Hell *Fuel Altered. Guasco moved to Funny Car in the 1970s and succeeded with several different drivers. Stan Shiroma is driving the car here at Tulsa. (Photo Courtesy Grant Bittner)*

It was an ugly scene at Tulsa in 1973 when John Wiebe's car crossed the centerline and careened into Jeb Allen. Both cars were heavily damaged, and both men's career were set back. (Photo Courtesy Don Gillespie)

Moody, Dale Funk, and Dwight Salisbury. Schwartz's best run during eliminations was a 6.32 ET, so one has to question what kind of final it would have been.

Funny Car

In Funny Car, the final round was a battle between Don Prudhomme and Jim "Superman" Nicoll.

Holding the number-one qualifying position was Gary Glenn in the Plueger & Gyger Mustang, which recorded a 6.488 ET at 214.79 mph. Final-round appearances were common for these guys, who took a runner-up finish at the season-ending World Finals at Fremont. (Photo Courtesy Michael Pottie)

Bobby Rowe wheeled the Wonder Wagon *for Don Schumacher at Tulsa in 1973. The Wonder Bread deal began with a Vega body, but poor handling resulted in the switch to a Barracuda. (Photo Courtesy Grant Bittner)*

When Nicoll's Vega sprung an oil leak, he was forced to shut off. At any AHRA race, the break rule would have gone into effect, but it wasn't used at this race. No one told Don Schumacher, who was the semifinal-round low-ET loser.

Schumacher fired and lined up to face Prudhomme without performing a single burnout. Well, he'd lose to Prudhomme's 6.565 ET. After discussions by officials after the run, it was determined that Schumacher should never have made the run, as the break rule wasn't in effect. Thus, it was decided that Nicoll was recognized as the runner-up.

Chrysler employees, with Don Carlton as driver, campaigned one of the more successful Mopars during the early 1970s. Their twin-plug Hemi-powered **Mopar Missile** *showcased newly developed factory parts. (Photo Courtesy Bob Martin)*

Pro Stock

In Pro Stock, Butch Leal held the low qualifying position with a 9.077 ET, while Les Swearengin's Chevy held the final spot with a 9.80 ET at 137.82 mph. Last year's champ (and the 1974 winner) Bill Jenkins returned in a new Vega and held the fourth position with a 9.127.

The final saw Leal and his Duster face Jenkins. Both cars had been running like clockwork, banging off 9-teen times, and a close race was expected. The eager crowd was not disappointed. Leaving the line together, it was a race to the finish that saw Jenkins taking it to Leal with a 9.081 ET at 150.00 mph to a losing 9.169 at 149.75.

Although the National Challenge carried on after 1973 (with disastrous results), this was the final year of AHRA involvement.

OCIR

Jim Tice jumped at the chance to take over the lease on Orange County International Raceway (OCIR) in July 1973 when the original leaser, Mike Jones, vacated. It was an expensive lease with the Irvine Company demanding a reported five figures per month. Jim Tice thought getting the track was a great score for the AHRA. Setting up shop in Wally Parks's backyard had to have brought

Butch Leal was back at Ron Butler's for a new Duster for 1973. That year, he won the Grand American at OCIR and the World Finals, defeating Bill Bagshaw both times. (Photo Courtesy Bob Martin).

Winning Top Fuel at the 1973 PDA Meet at OCIR were Gene Adams and Don Enriquez. The pair dominated Junior Fuel. (Photo Courtesy Stephen Justice/Robert Runne)

a smile to his face. It's just a shame that it never worked out. Tice walked away from OCIR after a year in which it seemed little went right.

Tice coaxed track operator C.J. "Pappy" Hart out of retirement, and the pair got off to a decent start by hosting OCIR's first ever national event, the Grand American West, in September. Pro category winners included James Warren, Tom McEwen, and Butch Leal.

Out of the northwest rode Herm Petersen to make a name for himself. He did just that, although maybe not in the way he'd have liked. Bremerton, Washington, restaurateur Sam Fitz gave financial support. (Photo Courtesy J.R. Bloom)

Before the 1973 season was through, Hart resigned from his position after repeated clashes with AHRA executive Rick Lynch. Blaine Laux, Tice's personal pilot, became the next track manager. Laux, a former Kansas City sportsman racer, had zero experience in managing a track.

"When Jim came to California, he brought his own crew, and they didn't really seem to know the market," said OCIR public-relations man Dave Wallace Jr. "Jim figured [that since] there were 10 million people here, they should be able to get 10,000. But, he was competing with so much: the beaches, mountains, so many other draws."

PDA 1973

Things went south in a hurry for Jim Tice and the AHRA. At its first Professional Dragster Association Meet, on the third weekend in July 1973, Herm Petersen, the defending Top Fuel champ, broke an axle and flipped his car on its lid. Sliding backward down the track, Petersen was soaked in fuel as it poured from the tank behind him. Things really went bad when sparks from the roll cage scraping on the track ignited the fuel and set Petersen ablaze.

As he laid upside down on fire, the fire brigade struggled to get extinguishers on him. When the fire was finally out, Petersen was rushed to the Orange County Burn Center (the same center that treated Gas Ronda two years before). He suffered from third and fourth degree burns over 55 percent of his body.

Petersen had little choice but to sue pretty much everyone (from the ambulance company to the chassis builder Woody Gilmore) to pay his hospital expenses. It spelled the end of Gilmore building any more drag cars, as once sued, he got out of the chassis-building business.

The AHRA organized many fine events during its brief stay at OCIR. The West Coast loved its Funny Cars, and although the East versus West meet may not have run the smoothest, it always drew a healthy crowd.

On top of that, the AHRA had no signed tech card from Petersen. Racers signed the card upon entry, basically waiving the track in case something like this happened.

California Jam 1974

The California Jam rock festival was Saturday, April 6, 1974, at Ontario Motor Speedway. A reported 300,000 people saw performances by the Eagles, Deep Purple, Rare Earth, and more. It was a great show that just so happened to fall on the same weekend that the AHRA booked its second Grand American West series event at OCIR.

David Wallace Jr. said it best when he stated that the one-day festival killed OCIR's hopes of drawing any crowd on Saturday. On Sunday, no one showed after ingesting whatever substances they had on Saturday while baking under the unusually hot April sun. The losses for Tice that weekend went into tens of thousands of dollars, and he reportedly saw a number of checks bounce.

The 1974 season was further handicapped by some of the worst weekend weather in local history. Even the well-attended sideshows that featured the likes of Evel Knievel, Bo Diddley, and Flash Cadillac failed to recoup losses. Tice walked away from the leases at both OCIR and its sister track, Fremont Raceway, which was being managed by Tice affiliate Richard Foley. Tice spent a little more than a year in California and it had cost him roughly $1 million. Both managers of OCIR and Fremont stayed on, and both tracks retained their AHRA affiliation under new lease holder Larry Huff.

Huff picked up the lease on the two tracks on June 1, 1974. He campaigned a pair of pro cars under the Soapy Sales name and was busted at Bakersfield trying to enter his Pro Stocker with an expired pro license. Although it was not an NHRA race, it was staffed by NHRA employees who embarrassed Huff by making a scene of it. Huff was clearly in the wrong, but he felt that payback for the public humiliation was in order. He was determined to show up Wally Parks and the NHRA.

Well, it never worked out as Huff planned. By the end of the summer, he had given up on Fremont, citing irreconcilable differences with the landlord. He held some

Four seemed to be a magic number for Don Garlits. In 1974, he drove his fourth rear-engine car to his fourth consecutive World Championship. (Photo Courtesy Rich Carlson/Grant Bittner)

Self-made millionaire Larry Huff was quite the character. What allowed him to campaign two cars and later manage OCIR was his Soapy Sales scheme and the cash that he made from his Dyna-Gym. It was all good until the checks started bouncing. (Photo Courtesy Bob Martin)

good races at OCIR but walked away from it in March 1975. The AHRA held its final race at OCIR, the Grand American West, in the spring of 1975. It saw James Warren win Top Fuel, Tom McEwen win Funny Car, and Ken Dondero in Grumpy Jenkins's Vega win Pro Stock.

Don Cook test-drove Garlits's Wynns-Liner *in Florida. It handled poorly enough that Cook refused to drive it after that. Butch Maas drove it at OCIR and failed to qualify. The experiment in streamlining was mothballed shortly after. (Photo Courtesy Steve Reyes)*

Kansas John, You Were Robbed

After winning the Top Fuel Championship in 1970, John Wiebe probably could have won it again in 1973. He had won the Grand Am race at Green Valley and was the leading point-getter, a step ahead of Garlits, as they broke for the National Challenge in August. Wiebe's crash with Jeb Allen at that

A dejected John Wiebe is consoled by Car Craft's *Fred Gregory (left) and fellow Top Fuel competitor Jim Nicoll. (Photo Courtesy Michael Pottie)*

Tracks Come and Go

Racetracks come and go. It's the nature of the business, and more often than not, outside factors play a part in their disappearance. One of those tracks was the short-lived Century 21 track in Colorado.

The track opened under NHRA sanction in 1971. Then, it switched to AHRA sanction for the 1972 and 1973 seasons before closing. Mother Nature played a part in the AHRA pulling up stakes.

Tom McEwen won Funny Car at the 1972 Spring Nationals at the Century 21 track in Colorado. McEwen defeated Bill Leavitt's Mustang in the final. (Photo Courtesy Paul Hutchins)

St. Louis Blues

St. Louis International Raceway Park was built in 1967 and hosted the AHRA's eighth-mile Spring Nationals that year. In 1970, the track was lengthened to a quarter mile and renamed St. Louis International Raceway. In 1971, the Gateway Nationals were born and remained part of the AHRA schedule through 1984.

Compounding issues, the AHRA faced mishaps in 1973 and 1974 that seemed to occur all too frequently. The Gateway Nationals was no exception.

The Grump Loses His Toy

At the Gateway Nationals from August 3 to 5, 1973, Grumpy Jenkins and his 331-ci Vega grabbed the number-one qualifying position with an 8.90 ET. Behind him was the flaming pink Camaro of Ed Sigmon (9.05 ET), Dick Landy, and Jack Roush, who was driving the ex–Barrie Poole Pinto. Satisfied with his lock on first, Jenkins and crew loaded up the Vega and headed out of town for an evening match race against Herb McCandless. After beating McCandless in three straight, the team grabbed a hotel for the evening and planned to head back to St. Louis in the morning. They stopped for a late breakfast in Collinsville, Illinois, and returned to the parking spot where they left the truck to find it gone.

The police were contacted, and an immediate search was launched. Back at St. Louis International Raceway, an announcement went out over the public announcement system notifying the crowd of what had happened. A request was made for any

Grumpy's Toy X ***was rushed into action when Larry Lombardo wrecked*** **Toy IX** ***in a February 1973 match race against Ronnie Sox. Jenkins's lone AHRA win of the season came at Dragway 42 in June. (Photo Courtesy Bill Truby)***

Jim "Superman" Nicoll won Funny Car at St. Louis in 1973. This was his last major event win. Nicoll was forced into retirement in 1976 when his car and equipment were stolen and sponsorship fell through. (Photo Courtesy Grant Bittner)

race appeared to put an end to any hopes of winning his second world title. But wait . . .

With Wiebe out of commission, good friends Warren, Coburn, and Miller stepped up to keep his hopes alive. AHRA rules stated that the earned points stayed with the car and not the driver, so Warren and Coburn dressed their car up in Wiebe likeness, name and all, and carried on for their friend. They won the Grand Am race at OCIR, putting Wiebe 450 points up on Garlits. Garlits appeared at the race with his short, 180-inch-wheelbase *Swamp Rat 18*, and his inventive but disappointing full-bodied Wynns Liner. Garlits bowed in the first round while the Wynn's liner, driven by Butch Maas, failed to qualify.

"Garlits was irate at the sudden development, and, ignoring the fact that the precedent for transfer of points due to driver injury had been set in his own case back in 1970, he began to attack the AHRA through the news media," according to *Car Craft* magazine. "To soothe Garlits's feathers, a plan was announced where double points would be awarded in Top Fuel at the World Finals in Fremont. When it was realized that Warren/Wiebe would still win the title if Warren made it as far as the semifinal round, Garlits was suddenly awarded 200 points for the OCIR race."

The *Car Craft* story went on to state that the points were awarded to Garlits because the streamliner qualified, which contradicts the race results. In the end, I don't think anyone was happy.

Garlits narrowly won the Top Fuel Championship in

witnesses to come forward. By mid-afternoon, an anonymous call led to the retrieval of the ramp truck but no car.

The following day, the police followed up on a lead and searched an isolated old farmhouse in Centerville. There in the garage was the abandoned Vega.

"Whoever stole the car had only taken the engine, transmission, and the aluminum motor mounting plates," said Ed Quay, who was a Jenkins team member. "They took the car apart with the same care we would have. They destroyed nothing, and the only real problem was that they had taken the motor plates, which at the time we didn't have duplicates."

Jenkins missed the remainder of the St. Louis race, which was won by Dick Landy. Landy's final-round opponent was Gary Kimball, who had been reinstated when his opponent Jack Roush crashed his Pinto and suffered a broken arm. Landy's winning time was a 9.16 at 150.26 mph.

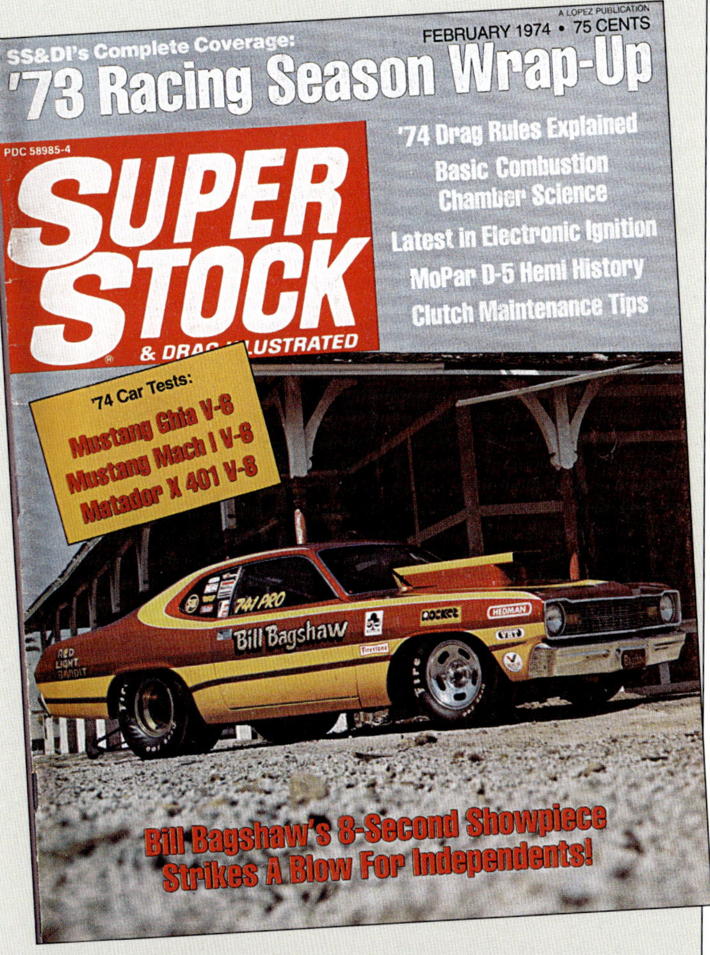
A LOPEZ PUBLICATION
FEBRUARY 1974 • 75 CENTS
SS&DI's Complete Coverage:
'73 Racing Season Wrap-Up
PDC 58985-4
SUPER STOCK
'74 Drag Rules Explained
Basic Combustion Chamber Science
Latest in Electronic Ignition
MoPar D-5 Hemi History
Clutch Maintenance Tips
'74 Car Tests:
Mustang Ghia V-8
Mustang Mach I V-8
Matador X 401 V-8
Bill Bagshaw
Bill Bagshaw's 8-Second Showpiece Strikes A Blow For Independents!

You know you've made it when . . . Bill Bagshaw's Dart Sport graced the cover of **Super Stock & Drag Illustrated** *before his crash. He'd returned to racing in 1976 with a new Ron Butler–built Dart Sport, which crashed that year at Irwindale. Bill took the hint and retired.*

Tragedy Strikes

Bill Bagshaw crashed his Pro Stock Dart Sport at the Gateway Nationals in 1974, leaving two dead and dozens injured. The incident happened when Bagshaw, racing to catch Shay Nichols's Dodge, had his Hemi come apart. The spilling oil got onto the slicks, causing Bagshaw to lose all control of the car. At approximately 120 mph, the Dart took a sharp turn to the left and launched over the guardrail into the bleachers. The car would have cleared the 6-foot grandstands, but the passenger door popped open, caught the top row of the stands, and dropped on the spectators.

Bagshaw, who at the time was the Pro Stock points leader, reportedly suffered a broken collarbone in the incident. He took the next year off, as he contemplated retiring from the sport, before returning with a new Ron Butler–built Dart Sport in 1976.

A Long Time Coming

It's been long established that "Jungle" Jim Liberman was one of the most entertaining gentlemen in drag-racing history. But has anyone ever questioned whether Liberman was also the hardest working man in Funny Car?

Little more than a one-man show with minimal sponsor support, Liberman did it his way, all the way. This made his 1973 Grand American win at Dragway 42 all that much sweeter. Liberman ran a 6.86 ET at 200 mph even to defeat Gene Snow, who limped across the line. This was Liberman's first major Funny Car win as a driver since the 1968 AHRA Winter Nationals.

"Jungle" Jim Liberman kicked off 1973, quite possibly his most successful season, with a runner-up finish to Don Schumacher at the Winter Nationals. Here, Liberman lays out Mart Higginbotham's **Drag-On** ***Vega early on. (Photo Courtesy J.R. Bloom)***

1973 by defeating Warren in the final at Fremont. Both were running the fairly new Milodon aluminum block, but Warren fried his in the semifinal and had to switch to his iron backup motor. Garlits's winning time was a 5.95 at 234.98 mph to Warren's 6.35 at 213.76.

Wiebe returned in 1974 from an off-season before winning back-to-back world championships. He retired in 1977 after running the East-West race at OCIR.

1974 Winter Nationals Recap

The Winter Nationals was always a great race. Excitement filled the air with the expectation of new cars debuting. Racers up north made the trek south to get a break from the long, cold winter, giving those in the south a look at some of what they had been missing.

Top Fuel

Don Garlits, the number-two qualifier with a 6.04 ET, managed to maintain a good 2-tenths to 3-tenths up on the competition over the weekend. In the semifinals, he lowered the boom and reset his own record with a 5.78 ET at 247.25 mph. His final-round opponent, *Enid*, Oklahoma's Mike Wagoner, may have been feeling a little intimidated.

Wagoner was a relative unknown but had all the right parts: a Gilmore chassis and a Donovan hemi to get the job done. But who's kidding who, right? Wagoner ran a best of 6.20 while facing Gary Beck in the semifinals. In the final, Wagoner took the win from Garlits, who had lost his brakes on a warmup burnout and coasted down the track. The easiest and biggest win of Wagoner's career came 6.20 seconds later.

Always a contender, Vance Thomas's F-3/EA Chevy II ran a 0.060-over 327 with a Crane roller cam, 12.5:1 compression, and a Braswell 650-cfm 2-barrel carburetor. A Powerglide and 5.57:1 gearing helped propel the car to a best ET of 12.09 at approximately 110 mph. (Photo Courtesy J.R. Bloom)

The surprise Top Fuel winner at the Winter Nationals was Mike Wagoner, who soloed when Garlits's brakes failed him. Wagoner's Woody Gilmore car was Donovan powered. (Photo Courtesy J.R. Bloom)

The Tommy Lisa and Vince Rossi Fueler featured a Gilmore chassis and had a few different drivers. Here, at the 1974 Winter Nationals, it failed to qualify with Randy Allison in the hot seat. (Photo Courtesy J.R. Bloom)

Prudhomme ran his John Buttera–chassis Vega at the AHRA and NHRA winter meets before he returned to his more successful 'Cuda, which paved the way to Prudhomme winning the AHRA Funny Car title in 1974. (Photo Courtesy J.R. Bloom)

Funny Car

Frank Hall and his *Green Elephant* Vega qualified number-one with low ET of the meet (6.34) but had the misfortune of facing Prudhomme in the first round. The Snake had a great weekend going with his new Army-sponsored, John Buttera–built Vega, until the semifinals, where he faced the Vega of Jim Nicoll. Prudhomme lost, but he was reinstated when Nicoll broke and couldn't make repairs. In the final, Prudhomme faced Raymond Beadle in Don Schumacher's red Vega and uncharacteristically drew a red light, handing Beadle the easy win.

Pro Stock

The Cleveland-powered Fords now ruled the roost in Pro Stock. Bob Glidden, a name that most Chevy die-hards are all too familiar with, defeated the Vega of Grumpy Jenkins in the final round on a clean hole-shot with an 8.93 ET at 152.08 mph to a losing but record-setting 8.86 at 154.01. In making rounds, Glidden defeated the Pinto of Ken Dondero, the Vega of Joe Satmary, and the Pinto of Gapp & Roush. Jenkins defeated Larry Huff, Mike Fons, and Sam Scott.

Other Action

In a refrain that was heard often,

After winning the AHRA world title in 1973, where he ran a three-car team, Don Schumacher returned in 1974 with two Vegas. Schumacher drove a yellow one, Raymond Beadle this one. (Photo Courtesy Michael Pottie)

Bob Glidden became the face of 1970s Ford Pro Stock. Here, at Minnesota, he carries the Pro 1 on the window for his first NHRA world title in 1973. (Photo Courtesy Gary Anderson)

Joe Satmary tried out a Vega Pro Stocker without much luck. A small-block and later a big-block could be found under the hood. Satmary debuted the Vega in 1972 and retired it in 1974. (Photo Courtesy Jimmy Murray)

Ken Veney won Pro Comp. His final-round victim was the Dave Mack–driven (Mack & Dorr) AA/D, which Veney dismissed with a phenomenal 6.98 ET at 194.38 mph. Modified went to Ron Buckley, Street to Rich Johnson, Super Stock to Gary Grame, and Stock to Glenn Erlandson and his trusty, world champ–winning Pinto.

Evel Knievel Jumps for the AHRA

In the mid-1970s, the AHRA looked at ways to broaden its appeal and get more spectators through the gates. With three sanctioning bodies and a gas crunch to contend with, it commonly hired side attractions, such as wheel-standers. On occasion, it hired stunt pilot Art Scholl, who in 1974 won the U.S. National Aerobatic Championship.

That year, Jim Tice paid Evel Knievel to jump at four events. To a kid growing up in the mid-1970s, there was no one as cool as Evel Knievel. Well, maybe Fonzie. Yeah, he was pretty cool too. Fonzie had his *Happy Days* TV show and Evel, well, he almost had a TV show. A pilot episode was filmed at the 1974 AHRA Winter Nationals, starring Sam Elliot as Evel Knievel. The show never got beyond the pilot episode, though, as Hollywood brass felt kids would try and mimic Evel's exploits back home—as if they weren't mimicking him already.

Looking to finance his upcoming Snake River jump, Evel reached out to Tice, who agreed to book him for four shows at $25,000 each. The jumps took place in April and May at Fremont, OCIR, Kansas City, and Tulsa. Each show consisted of Evel jumping his Harley-Davidson XR-750 over 10 Mack trucks. To the delight of the spectators, well most of them, each jump was performed flawlessly. Evel's Snake River jump didn't go as well and was considered a bust when the chute deployed upon takeoff.

Evel Knievel was one of the coolest cats going in the early 1970s. Jim Tice knew it and booked the daredevil in to numerous shows to everyone's delight.

Between Jed Dahar and partner Mike Bailey, this '57 Chevy wagon saw plenty of trips down the track. Between 1973 and 1975, the wagon won numerous series events, including the World Finals in 1974. (Photo Courtesy J.R. Bloom)

Ed Smith proved again that six in a row can be made to go. His Falcon held numerous class records with engines ranging in size from 144 ci to 200 ci. Smith painted the Falcon by dipping it down the middle. (Photo Courtesy J.R. Bloom)

1974 World Final Recap

It was the season finale, but was it really necessary? Outside of a healthy payday, the season champs had pretty much all but been decided. By the fall, Don Garlits, Don Prudhomme, Larry Huff, and Dale Armstrong in Pro Comp all had the series championship in their pocket.

Top Fuel

Garlits had the series wrapped up in July. Which makes it sound like he had a pretty easy go of it, and he did, winning a total of six series races. Gary Beck, an American who moved to Edmonton, Canada, to find fame (how does that work?!) defeated Don at the Spring Nationals. Beck was the class record holder through the summer with a 5.91 ET at 244.00 mph.

At Kansas City, Garlits lost to John Wiebe, which no doubt brought Wiebe a little satisfaction. At Dragway 42, Garlits ran low ET and the top speed of 6.18 at 241.28 mph but bowed early. He had to watch the versatile Paul Longenecker (having previously run Gas, S/S, and Modified Production) defeat John Wiebe in the final.

Nothing Like Stirring the Pot

Steve Gibbs, who was long associated with the NHRA, relayed the following story from 1974.

Jim Tice stopped by the NHRA office on Riverside Drive in Hollywood for a friendly visit with Wally Parks. Gibbs walked into the office just as Tice was leaving and was asked by Parks if he'd mind giving Tice a ride to the airport.

Gibbs suggested that maybe they'd have a little fun first. Gibbs knew that Ed Pink was holding his annual Christmas party at his shop for customers and friends, and it would be well attended. He suggested that they all ride over and the two of them walk in together unannounced. Tice and Parks agreed that it would be fun and maybe spread some rumors. Gibbs said the look on the faces of the drag racers as they walked in was hysterical. Jaws just dropped. A photo was taken, and it got back to the IHRA's Larry Carrier, who wrote an article about his two rivals about to merge. The pair stayed for about a half hour, enjoying themselves.

Richard Parks, the son of Wally, contacted Ed Pink, who told him everyone who was there: Prudhomme, McEwen, et al. A limousine pulled up and out stepped Gibbs, Tice, and Parks. Pink said that it caused quite a sensation to see the two most powerful men in drag racing together like that. Gibbs added that Tice and Parks respected each other even though they were ardent rivals in the sanctioning wars.

Few dominated Pro Comp in the mid-1970s the way that Dale Armstrong did. Whether teamed with Jim Foust running this Donovan-powered Satellite or with Ken Veney running an A/FD, Dale seemed to win everywhere. (Photo Courtesy Michael Pottie)

Gary Beck seemingly came out of nowhere to win the NHRA U.S. Nationals in 1972. Seen here at Spokane in 1974, Beck won his first AHRA event that year by defeating Garlits at the Spring Nationals. (Photo Courtesy Rich Carlson/Grant Bittner)

Garlits was in his prime during the mid-1970s, and no one could touch him. He had the uncanny ability to run as well as anyone, even a little bit better, and not destroy his engine while doing so.

"My famous trick at the AHRA tracks was to win the event, refuel the engine at the other end, wind the chute up around the wing, pull out on the drag strip, start the motor, and drive my car to the victory circle in front of all the competitors and fans," Garlits said. "It made them crazy when I did that. I did it because I wanted them to know I didn't blow up my s—— to win the race."

Garlits never had the opportunity to pull the move at the World Finals, as he was bumped early by Wiebe. In the final, "Starvin'" Marvin Graham, the Oklahoma TV repair man, defeated Dwight Salisbury with a 6.36 ET at 225.00 mph.

Tom "the Mongoose" McEwen campaigned two AA/Funny Cars in 1974 with Russell Long driving the second car. McEwen won three AHRA series events that year, and he won the world title in 1975. (Photo Courtesy Rich Carlson/Grant Bittner)

Funny Car

Tom McEwen won the Northern Nationals, where he defeated Tom Hoover's *Showtime* Vega with a 6.57 ET to a 6.65. At the World Finals, McEwen faced the points champ: Don Prudhomme. Prudhomme was one of the paid seeded drivers and was liked by Jim Tice. He negotiated his own pay with Tice, and it must have been some astronomical number, as Tice told him, "You better not lose!" Prudhomme rarely did, winning five series events in 1974. Prudhomme had nothing but praise for Jim Tice and the AHRA.

"Jim was a wonderful guy and kept the Mongoose and I in business by paying us to run their national events," Prudhomme said. "Some of the best times in my life were racing for Jim. If the AHRA could have weathered the storm, we could really use them today."

Pro Stock

At 7.3 pounds per cubic inch, only the Hemi Colts carried more weight than the 7.2 of the Hemi Dodge or Plymouths. Larry Huff and his *Soapy Sales* Dodge Dart still managed to win the World Finals and the series championship as well. Through the season, Huff faced stiff competition from Joe Satmary, Bill Bagshaw, and Ken Dondero, who was driving AHRA events for Bill Jenkins. Dondero had spent the 1973 season teamed with Don Nicholson.

At the World Finals, both Dondero and Nicholson were tossed due to weight infractions, allowing Warren Johnson and his big-block Vega and Sonny Bryant and his big-block Camaro back in. In the final, it was Huff over Satmary with a 9.11 ET at 148.51 mph.

Other Action

Pro Comp, a new heads-up category introduced in 1974, consisted of cars running in classes AA/GD, A/FD, B/FD, AA/FA, A/FC, and BB/FC. World-champ Dale Armstrong, in the Faust & Armstrong Altered, qualified number-one, followed by Ken Veney's Vega in the number-two spot with a 7.26 and a 7.30. The pair would meet in the final with Veney taking the win with a 7.26 to a 7.59.

Walt Niesen and his *Dictator* B/GD won Modified and the first of two straight points championships. Street went to defending champ Allan Patterson and his Braswell 2-barrel-equipped Camaro. Patterson would see Larry Spitali in the Whatley brothers (Bill, Stan, and Bob) car win the title this year.

Colorado's Herman Chapman and his 1965 Nova won

George Wepplo fabricated this Vega from Warren Johnson's plans. A big-block engine and 4-speed transmission moved the Vega to 8.60 times. He earned a runner-up finish at the Green Valley and St. Louis series events. (Photo Courtesy Tommy Shaw)

Tough West Coast competitor Sonny Bryant was runner-up to Bill Bagshaw at the Northern Nationals in 1974. His big-block Camaro was good for 9.20 times.

Larry Spitali won the 1974 Street World Champion driving the Whatley brothers' 1967 Camaro. The Camaro ran a best ET of 10.86 at 126 mph with 2-barrel-equipped 354 in C/HR, and an 11.12 ET at 124 mph with a 2-barrel-equipped 329 in D/HR. Ed Smith sponsorship replaced Rundles in 1974. (Photo Courtesy J.R. Bloom)

What can be said about Ken Veney that hasn't been said already? His injected big-block Chevy Vega opened the season with a Winter Nationals win and closed it with a World Finals win. (Photo Courtesy Michael Pottie)

A decade of bracket racing and a year with Sox & Martin helped Glenn Erlandson develop a strategy to win back-to-back world titles. Here, he poses with Firebird track owner Bill New and an unknown beauty. (Photo Courtesy Rich Carlson/Grant Bittner Collection)

Super Stock, and Gary Grame won the world title. In Stock, Jed Dahar driving Mike Bailey's well-traveled 1957 Chevy wagon won the meet, while Glenn Erlandson and his 17-second *TraveLodge* Pinto took home the Stock world title.

1975: Bye-Bye Bee Line

The AHRA lost Bee Line Dragway in 1975 when talks with the landowners, the Pima Indian Reserve, broke down. The final AHRA race at the track was the season's opening Winter Nationals. Bee Line Dragway had its ups and downs over the years, the latest being the tragic loss of Pro Stock racer Irv Beringhaus in 1974. Beringhaus, a popular racer from Denver, died when his Pinto crashed at speed during a qualifying run.

The Winter Nationals were moved to Tucson Dragway for 1976, an "adequate" track some 100 miles south of Phoenix, where it would remain through 1984. The NHRA picked up the lease on Bee Line Dragway in 1976 and made numerous upgrades before running the Winter Classic. By the early 1980s, the NHRA was out of Bee Line Dragway, and the track closed for good in 1982.

1975 Winter Nationals Recap

By 1975, Bee Line Dragway was showing its age. As a track that hosted a major event, it was lagging by the day's standards. The pits needed work, crowd control wasn't the greatest, and the track surface was due for

The James Warren–Roger Coburn team was a West Coast threat going back to the 1960s. Their Warren-Coburn-Miller Rain for Rent *was runner-up at the Winter Nationals in 1975 before winning at OCIR and Tulsa. (Photo Courtesy Michael Pottie)*

Raymond Beadle and Harry Schmidt made a formidable pair when they clicked in 1974. Success immediately followed, and through 1981 the Blue Max *remained one of the sport's most dominant Funnies. (Photo Courtesy Dan Williams)*

a working over. But it was still the first major race of the season and continued to draw the masses.

Top Fuel

After winning the 1974 World Finals, Marvin Graham was back for more. Graham seemed to come out of nowhere to win the U.S. Nationals in 1974. He returned to Bee Line Dragway for the Winter Nationals and defeated James Warren in the Top Fuel final.

Graham had defeated Garlits in convincing fashion in the semifinals with a 6.64 ET at 229 mph to Garlits's lagging 6.82 at 216. Leading up to the final round, the team of Warren-Coburn-Miller was in a major thrash after destroying the engine while defeating Gary Beck in the semifinals. Against Graham, the Warren-driven *Rain for Rent* saw a repeat of their previous-round carnage as the Donovan Hemi went up in flames, giving the fans quite the sight in the darkened skies. Graham soloed for the win with a 6.57 ET.

Funny Car

NHRA World Champion Shirl Greer qualified fourth but won the Funny Car final in his new Mustang II by defeating the Mach 1 Mustang of Jim Terry, which was driven by veteran Neil Leffler. Leffler qualified number-one with a 6.32 ET and earned his final-round birth by defeating Gordie Bonin, Dale Pulde, and Billy Meyer, who was driving for Gene Snow. Greer eliminated Richard Tharp, Jim Dunn, and Mike Miller to earn the right to face Leffler. In a match that was too close to call, Greer took the win with a 7.03 ET at 218.96 mph to a 7.08 at 220.58.

Defending AHRA World Champ Don Prudhomme debuted his Monza at the Winter Nationals. Prudhomme qualified number-two with a 6.40 ET but failed to make an early dent, falling to Billy Meyer in the second round. Prudhomme's initial pass saw him break the rear end and spill gear oil all over the track. In no time, crewmen Bob Brandt and Harlan Fagan had the Monza back in action. Without question, the Monza was Prudhomme's best car. He spent the next four years winning NHRA Funny Car titles with it.

Pro Stock

Unfavorable weight breaks saw Indiana's Bob Glidden park his NHRA-world-champion Pinto and start the year with a new Don Hardy–built 1970 Mustang. Glidden qualified the Mustang number-one with an 8.96 ET and

As Bob Glidden focused his attention on running NHRA races, his AHRA wins were rare. In 1975, the Winter Nationals was his only AHRA win of the season. (Photo Courtesy Todd Wingerter)

ran top speed of the meet at 153.641 mph. The Mustang was the only Pro Stocker in the 8s all weekend.

Drag racing's *Mad Dog* powered his way to the final, where he defeated the AMC Hornet of Wally Booth with an 8.99 ET at 152.28 mph to a 9.12 at 149.25. The Winter Nationals win would be Glidden's only AHRA win of the season.

Mike McCloskey and Greg Jordan couldn't lose. Their success goes back to the early 1960s when McCloskey started with a flathead. McCloskey won a pair of world titles in the mid-1970s. (Photo Courtesy Rich Carlson/Grant Bittner)

It was a different story in the NHRA, where he campaigned five different cars and won another NHRA Pro Stock title. Booth returned to the finals at the AHRA Drag Nationals in Kansas City and defeated Warren Johnson.

Other Action

Pro Comp honors were earned by Frank Harris, who drove the BB/FC *Hawkeye* Vega of Zig & Dietz to a 7.20 ET to defeat a broken Wayne Stoeckel. Mike McCloskey, for the umpteenth time, won Modified by defeating Walt Niesen with 8.70 ET at 166 mph to an 8.88 at 150.75. Allen Patterson, searching for a third world title that would never come, won Street with his Camaro. Herman Chapman won Super Stock, Glenn Erlandson won Stock, and George Wagner won Selectra class.

Larry Kimball ran his 1969 Camaro in both AHRA and IHRA competition through the mid-1970s. Things were never the same after his brother Gary lost his life due to an on-track incident. (Photo Courtesy Todd Wingerter)

The World Finals Settles in Spokane (1975)

Spokane's Raceway Park opened in 1974 under the management of Orville Moe. The track became a reality thanks to investors who coughed up a couple million to make it happen. The AHRA held its Spring Nationals there in 1974, and the track became home of the World

Hank Johnson, seen here in Edmonton, Alberta, Canada, had his share of Top Fuel success, dating back to 1971 when he won the Super Nationals, the first national event that he ever entered. (Photo Courtesy Bob Jackson)

There's no keeping a good man down. John Wiebe returned in 1975 to win his third world title. Victories would come for Wiebe in AHRA, IHRA, and NHRA competition. (Photo Courtesy Mike Sopko Sr.)

Finals beginning in 1975. There the event remained through 1983 to the approval of the large crowds that it drew annually.

Top Fuel

Don Garlits saw his streak of four world championships come to an end, as this year's honors fell to John Wiebe. Wiebe had the title sewn up early on the basis of three series wins: Tulsa, Dragway 42, and the inaugural race in Minnesota.

At the World Finals, mechanical ills sidelined Garlits early. He watched as Hank Johnson defeated Marvin Graham in the final. Johnson's Al's Auto Supply fueler ran consistent and held low ET with a 6.13 and ran consistent 6-teens all weekend, saving a 6.16 ET at 233.66 mph for Graham, who shut off with a 6.92.

Funny Car

Tom McEwen was in a similar situation as Wiebe. McEwen won three series events: OCIR, the Drag Nationals at Kansas City, and the North American Nationals at Minnesota. Giving McEwen a run for his money was crowd favorite Jim Liberman.

Liberman was pure entertainment, and win or lose, he never failed to brighten a program. In 1975, he was having the best year of his career. He won races at Dragway 42 and Tulsa and was runner-up in St. Louis to the Mustang of Dick Custy. On top of that, Liberman found time to win the NHRA Summernationals.

The World Finals overlooked both men and saw Gordie

In a scene that repeated numerous times since the early 1960s, Tom McEwen faced off against Ed McCulloch. In 1975, the AHRA went to a minimum 62-inch body width for the Funny Cars (reduced from 64 inches). (Photo Courtesy Terry Gilkes)

A win at the World Finals for Canadian Gordie Bonin was only the beginning. Bonin went on to earn the nickname "240 Gordie" for having the knack of breaking the mile-per-hour barrier with ease while others were still knocking on the door.

Bonin in his *Bubble Up* Monza take it to Jake Johnston, who was driving the Vega of Pisano & Matsubara. The main driver, Joe Pisano, was sidelined with a broken leg and retired instead of returning to the seat. Pisano remained a staple in Funny Car for years to come. In the Funny Car final, Johnston's 6.58 ET came up short against Bonin's quicker 6.46, which was low ET of the meet.

Ken Dondero, one of Pro Stock's most versatile drivers, won two AHRA world titles driving for Grumpy Jenkins. Dondero also drove for Bob Panella, Dick Landy (twice), Don Nicholson, and Gapp & Roush.

Pro Stock

Ken Dondero in Grumpy Jenkins's Monza owned the season. He began the year in Grumpy's Vega before switching to a Monza midseason. Of the dozen series races in 1975, Dondero won seven, including the World Finals. In between were series wins by the Mustangs of Bob Glidden and Don Nicholson, the Vega of Tom Haller and Royce Freeman, and the AMC Hornets of Wally Booth and Dave Kanners (Maskin-Kanners).

Dondero's final-round victim at the World Finals was former world champ Larry Huff, whose only other final-round appearance in 1975 came at Tulsa where he'd come in second to . . . Ken Dondero. At the finals, Dondero took the win with a 9.04 ET at 148.51 mph to Huff's 9.10 at 147.54 mph.

In the mid-1970s, Hot Rod *magazine featured a series of articles that focused on the build of C.J. Baker's 1969 Chevelle. Baker prepared the Chevelle for AHRA competition, where he ran the car in multiple 2- and 4-barrel classes, capturing records and class wins along the way. (Photo Courtesy Rich Carlson/Grant Bittner)*

Other Action

Wayne Stoeckel went home a happy camper having won the event with his Pro Comp dragster and the world title as well. Walt Niesen had a

Heading into the World Finals, the S/S title was still up for grabs with four racers in the running. Billy Ray would pull it out with his 1968 Camaro. Ray ran a C&S 2-barrel carburetor atop his 331 engine. (Photo Courtesy Christian Ray)

tough go of it, winning Modified when he beat the A/MP Plymouth Barracuda of Bob Lambeck.

Jeff Schmidt, who could row a Nash transmission like no other, drove his small-block *Black Acid* Camaro to victory in Street. Billy Ray and his 1968 Camaro won Super Stock, and the first of two championships with an 11.90 ET. It was an amazing feat, considering the caliber of cars that he had to defeat, including C.J. Baker and future world champs Noel Zweigler and Larry Mitchell. Rounding out the action was Glenn Erlandson and his *TraveLodge* Pinto winning Stock and his second consecutive world title.

1975–1977 Pro Stock World Champs

There's no denying that Bill "Grumpy" Jenkins built the most potent Pro Stock Chevys in the 1970s. Jenkins and his two drivers, Larry Lombardo and Ken Dondero, won three AHRA World Championships and two NHRA World Championships.

Dondero was hired by Jenkins after spending a few successful years driving for Nicholson. With Jenkins's plans to campaign two cars in 1975, Dondero was a welcome addition. But almost immediately, friction between Dondero and Lombardo developed. Lombardo, maybe suffering insecurities after crashing Jenkins's Vega early in 1973, felt that Dondero was hired to replace him. Jenkins seemed amused by the friction, which only took a few months to boil over. Dondero was an easy-going guy who finally had enough and came to an agreement with Jenkins. He would run the AHRA races with crewmember Dave Christie, while Jenkins, using the new Monza, would run the NHRA races with Lombardo.

Dondero's first national event win came at OCIR in March 1975, where he defeated the Vega of Gary Hansen in the Pro Stock final with an 8.83 ET at 156.79 mph. Jenkins's go-to engine during the 1970s was the 327-derived 331.

"Bill always took the first four good engines to run the NHRA with, [and] I would get engine number-five and whatever was left," Dondero said. "Bill would jokingly say, 'You don't think I'd give you the good stuff?' But even Jenkins's fifth engine was better than most team's number-one engine." Dondero won the AHRA world championship in both 1975 and 1976, and Larry Lombardo won it in 1977.

1976: Tucson, Home of the Winter Nationals

Tucson, the new home of the Winter Nationals, opened in 1964 and was an AHRA-sanctioned track from Day 1. Although it was not intended to host major events, owner/operator Bob Huff saw to it that the track was brought up to snuff prior to hosting the Winter Nationals when it came to town from January 16 to 18.

The AHRA always had its dedicated racers, who were

Ken Dondero was in his prime during the mid-1970s. His two world champ titles didn't come easy, not while battling the likes of Dave Kanners, who is seen here in the far lane. (Photo Courtesy Gary L. Anderson)

Bob Pickett gave Mickey Thompson a win at the Nationals at Spokane in 1976. Although on the heavy side, as it appears, the Pontiac Grand Am body was used by Thompson with various drivers over four years. (Photo Courtesy Bob Snyder)

Paul Longenecker competed at all levels. In 1974, he made the move from running door cars to Top Fuel, and he won the Grand American race at Dragway 42. A few runner-up finishes followed. (Photo Courtesy Michael Pottie)

stars of the sport in their own right. Many of these people never became household names because they avoided racing in the NHRA due to rules that were more restrictive as well as the politics that were involved. Thus, they never received the ink that they should have. As often was the case, here at Tucson, the AHRA die-hards collected their share of gold.

Top Fuel

In Top Fuel qualifying, journeyman Paul Longenecker surprised many by grabbing the number-one position with a 6.03 ET. Slipping into the number-two spot was Frank Bradley with a distant 6.15. Securing the final spot in the 16-car field was Colorado's Bob Williams with a 6.47. In between fell several racers who could make life miserable for the leaders: Shirley Muldowney, John Wiebe, and Jim Plummer (to name a few).

Eliminations saw the two leaders meet in the final round after Longenecker defeated underdog Bob Struksnes in the semifinals. Bradley took care of his opponent, Jim Plummer. Bradley was able to choose his lane due to his quicker previous-round ET. He chose wisely, and it paid off. Bradley sailed on to his first-ever national event win, turning a 6.15 ET at 222 mph to Longenecker's 6.31 at 224.43. Longenecker got his taste of victory later in the year when he won the Gateway Nationals by defeating Bill Pryor in the final round.

The ex-Stone-Woods-Cook Mustang saw many trips down the quarter mile by Mighty Mike Van Sant. No wins were bigger than the Winter Nationals in 1976. (Photo Courtesy Michael Pottie)

The Mongoose debuted a new Duster in 1976. He retained his old car and had John Collins drive it. It proved to be a dry year, as McEwen's best showings were a few runner-up finishes. (Photo Courtesy Bob Snyder)

Funny Car

A surprise in Funny Car saw Mighty Mike Van Sant in the well-worn ex-Stone-Woods-Cook Mustang take honors by defeating Shirl Greer. Like Top Fuel, the Funny Car field was loaded with all of the heavy hitters. Liberman showed up with his new Monza and laid down the low ET while qualifying number-one with a 6.44. Liberman lasted to the second round before falling to Greer.

Gene Snow in his own Monza fell in the first when he got out of shape and crossed the centerline. Snow was reinstated on the break rule and fell in the next round to Tom Hoover's *Showtime* Vega. Others that came and went included Dick Custy, Gary Burgin, and Tom McEwen.

In the semifinals, Greer disposed of McEwen, and Van Sant sent Tom Hoover packing with an oh-so-close 6.82 ET to a 6.84. The final round proved to be anticlimactic, when on the green, Greer lost traction and watched his race go up in smoke. Van Sant took the win, which was his only national event win with a 6.84 ET at 207.85 mph.

Pro Stock

Lee Edwards in his big-block Camaro grabbed the number-one qualifying position by laying down a record-setting 8.67 ET. Close in the number-two position was 1975 world champ Ken Dondero with an 8.71 ET. Threatening the leaders were Lee Hunter, Shelby Jester, Warren Johnson, Roy Hill, Gordie Rivera, and Dick Landy, whose Dart held top speed of the meet at 153.58 mph.

Round action saw Edwards eliminate Kevin Rotty's Camaro in the first and the Claude Hodges *Shag* Monza in the second with a pair of 8.96 ETs. Dondero was losing no ground as he defeated Scott Behar's Vega and Roy Hill's Duster in the first two rounds. That was the end of the line for the Jenkins's Monza, as Dondero then fell to Johnson. Rivera was sent packing by Edwards, setting up an all-Camaro, all-big-block final.

Landy's Kent Fuller Dart was initially campaigned by Larry Huff, which Landy purchased in 1976 after wrecking his own Fuller car. Landy raced the Dart into 1978, at which time he took a hiatus from drag racing to focus his attention on Dick Landy Industries. (Photo Courtesy Dan Williams)

Warren Johnson had his best year yet in 1976, earning wins at the Winter Nationals and the Southwest Nationals at Tulsa. Powering the Don Ness–built Camaro to record 8.80 times was a de-stroked 427 that measured 397 ci. (Photo Courtesy Michael Pottie)

The nation's quickest Street Roadster belonged to Ed Sigmon. Sigmon battled in the new Top Comp category and ran well into the 8s with 394 ci of big-block Chevy. (Photo Courtesy Michael Moore)

Lights Out

It was previously mentioned that mishaps seemed to happen all too frequently at AHRA events. Well, here's another that took place during the Funny Car final at the 1976 Grand American race at Detroit Dragway on the weekend of May 22 to 24.

The season points race was close with Minnesota's Tom Hoover swapping the lead back and forth with Gene Snow. Entering the race at Detroit, Snow had a slight lead. Luck would have it that the two combatants would meet in the final round.

"My first inkling that something was wrong came when the announcer's voice cut out mid-sentence," said author Tom Bonner, who witnessed the event. "I glanced at the silent tower to see that all of the windows appeared to be dark. I turned my attention to the Christmas tree, to see that it looked dead. The staging beams were out as well. How could a power failure happen at this exact moment, just before the most important run of the weekend?"

Track manager Tom Gilmore may have been wondering the same thing, but he didn't hesitate and quickly took control of the situation. Gilmore lined the two cars up by hand, figuring on flag-starting the race. First, he lined up Hoover, and then he turned to Snow.

"I'm not sure what happened, but all of a sudden, the *Showtime* Vega exploded off the line and launched on an all-out pass," Bonner said. "From the starting line, you could see the death smoke hanging above the Vega as Hoover burned up everything he had on the run. The problem was that Snow watched all of this through the windshield of the not-yet staged Monza."

So, what next? Well, it was decided by officials that the winner would be determined by adding up the weekend's ET slips of each racer. Whoever had the lowest ET would be the winner. Hoover came up on the short end, and Snow was determined the winner.

"Of course, the AHRA realized that this was an unfair method to distribute the championship points," Bonner said. "So, they took all the points for the winner and runner-up positions, added them together, and then awarded half to Snow and the other half to Hoover. Thus, after three days of hard runs, the points contest was exactly the same with Snow still leading Hoover by the same amount. The only consolation was the two drivers had put a comfortable margin between themselves and whoever was in third place."

What do you do when the power goes out? You revert to the old way of doing things. Tom Hoover, in the ex–Don Prudhomme Vega, and Gene Snow wait for the flagman. Well, one of them waited. (Photo Courtesy Tom Bonner)

The power outage that led to this mess was due to a kid in the pits who decided to get a better view of the race by climbing up on the main power transformer, ignoring the "Danger, High Voltage" sign. Inadvertently, he stepped on the power-lever switch and killed the power to all of the track.

Tom Hoover surpassed Snow in points and went on to win the Funny Car Championship in 1976 and repeat in 1977.

Tom Hoover's* Showtime *Monza was built around a Jaime Sarte chassis and was powered by a Keith Black 484. Hoover earned his second consecutive world title with the Monza. (Photo Courtesy Mike Dimery

You couldn't ask for a closer, more evenly paired race. The two left the line like they were tied together and remained that way through the top end. The clocks would tell the tale, as Johnson nipped Edwards with a 9.01 ET at 153.32 to a 9.00 at 149.75.

Dave and Carol Kaercher's 283-powered '57 Chevy won a lot more than it lost. Sponsorship for the* Strip Teaser *came from Tucson, Arizona–based Speed Hut. (Photo Courtesy Jim Kelso)

Other Action

Let's start with Top Comp, a new category introduced at the Winter Nationals. It was billed as a "run what you brung, dial your own ET" class that saw a variety in the 32-car field: Ed Sigmon's A/Street Roadster, Dick Krieger's Econo Dragster, and Mike McCloskey's flathead-powered dragster. The inaugural win went to McCloskey, who defeated Walt Niesen with a 9.16 ET at 155.44 mph. Niesen broke out when he ran an 8.63 ET trying to catch McCloskey.

Pro Comp went to Dale Armstrong, whose *Alcoholic* Plymouth recorded a 7.09 ET to defeat Wayne Stoeckel's tire-smoking 9.49. Modified Street was won by Larry Spitali, Super Stock went to Glen Pucilowski, Super Street went to Scott Strachan, and Stock honors went home with Dave Workman.

Jeb Allen's Triumphant Return

Outside of a win at the 1976 NHRA Fallnationals, Jeb Allen all but disappeared from the winner's circle after his fiery crash with John Wiebe at the National Challenge in 1973. In 1977, he bounced back in dramatic fashion and won the AHRA Top Fuel world title. In the abbreviated seven-race season, Allen started off by winning the Winter Nationals, defeating Rance McDaniel in the final with a 6.36 ET. He followed with wins at Tulsa and St. Louis by defeating Tom Dumbell and Gary Beck.

A natural-born racer, Allen earned his Top Fuel license at the age of 17. In 1972 at age 18, he won his first national event: the NHRA Summernationals. In winning the AHRA title in 1977, Allen became the youngest person in the history of the sport to win a Top Fuel world title. In 1980, he won the IHRA world title. In 1981, he won the NHRA title, becoming the first ever to win the championship in all three sanctioning bodies. He did this all before the age of 30.

It was a long road back for Jeb Allen after the incident with John Wiebe at the National Challenge 1973. It all paid off in 1977. (Photo Courtesy Mike Dimery)

1977–1979: Some Wins and Some Losses

The late 1970s were lean years for the AHRA, as annual series events hovered at 7 and 8, down from the regular 10 that ran through 1976.

"Too many track leases put us into terrible financial trouble, and the races that were money losers were cut," Ruth Tice said.

Races that were money losers were cut.

In December 1976, NHRA president Wally Parks sent a letter to Jim Tice suggesting that he "dissolve the AHRA sanction activity, allowing some of your [AHRA]-affiliated tracks to consider sanction by the NHRA."

Parks looked to absorb Spokane and Green Valley. In exchange, the NHRA would support Tice's Grand American series of events. Parks's assumption wasn't too far off when he stated that the "AHRA's sanctions can't be too lucrative a source of income under present circumstances."

Obviously, Tice shunned the suggestion and soldiered forward.

In 1978, Don Garlits was recognized by the AHRA as drag racing's man of the century. With a new crew chief, Herb Parks, pulling wrenches, the pair won both the AHRA and the IHRA world titles in 1978. (Photo Courtesy Bob Snyder)

Top Fuel Action

After Jeb Allen won the Top Fuel world championship in 1977, Garlits took it the next three years on the strength of over a dozen series wins. There was no topping Garlits. He ran a 5.63 ET in October 1975, and the mark stood through July 1982 as the quickest ET turned by a Top Fuel car.

Garlits appeared at the 1978 Winter Nationals with a Donovan 417 replacing his standard Keith Black mill. A new sponsor in the U.S. Navy was also onboard. Garlits had repainted *Swamp Rat 24* in a new blue and white paint scheme with a Holy Cross and "God Is Love" adorning the cowl.

Larry Frazier pulled wrenches, and John Abbott laid down times that made the Jet X Fueler *tough on the competition. The team opened the 1979 season by winning the Winter Nationals, defeating Frank Bradley in the final with a 6.92 ET. A 488-ci Milodon got the job done. (Photo Courtesy Teri Abbott Vanderhoof)*

In his own book, Garlits wrote, "The Navy was unhappy; they wanted the cross removed at once or moved into the cockpit where it couldn't be seen by cameras. I wouldn't comply, and the Navy withdrew the sponsorship . . . I'm a Christian and I figured God would work it out—and did God ever!"

Giving Garlits a run for the money during this period were the usual suspects: Jeb Allen, John Wiebe, Gary Beck, and Frank Bradley. Not to take anything away from Bradley, who had a magnificent career well into the 1990s, but he somehow managed to have never won a world title. Some say 1976 was his best season, where he won multiple events.

In front of the usual sold-out Spokane crowd, Tom McEwen won the 1979 World Finals and the season championship. His final round opponent was Gordie Bonin. (Photo Courtesy Rich Carlson/Grant Bittner Collection)

Few have made the transition from Top Fuel to Funny Car (or vice versa) with success. However, veteran Bill Graham did it with his Donovan-powered Million Dollar Baby *Monza. (Photo Courtesy Mike Dimery)*

John Collins and Tom Hoover came face to face at the Winter Nationals in 1979. Hoover won this one and the event by defeating Gary Burgin in the final. A year later, Collins switched to a Datsun 280-Z body. (Photo Courtesy Ruth Tice)

After wrecking Andy White's Shag *Monza Pro Stocker through no fault of his own, Shelby Jester returned in 1978 driving for Claud Hodges. Success followed with Jester accumulating two world championships.*

Funny Car

Although Gene Snow and Tom McEwen won the world championships in 1978 and 1979, Lord knows that they didn't come easy. Tom Hoover, Don Prudhomme, Billy Graham, and John Collins all made life difficult. Graham made the move from Top Fuel to Funny Car in 1977 and the move paid immediate dividends when he drove his *Million Dollar Baby* Monza to a win at the Spring Nationals, followed by a win at the Ozark Nationals in 1978.

Collins, who started campaigning Funny Cars back in 1970 with partner John Bateman, was hired on to drive McEwen's second car and used it to win the 1977 Winter Nationals. A sponsorship deal with Pioneer stereos helped Collins, as he established his own program running a Duster and a Trans Am before he debuted a Datsun 280Z in 1980. During the period, Collins would make numerous final round appearances.

One of the many underdogs still chasing the Pro Stock dream was Tom Chase. Chase would bookend the 1977–1979 period by winning the World Finals each season. Chase and his Alston Mustang beat out Rick Rader and Billy Wash in doing so. (Photo Courtesy Tom Chase)

Pro Stock

After Larry Lombardo brought Grumpy Jenkins his third consecutive crown in 1977, Shelby Jester brought it home in 1978. After a wreck in 1976 and again in 1977, Shelby took time off before returning in 1978 driving the ex-Kelly Chadwick Vega for Claud Hodges.

A mechanic and gas station owner from Lawton, Oklahoma, Shelby knew how to build a 331-ci motor from his experience working on the Monza of Reher & Morrison. His experience proved out when he won the Pro Stock championship for the second time in 1980.

The (Not So) Little Guys

Let's start with the Comp categories. In 1977, the AHRA divided Pro Comp and created the Pro Comp Dragster and Pro Comp

Frank Cook was a seasoned veteran by the time this photo was taken in 1977. With Chuck Landers pulling wrenches, and the most wonderful helpers, Cook won his share of Pro Comp races. Cook later made a move into Top Fuel. (Photo Courtesy Bob Aberty Jr.)

World Champ Simon Menzies, driving Jim Jackson's Racing Enterprises 1978 Corvette BB/FC, dominated the season. Menzies often qualified at shows running AA/FC to fill programs. (Photo Courtesy Michael Pottie)

Funny Car categories. Championships were won that year by veterans Richard Ogg and Mike Savage. Savage relinquished the title to Simon Menzies in 1978. Menzies, along with the likes of Dale Armstrong, who prepped the Donovan hemi in Jackson's Corvette; Wilfred Boutilier; and Ken Veney, dominated mid-1970s' Pro Comp Funny Car action. Top Comp Dragster saw Brian Raymer and Porter Dunn walk off with championships.

Door Slammers

In 1978, Super Street became the AHRA's first dial-your-own-ET bracket for cars running 14.99 or quicker. Richard Wegner won the championship that year in a class that was dominated by Wegner, and "Missouri" George Montgomery through 1979. Super Stock was a real toss up with Championships won by Roy Kempe, Noel Zweigler, and Larry Mitchell, who repeated his 1976 Super Stock title.

In 1977, Mike Burger showed that there was still life in the old Chevy when he ran a 12.15 ET to defeat Don Anderson in Modified Street at the Grand American at Dragway 42. (Photo Courtesy Todd Wingerter)

Stock read like a who's who list. Don Spencer and partner Ron Knape were quite possibly the winningest team in the sportsman categories. With Spencer at the wheel of his 327-powered 1962 Corvette, they campaigned the car in AHRA competition. Between 1972 and 1984, they had 76 class wins, 15 eliminator wins, and the 1977 Stock World Championship.

Bob Bowe began racing his 1957 Chevy wagon in 1974, and in 1978 he won the Stock world title. A high-revving punched-out 283 was backed by a turbo 400 and a 6.17-equipped Dana. The wagon, which is still in use, has managed 11.70 ETs and held records in multiple classes. There's lots

World Champ Bob Bowe and his '57 Chevy wagon held the AHRA elapsed time and top speed records in three classes. To do so, he ran a Holley 750-cfm double pumper atop the 283 in F-2, a Holley 650-cfm 2-barrel in F-3, and two Holley 500-cfm 2-barrels on a custom adapter in F-1. (Photo Courtesy Bob Bowe)

Rick Ducusin's 1958 Chevy was another wagon that turned on the win light more than not. Ducusin was a two-time Stock World Champ. A 283 propelled the wagon to mid-13 times. (Photo Courtesy Sally Ruble)

Don Spencer was the Stock World Champ in 1977 and the runner-up in 1979. He and Ron Knape began campaigning this E/V Corvette in 1972 with a 283. An unheard-of streak saw Spencer set class records each year between 1972 and 1984. In 1965, "X" classes were introduced by the AHRA for American Sports Cars. In 1972, "V" classes were introduced for Stock-class Corvettes. (Photo Courtesy Don Spencer)

The Ozarks

Sanctioned tracks frequently came and went. One AHRA track that came, went, and came again was Springfield-Ozark Raceway near Springfield, Missouri. The AHRA began hosting meets at that track back in 1963.

Tragically, it's at this track that Lou Cangelose lost his life in 1965, driving his Fuel Dragster off the end of the strip when his chute failed. A year before the track closed in 1974, veteran racer Gary Kimball was fatally injured when he was struck by flying debris thrown by another car.

Demand from local racers saw a new track (the Springfield-Ozark International Raceway built in 1977), and the AHRA was there to sanction it. The new track was built in nearby Rogersville. It was there that the AHRA ran its Ozark Nationals at the end of June in 1978 and 1979. The track closed at the end of 1979 and reopened under IHRA sanction in 1985.

Two Sportsman greats, Ollie Dean (left) and Don Spencer (right) battle at the Ozarks in 1978. Spencer took the win as well as the eliminator final over Bob Bowe with a 13.40 ET. (Photo Courtesy Don Spencer)

to be said about the small-block Chevy in an early wagon.

Rick Ducusin ran a 283 in his 1958 Chevy wagon and earned world titles in 1979 and 1980. In 1979, it was quite the points chase between Ducusin, Don Spencer, and Jim Parmenter. At the Gateway Nationals, these were the three racers remaining heading into the semifinals. Spencer got the bye run, and Ducusin raced Parmenter. Parmenter took the win light but, upon hitting the scales, he was 70 pounds underweight. So, the winning points went to Ducusin. Spencer was given the runner-up points. The season ended with Spencer and Parmenter finishing second and third behind Ducusin.

With Bobby Marriott at the wheel, the Marriott brothers' Camaro was fierce. The Don Hardy–built car was purchased from Pat Musi and ran a Musi 366-ci engine. (Photo Courtesy Bobby Marriott)

The 1979 Pro Stock World Champ

The 1979 Pro Stock season was dominated by two teams: the team of David Reher, Buddy Morrison, and Lee Shepherd (RMS), and the Marriott brothers, who ran a family team of Bobby Marriott Sr., Bobby Jr., Uncle Johnny, Cousin Bubba, and one outsider, wrench man Jimmy Walker.

RMS debuted a new Don Ness Camaro in 1979 that used a 331-ci engine to win four AHRA series events. Shepherd ran a quick 8.48 ET at 160.71 mph to grab the NHRA class record. The Marriotts' Camaro was a fresh Don Hardy car that they purchased through Pat Musi. Under the A&A Fiberglass hood was a Musi-built 366-ci engine. According to Bobby Sr., who pulled the levers on the Lenco, the Camaro ran some 8.40 ETs in good air and good track conditions, but it usually ran in the 8.60s.

Leading up to the World Finals, RMS won the proceeding Summer Nationals at Kansas City by defeating Bobby Marriott in the final with an 8.77 ET to an off-pace 9.01. The victory put the two teams in a tie with 3,200 points each, with just the World Finals remaining.

Due to distance and scheduling, neither team attended the World Finals. So, one would think that a tie (or maybe a tie-breaker) would have been used. Reading through the results in the October 30 issue of *Drag World*, the AHRA gave the title to the Marriotts by "a whisker." History buffs are left to ponder what that "whisker" was, as no exclamation was provided. Rounding out the top five were Shelby Jester, Bill Wash, and Don Nicholson.

No matter your brand preference, Lee Shepherd was one of Pro Stock's best. The RMS Camaro was built on a Don Ness chassis and housed a 331-ci engine. (Photo Courtesy Joe Webber/Todd Webber)

With Sid Reed at the wheel, Ed Bottom's Chevette was the 1981 Pro Gas World Champ. The Glendale, Arizona–based bullet is running a 4-barrel-equipped big-block Chevy and a Powerglide. (Photo Courtesy Bob Snyder)

Chapter Six

The 1980s: The Sun Sets

For the AHRA, the 1980s opened with 12 stops on the Grand American series trail and closed with a planned 7 stops in 1984. In 1983, the AHRA did away with "buying in cars" and put up an even $10,000 for the pro category winners, thanks in part to the Coors series sponsorship.

The AHRA continued its move toward ET-based categories with Super Comp, Pro Gas, Modified Gas, Super Street, and ET Stock all running off a set index by 1984. New tracks were sanctioned, including Bonneville Raceway in Salt Lake City, Firebird Raceway in Boise, Portland International Raceway in Oregon, and Seattle International Raceway in Washington.

There was a lot to celebrate as the decade began. Racers came out in droves, and fans continued to fill the bleachers at major events. By 1982, the three sanctioning bodies held a combined total of 30 annual national events, and it was becoming questionable as to whether the numbers could be sustained.

Pro Stock Gets an Overhaul

With Pro Stock struggling to field an eight-car program at some series events, changes had to be made if the category was to survive. In 1980, beginning with the Grand Nationals at Dragway 42, the AHRA adopted IHRA-style category rules.

In 1977, the IHRA had gotten away from the fluctuating weight breaks that penalized winning combinations and adopted an "any cubic inch goes, minimum 2,350-pound weight" format. At the Summer Nationals in Kansas City, Sam Carroll won Pro Stock with an 8.27 ET. It was a vast improvement over Lee Shepherd's 1979 winning ET of 8.77.

The AHRA's revised rules entering 1981 had small-block-equipped cars running at a minimum 2,150 pounds and big-block-equipped cars running at a minimum 2,350 pounds. The AHRA took things a step further when it welcomed nitrous oxide to Pro Stock, becoming the first sanctioning body to run a nitrous door-car category.

Mike Thermos of NOS should be thanked for campaigning hard for nitrous to be allowed. Thermos reasoned that nitrous would help to level the playing field. The AHRA agreed with the stipulation those cars running the bottle had to carry an additional 200 pounds.

At the Winter Nationals, Lee Hunter's Mercury Zephyr, powered by a 400-plus-ci Cleveland plumbed with a Lazar nitrous system set low ET of the meet with

"Animal" Jim Feurer was a heavy hitter during the nitrous small-block era. Cliff Sturm pulled wrenches on the Mercury Zephyr, which featured a Woody Mays chassis. (Photo Courtesy Bob Snyder)

Dave and Karen Smith's Oldsmobile-powered 1980 Trans Am had their peers up in arms. Many considered the large-bore, short-stroke engine to be a big-block and felt that it shouldn't have been allowed to run with nitrous.

an 8.228. Hunter made it to the second round before being eliminated by Dyno Don Nicholson's big-inch Boss Mustang.

Jerry Haas ran the only other nitrous car at the meet and loaded up his Monza after a first-round defeat by Nicholson. Pat Musi in his big-block Camaro won the event, defeating Nicholson in the final with a 7.22 ET. Haas proved the nitrous-small-block combination's worth when he won the 1981 AHRA Pro Stock World Championship.

The team of Dave and Karen Smith caught fire after replacing their nitrous Pontiac Starfire during the 1981 season with an Oldsmobile-powered 1980 Trans Am. The Pontiac made use of a 410-ci diesel block and ran a nitrous-oxide system designed by Mike Thermos. Many competitors screamed foul, insisting that Smith's engine was a big-block and shouldn't be allowed to run nitrous. General Motors labeled it as a small-block, and the AHRA accepted it as such.

With Tom Chelbana at the wheel, the Pontiac won the Nationals in 1981 at Alamo Raceway. Wins at the 1982 Winter Nationals, the Alamo (again), and Bonneville, helped the team secure the season's Pro Stock championship. The Smiths replaced the Trans Am in 1983 with a Willie Rells–built Cutlass, which took them to a second-place finish in points that season.

Muldowney's 1981 World Title

Shirley Muldowney, runner-up to Garlits in the 1980 points chase, went all the way in 1981 to become the first woman to win an AHRA World Championship. It was a feat that took Muldowney until the World Finals to accomplish. Entering the race, it was a toss-up between her and Garlits as to who would be crowned the King or Queen of Top Fuel. In the mix was Jerry Ruth, who was determined to ruin someone's weekend, namely Garlits's.

Ruth let the reigning champ know he meant business when he laid down a track-record 5.577 ET during Friday's qualifying. During elimination, Ruth first defeated Chris Karamesines in the quarterfinals before facing Garlits in the semifinals. A loss by Garlits would mean a world championship for Muldowney.

With the burnouts complete, neither racer was prepared or willing to stage first. Of course, the fans ate it up while starter Jim Tice Jr. grew impatient. He waved the drivers on, and Garlits crept into the lights first. Showing impatience of his own, Garlits drew a red light, handing the win to Ruth and the title to Muldowney.

When asked about the red light, Garlits had no comment. After winning the previous three World

Malfunctioning Lights

The 1981 AHRA Nationals at San Antonio, Texas, provided one of those less-than-stellar moments that occasionally inflicted the sport. The scene was the Alamo Dragway, which was a less-than-ideal place to hold a national event, but the AHRA managed to pull it off with malfunctioning lights and all.

It was those malfunctioning lights that led to chaos in the second round of Top Fuel eliminations. Local Texan Jody Smart was lined up against Garlits, and as Garlits's side of the tree flashed down to green, Smart's side was delayed. Garlits took off, and as far as he was concerned, his 6.21 holeshot beat Smart's 6.02. Of course, an expected rile-up ensued between Smart, Garlits, and the officials, but the results stood.

Jody Smart was born to drive. He made the move from running an injected dragster to Top Fuel in 1980 with this Tony Casarez–chassis car. Veteran J.E. Kristek kept the Keith Black engine in tune. (Photo Courtesy Michael Pottie)

Smart was offered $1,000 to rerun Garlits but refused, as win or lose he was out anyway. Well, showing his displeasure with his options, Smart stormed back out onto the track and attacked the Christmas tree, leaving it out of commission and laying on the ground. Smart then drove off, promising never to run another AHRA race. Garlits, once the tree was cobbled back together, fell to Shirley Muldowney in the final, after defeating her just three weeks earlier at the Gateway Nationals.

Championships, Garlits, showing he was just a little peeved at the results, said, "This is it for me. I'll be 50 years old next year. I'm going to get out of it."

Garlits returned and won the next three AHRA world titles.

If Don Garlits is the king of drag racing, then Shirley Muldowney is the queen. Among the AHRA, IHRA, and NHRA, Muldowney won five world titles. (Photo Courtesy Mike Dimery)

Garlits complimented Muldowney by stating she was the toughest of them all.

"She wasn't the longest competitor, but she was tough when she was out there," he said. "Most of the time, we made our money match racing, and we didn't try to run as hard as we could run because we didn't want to blow the engine up. We wanted to make money. But with Shirley, every run was do or die. She wasn't going to let Big Daddy put a wheel out on her."

Muldowney made the final round after defeating Rob Bruin in the semifinals with a 5.71 ET. Against Ruth, she recorded an off-pace 5.89 ET at 202.24 mph as oil pressure went away. Ruth repeated his 1980 World Finals win with a 5.74 ET at 238.72 mph.

Muldowney's season didn't get off to a good start, as she opened with a loss at the AHRA Winter Nationals, falling to Dick LaHaie in the first round. However,

Garlits's run of world titles from 1978 through 1984 was interrupted by Muldowney in 1981. Garlits's Kendall sponsorship was picked up in 1979. (Photo Courtesy Bob Snyder)

things quickly improved, as she won the March Meet at Bakersfield, becoming the first and only woman to do so. At the Spring Nationals, she garnered her first AHRA win of the season, defeating Karamesines in the final round. She won the Nationals in San Antonio and was runner-up at Bonneville and St. Louis.

After the World Finals, Muldowney entered her aging car in meets at Portland and Seattle, as the points earned at those races counted toward the 1982 season.

Other 1981 World Finals Action

Although the World Finals didn't hold a lot of surprises, a few new names joined the fray in the winner's circle, one being Al Young. Young, the pride of the northwest, won Super Street at the Western Nationals at Salt Lake and made it two in a row by winning the World Finals.

Young topped his season by winning the World Championship title with his 440-equipped Dodge Challenger. Bucky Austin, who was making a name for himself, won Pro Comp. Andrew Lee won Top Comp by defeating Walt Niesen. In BB/FC, San Diego's Chuck Beal, coming off a win at Salt Lake, soloed for the win at Spokane when opponent Jack Holsey failed to appear.

In the early 1980s, Jerry Ruth contended for the World Championship most years. This is a 1982 photo from Portland, where he's hazing the tires against the team of Arnold Birky, Jim Murphy, and Wendell Trappe. Murphy took this one with a 5.95 ET at 231.73 mph. (Photo Courtesy Ruth Tice)

Unbelievable as it may sound, only four cars were entered in Pro Stock. Jerry Haas and his Chevy Monza took the win on a solo, and the World Championship from Lee Hunter, who failed to qualify his Mercury Zephyr. Hunter, a longtime Ford proponent, closed his career at the end of the season.

In Funny Car, World Champ Don Prudhomme took it to "240" Gordie Bonin with a 5.98 ET at 239.36 mph. Prudhomme was in the midst of his

Seattle's Al Young and his 440-powered Dodge Challenger was a force in both AHRA and NHRA competition. In 1983, beyond the World Championship and in between bracket racing, Young won the Spokane National Open, North Central Open, and the World Finals. (Photo Courtesy Al Young)

With Boyd Newby at the helm, the (Ron) Chambers & Newby *333-ci Chevy-powered rail was a serious Top Comp threat. During the 1981 season, they were runners-up at the Spring Nationals and Gateway Nationals. (Photo Courtesy Ruth Tice)*

three-year run as World Champ and gave a lot of thanks to a good crew.

"We had good clutch management and fuel delivery," Prudhomme said. "Me and (crew chief) Bob Brandt worked hard at it."

Chuck Beal and his Bealmobile *Plymouth Arrow was a much-feared car in both AHRA and NHRA alcohol Funny Car racing. Beal tried out fuel Funny Car in the 1990s. (Photo Courtesy Grant Bittner)*

Much the same way that Garlits ruled Top Fuel, Prudhomme ruled Funny Car. Prudhomme was the NHRA World Champ from 1975 through 1978 and was the AHRA World Champ from 1980 through 1982. (Photo Courtesy Mike Dimery)

At the last race that Jim Tice attended, the 1982 Winter Nationals, John Muldowney presented him with a replica of Don Garlits's car that he worked on during 1981. The replica is now in Garlits's museum. (Photo Courtesy Ruth Tice)

The Declining Health of Jim Tice

In February 1981, AHRA president Jim Tice began showing symptoms of the pancreatic cancer that eventually took his life. He and his wife, Ruth, flew to the Mayo Clinic in June, where he received the diagnosis. At that time, they were told that Tice probably had only six months to live. He put up a good fight, and as the year wound down, he appeared to be doing well.

Ruth recalled that late in December she got a migraine headache, a first for her, and could not get out of bed.

"But Jim got up and started packing his suitcase." Ruth said. "I asked him, 'Where are you going?' 'To the Winter Nationals in Tucson,' he said. And he did!"

Chemotherapy and trips to the Mayo Clinic followed. He received experimental surgery at Mayo, but the cancer spread. Tice returned home to continue the fight.

"He actually did great for months, but it finally got him on August 27, 1982," Ruth said. "He lived over a year with this type of cancer, which was rare at that time. We were so blessed to have two doctors as neighbors who stopped in every day to check on him."

Tice left controlling interest of the AHRA in the hands of Ruth, who carried on under less-than-ideal circumstances. She received support from several track operators, but as Jim lay on his death bed, the storm clouds were gathering.

The 1982 World Finals

Jim Tice had never missed a World Finals, but with death imminent, there was no way he was going to make Spokane. The race was August 19 to 22, and five days later, Jim Tice passed away. It seems appropriate that preacher Billy Graham made an appearance at Saturday's race, where he led the attendees in prayer.

Graham invited everyone out to his crusade that would be taking place the following day at Spokane's Joe Albi Stadium. Based upon reports of Sunday's Finals turnout, I think a good many of them took him up on the offer. Graham's crusade drew a sold-out crowd of 33,000 people, while Sunday's final had one of its smallest turnouts on record.

Jim Tice's Vision

Jim Tice was always thinking of ways to better the sport of drag racing. He envisioned and worked at making AHRA events a show that could be enjoyed by a wider spectrum of people. He worked to make the sport easier to understand by going to index-orientated classes. In his eyes, this would eliminate the whole issue of rule books and tech inspectors, which were the things he never really cared to deal with.

Tice also envisioned an AHRA where he could have better control if his staff was only in the Kansas City office. Each track operator would become an AHRA representative with some decision-making authority (i.e., procedures on race day [local]). Tice's full-time pilot, Blaine Laux, flew with staff to any track needing help with its weekly races. The major series events would have Tice and his staff fly in, run it, and return to Kansas City after the event was wrapped up.

"Everything changed when Jim was given the death sentence in 1981," Ruth Tice said. "All of a sudden you see life very differently. I am sure he knew what would happen to me running the AHRA, and the travel was seven days a week. Jim was very concerned about who would raise [our daughter] Michelle through her teenage years. He said to sell the company [to] raise Michelle if you have to. Guess what? She has turned out to be a wonderful person and a great mother of two boys. Now, she is guiding them through school and life and teaching them to respect all people."

Spokane track manager Orville Moe congratulates Don Garlits after winning the World Championship in 1982. To Garlits's right is his wife, Pat, holding their Yorkshire Terrier named Schultz. (Photo Courtesy Ruth Tice)

Although Frank Bradley qualified in the number-one position at the World Finals, he failed to make rounds. Bradley's career included membership in both the Cragar 5- and 4-second club. (Photo Courtesy Ruth Tice)

When it came to the racing, three seemed to be a popular number in the pro categories. Don Garlits won his first of three World Championships in a row, Don Prudhomme won the last of his three in a row, and Karen and Dave Smith with Dave Chelbana, driving their nitrous Oldsmobile-powered 1980 Trans Am, won their third national event of the season.

John Abbott was always in the thick of battle, be it in the AHRA, the IHRA, or the NHRA. He came close to winning the AHRA World Finals in 1981 as well as the NHRA World Championship. (Photo Courtesy Mike Ball/David Ball)

Top Fuel

The Top Fuel field was led by Frank Bradley, who set the pace by qualifying number-one with a record 5.53 ET. Close behind was Garlits with a 5.56 ET. Bradley, who had last won at the Chi-Town Nationals in July, made it to the second round before the shadow-ladened, cool left lane saw him smoke the tires against eventual runner-up John Abbott.

The same fate awaited Abbott in the final against Garlits. Garlits, after defeating Jerry Ruth in the semifinals, chose the good right lane in the final and bested Abbott's tire-smoking 5.91 ET at 244.56 mph with a 5.66 at 251.39.

Funny Car

Heading into the World Finals, Don Prudhomme and his Pepsi Challenger–sponsored Firebird had already wrapped up the world title by winning the Spring Nationals, Chi-Town Nationals, Grand Nationals, and Bonneville, which made him the odds-on favorite to win the World Finals.

What no one expected to see was Prudhomme falling in the second round to underdog Gary Densham. Densham, who'd been looking for a big win since join-

Good times call for good celebrations. Tom McEwen seems to eye John Force as he tries to steal his Coors sponsorship. I wonder who got the most out of the sponsor this night. (Photo Courtesy Ruth Tice)

ing Funny Car back in 1973, took a holeshot lead and never looked back. He defeated a tire-smoking Prudhomme with a 6.08 ET at 233.76 mph.

Densham's final-round opponent was Tom McEwen, who previously defeated Hank Johnson, and Ed McCulloch. In the final, it was McEwen and his Coors-sponsored Corvette in the good right lane, taking the win with a 6.11 ET at 204 mph even to Densham's slowing 6.49 at 196.50.

Pro Stock

Chuck Aronson and his 588-ci Fairmont (Bob Glidden's old undefeated NHRA World Championship car) pretty much owned Pro Stock from start to finish. He opened up by polishing off Brad Yuill in the controversial Pontiac J-2000 of the Yuill brothers and closed by defeating the Oldsmobile Cutlass of Dave and Karen Smith with a 7.90 ET at 167.71 mph to a red-light 7.78 at 171.48.

Other Action

The list of category winners contained many previous-event champs: BB/FC went to Chuck Beal, the Pro Comp winner was Doc Liscombe, and Top Comp honors went

Through the late 1970s and into the 1980s, brothers Larry and Bill Mitchell were dominant in their chosen categories. It wasn't unusual to see Larry's Corvette and/or Bill's Camaro in the winner's circle at any given race. (Photo Courtesy Bill Mitchell)

In 1983, Chuck Aronson won the AHRA World Championship, which was in addition to being the AHRA and IHRA Rookie of the Year. Aronson relied upon Jon Kaase engines that measured 588 and later 605 ci. (Photo Courtesy Cale Aronson)

Doc Liscombe's **Whiplash 3** *Top Alcohol Dragster won Pro Comp at the 1982 World Finals with a 6.77 ET and was runner-up in 1983 to Ken Sitko. Power came by the way of a Rodeck Chevy. (Photo Courtesy Vern Scholz)*

Larry Peternel's 1981 Chrysler Imperial may be the epitome of the phrase "dare to be different." A 496-ci Hemi made the car competitive. Here, Peternel faces Chuck Aronson. (Photo Courtesy Richard Kluk)

home with Mike Ferderer and his Roadster. Pro Gas belonged to Bill Fetter, Modified Gas went to Bob Kerslake, Modified Super Stock (a category the AHRA created in 1982 by combining Super Stock with Modified Street) went to Larry Mitchell and his Corvette. Ron Zeller took Super Street, and Steve Jackson took ET Stock.

1983: Racing Among the Turmoil

The AHRA offered some stellar shows through the 1983 season, holding series events in Tucson, Arizona; Tulsa, Oklahoma; St. Louis, Missouri; San Antonio, Texas; Gary, Indiana; West Salem, Ohio; Kansas City, Missouri; Salt Lake City, Utah; and Spokane, Washington. Helping Ruth Tice run operations were several people who shouldn't be overlooked, including Janice Stuteville and Norma Brooks, who ran the main office in Leawood, Kansas.

Georgia Miller joined the AHRA in the 1970s. In later years, she carried the title of manager of driver scheduling and pit credentials. Without Miller, there would have been no racing. She made things happen, period.

"She was one of the most important people we had," Ruth Tice said about Miller. "She was actually a representative for all of the racers, like a lobbyist for them. She and Jim would go over who to book for the big meets and she would work with track operators and racers to lock them in—no contracts, just by word! Then, we could cut radio and TV spots with names."

In the field was tech manager Vance Brady, who took over the position from Don Wormsley in the mid-1970s, and Jim Tice Jr., who carried the title of race director. In hindsight, Ruth says she probably should have fired Jim Jr.

Jim Jr. was Tice's son from a previous marriage. Try as she might, Ruth never was able to establish a relationship with him.

"Jimmy was stabbing me in the back every chance he got to make himself look better," Ruth said.

It was shame, as Ruth stated that maybe if they were on the same page, they could have made the AHRA work.

The ongoing stress, along with the constant travel and worrying about her daughter at home became too much. Inevitably, a change had to come. In the meantime, there were scheduled events to be run.

1983 Winter Nationals

To know Ruth Tice is to know she is a woman possessed with a positive disposition and one who thinks before reacting. It's just who she is. At Tucson, Arizona, from January 14 to 17, Ruth was tested, as she hosted her first national event as the president of the AHRA.

Action was to get underway on Thursday, but Mother Nature had other plans. Due to freezing temperatures

Between-round thrashing was and remains a common practice. Unresolved mechanical issues sidelined Frank "the Beard" Bradley here at the Winter Nationals. (Photo Courtesy Mike Dimery)

that brought rain that turned to hail and a little snow, warmup runs were delayed until Friday. When the racing began, the combination of a poor track surface and a high altitude (2,300 feet) saw ETs suffer.

Top Fuel

Finding enough bite to make the eight-car field were (in qualifying order) Garlits, Snow, Ruth, LaHaie, Karamesines, Abbott, Bradley, and a re-energized Lyle Fisher. Fisher had been around since the mid-1950s when he raced the mid-engine Speed Sport Modified Roadster with partner Red Greth. It was a shame that his weekend came to an early end.

Garlits led the field from beginning to end. He set the low ET and top speed of the meet with runs of 6.08 and 240.64 mph. Sunday eliminations saw Garlits run low ET in each round. Keeping pace with Garlits (albeit at a slower pace) was Gene Snow, who was Garlits's opponent in the final round. Saving the best for last, Garlits took the win with another 6.08 ET, besting Snow's 6.12.

Although always in the thick of battle, 1983 was a dry year for Jerry Ruth, as he went without a series win. His career came to an end in 1984, when it was discovered that he had been supporting his drag racing with illicit funds. (Photo Courtesy Ruth Tice)

Funny Car

The show proved to be little more than a walk in the park for number-one qualifier Don Prudhomme. His 6.80 ET was unmatched all weekend. The only real battle, if you want to call it such, was a first-round win over Tom Hoover, where the Snake slowed to a 7.32 but still defeated Hoover's 7.67.

Popular Southern California racer Gary Burgin was coming off a great 1982 season, having won the Gateway and Summer Nationals. However, he ran dry in 1983, his final season in competition. (Photo Courtesy Jack Muller)

In the all-Firebird final, Prudhomme faced Gary Burgin, an independent who made good, and defeated him with a 7-flat ET. Burgin fell with an 11-second time. As I said, it was a walk in the park.

Pro Stock

A total of 13 cars showed with hopes of making the 8-car field. It was a vast improvement over 1982's Winter Nationals, where only four cars showed for Pro Stock (Tom Chelbana defeated Jim Feurer in the final). Leading the field in 1983 was Feurer, who recorded an 8.74 ET with his nitrous Mercury. Rounding out the pack was the Camaro of Rick Rader, which managed a 9.70 ET before disappearing in the first round.

Dale Shafer raced his Mustang as far back as 1977, focusing his attention on AHRA and circuit races, where he did pretty well for himself. By 1983, he was running a 422-inch Cleveland. (Photo Courtesy Ron Berges)

Chuck Nuytten has been building performance carburetors since 1972, and what better way to advertise your work than to build a winning race car. Nuytten won at San Antonio in 1983, handing Chuck Aronson a rare loss. (Photo Courtesy Larry Fulton)

The surprise of the meet was Benny Flowers, whose 1981 Camaro sailed on to a Pro Stock victory after improving from his initial 9.13 qualifying time with a pair of 8.73s. In the first round, Flowers took an easy win when number-two qualifier Dave Shafer failed to show. In the semifinals, Flowers defeated the Charger of Chuck Nuytten before facing and defeating Feurer's quicker 8.69 with his second 8.73.

Other Action

Other action centered around the BB/FC Corvette of Rick Ruiz. Ruiz's Corvette was sporting a three-stage, 900-hp nitrous system built by Internal Combustion Engineering (ICE), which was a new AHRA sponsor for the 1983 season. Although it was legal in AHRA BB/FC, nitrous wasn't legal in AA/FC, but Ruiz received prior approval from Vance Brady (head of AHRA tech) to run with the AA cars during Saturday's qualifying. But first there were the BB cars Friday, where Ruiz ran a 7.91 ET for the number-one qualifying position.

Saturday morning, Ruiz lined up with the AA cars and ran an off-pace 8.48 ET on the poor track. This netted him the number-seven spot in the eight-car field, one ahead of Tom McEwen. John Force, in his first race with his new Jolly Rancher sponsorship (who was also an AHRA sponsor) was bumped from the field. In protest, half of the AA racers threatened to leave if Ruiz wasn't tossed.

Boy did Rick Ruiz shake things up with his nitrous Corvette. At the Winter Nationals, he had the Double B field covered, and only human error prevented a win. (Photos Courtesy Bob Snyder)

Rules limited Gene Fiore's Maverick to bolt-ons, which included an Edelbrock intake, 600-cfm Holley carburetor, Hooker headers, and a Mallory ignition. The transmission was a C-4 with a 4000-stall Hughes convertor, and a 5.14:1 gear filled the rear. (Photo Courtesy Gene Fiore)

Category winners at the winter meet included Larry Smith in Top Comp, Vic Phillips in Top Comp Dragster, Walt Replogle and his Vega in Pro Gas, Rick Ducusin's Camaro in Modified Gas, Bill Mitchell in Super Stock, Dan Kibler and partner Vic Hobbs with their 1965 Plymouth in Super Street, and Gene Fiore with his *Yellow Fever* 1971 Maverick in ET Stock.

Led by Garlits, the Top Fuel guys offered to stand with Ruiz and were prepared to go as far as boycott the race if Ruiz was bumped. Ruiz wanted no part of that, and cooler heads prevailed. After a meeting of AHRA representatives, Ruiz was approached by Jim Tice Jr., who basically told him he'd have to return to BB or be tossed.

"Jimmy told me that he'd rather piss off one guy than eight," Ruiz said.

Ruiz was upset but could see Jimmy's point. Sponsor ICE was not happy at all with the terms and immediately withdrew its AHRA sponsorship. After the event, Jim Tice Jr. announced that from this point forward, nitrous would be allowed in Top Fuel and AA/FC.

Back in BB/FC, Ruiz almost won class. After defeating a not-too-pleased World champ Chuck Beal in the semi-finals, Ruiz faced Dale Van Gundy in the final. Ruiz came up short after mistakenly hitting the second stage of his three-stage nitrous system.

"The track was so poor that I hadn't planned on hitting the buttons till the third stage," Ruiz said. "I got a little excited, went off script, and hit the second button and the car broke loose."

Ruiz tried his nitrous combo at the NHRA Winternationals but failed miserably, splitting his Keith Black block after snapping a valve. That was pretty much the end of the nitrous experiment.

1983 World Finals

The World Finals was August 19 to 22 at Spokane and was the last World Finals with Ruth at the controls. From its first race back in 1974, Spokane had no issue filling the bleachers, and the World Finals in 1983 was no exception. A reported crowd of 125,000 rolled through the gates over the four-day event to take in the sights and sounds of 500 entries.

Multi-talented Randy Meyer won the Pro Comp world title in 1983 with his home-built car. He made the move to Top Fuel in 1988, again with a chassis of his own design. (Photo Courtesy Grant Bittner)

Top Fuel

Frank Bradley grabbed hold of the number-one qualifying position with a 5.55 ET, which was just short of his 5.53 class record. Behind him was relative unknown George Tolon, who ran a 5.63 ET at 254.95 mph for the top speed of the weekend.

Chris Karamesines held the final number-eight spot with a 5.84 ET. In between were Don Garlits, Dwight Salisbury, Arley Langlo, Danny Danell, and Butch Blair. The biggest surprise in Top Fuel was the inability of the King of the Northwest (Jerry Ruth) to qualify. Ruth tossed a blower during a qualifying attempt and was never able to get his combination dialed in.

Round action started off bad for Karamesines, who blew his engine against Garlits, handing Big Daddy the easy win. Salisbury next ran a 6.17 ET to defeat the fading *Zip Code* of Langlo. Bradley then laid to waste Danell before Tolon recorded a 5.80 ET to send Blair packing.

In the semifinals, Tolon dropped a few jaws when he opened the round by defeating Garlits. It was a close one, but Tolon's 5.78 ET at 250 mph was just enough to beat Garlits's 5.82 at 252. On the other side of the fence, Salisbury was left to watch Bradley solo after a leaky pan sidelined him.

In the final, Tolon went up in smoke and recorded a losing 6.04 ET. Bradley, suffering traction problems of his own, ran a hazy 5.92 ET at 221.87 mph for the win.

In a smoke-filled final round, Frank Bradley laid to waste George Tolon. It was another good year for the strong independent, having won a pair of series events, and he was runner-up at another. (Photo Courtesy Ronald Kluk)

George Tolon was another tough independent racer. He always qualified well, and in 1983, he finished third in points. Tolon counted on a Chuck Kurzawa chassis and a 484-ci Keith Black engine. (Photo Courtesy Jon T. Hoffman)

Funny Car

Funny Car should have belonged to John Force, and for the most part it did. He opened qualifying with a 5.77 ET and later improved with a record-setting 5.70 at 254.23 mph. During first-round eliminations, Force ran a 5.79 ET at 253.52 mph to defeat a trailing John Collins, whose JVC Camaro could only manage a 6.17.

Other first-round action saw points-champ Tom McEwen defeat an ailing Mike Miller, who was wheeling Jerry Verheul's *Pacemaker*. Raymond Beadle defeated a tire-smoking Gary Densham, and Johnny West defeated Henry Harrison with a 6.04 ET.

Semifinal action began with Beadle stepping up his game and improving with a 5.92 ET to defeat McEwen, whose smoke-filled run netted him a 6.39 ET. Force was up next to face West, and he sent West home in defeat with a 5.79 ET at 254.23 mph.

In the final round, Beadle surprised many by defeating Force's Mountain Dew, Don Steve's Chevrolet–sponsored Camaro with a 5.78 ET at 247.97 mph. Force hazed the tires and slowed to a 5.91 at 220.04.

Long before his first NHRA national event win in 1987. John Force gained experience and won AHRA meets. His first came in 1983. (Photo Courtesy Hector Leal)

Tom Chelbana in Dave and Karen Smith's Firebird won a few series events in 1983 but failed to repeat his 1982 Championship. (Photo Courtesy Grant Bittner)

Tom McEwen's 1983 AHRA Funny Car world title was his second with the sanctioning body. McEwen's Coors sponsorship was very rewarding and ran eight years. (Photo Courtesy Ronald Kluk)

Pro Stock

Bob Glidden's presence was felt, as it had been all season, as Chuck Aronson drove Glidden's old Fairmont to a World Championship title win. Aronson's dominance continued at the World Finals, where he grabbed the number-one qualifying spot with a 7.80 ET. Behind him was Tom Chelbana, who ran a 7.82 ET in the Trans Am of Karen and Dave Smith.

Round action went pretty much as expected. Although, in the semifinals, Aronson, asleep at the wheel, had to come from behind with a 7.93 ET at 171.10 mph to defeat underdog Rich Marino, who ran an 8.18 at 169.49 in Ron Grose's Camaro. Chelbana had little trouble defeating Chuck Nuytten's Charger with a 7.91 ET.

In the final, you couldn't ask for a better, more evenly matched pair. Both Aronson and Chelbana had been running within a tenth of a second of each other all weekend. Off the line, it was Chelbana who reacted first, and it made the difference. Through the lights it was Chelbana taking the win, running an ET of 8 seconds flat at 166.97 mph to Aronson's 8.03 at 170.77!

Other Action

Pro Comp Funny Car eliminator was won by the Camaro of Steve McGee, who defeated the Firebird of points champ Hank Johnson in the final round with a 6.55 ET at 211.76 mph.

Randy Meyer won the Pro Comp Dragster championship. However, at Spokane, it was an all-Canadian final that saw Kenny Sitko in Brad Ennis's *Artic Traveller* defeat Doc Liscombe with a tire-smoking 7.11 ET at 205.47 mph.

Mike Ferderer and his Chevy rail won Top Comp and the championship. Gary Herberger won Pro Gas, Modified Gas was won by Darryl Vigger, and Mike Stoken and his Chevy Vega won Modified Super Stock. Former World Champ Al Young (1981) drove his 440-equipped Dodge Challenger to a win in Super Street, and Keith Daly went home with ET Stock honors.

The Pro Comp Dragster final was all-Canadian at Spokane. Ken Sitko faced fellow Albertan Doc Liscombe and won the race. (Photo Courtesy Ken Sitko)

Closing Out 1983

By the end of 1983, Ruth Tice was all but done. Running the AHRA was eating up her savings and sinking her both physically and mentally.

"Jim never intended for Ruth to take over," Don Garlits said. "I was supposed to take the reins and run with the company. However, it's questionable that I could have done any better. I doubt the operators respected me any more than they did Ruth Tice. It's sad but true! We were just on the verge of getting National TV when Jim got sick. We had done a few TV shows already."

Minnesota-based Tom Hoover moved from running a fuel rail in 1969 to Funny Car (White Bear Dodge), and AHRA and NHRA success followed. With his father, George, on the wrenches, Hoover's Corvette was one to beat in 1983. (Photo Courtesy Ronald Kluk)

Spokane's Orville Moe and Tulsa's Gerald Pritchard (among others) had visions of taking control.

"I was talking to Orville regarding selling to him and a partner of his, Frank Duval, a gentleman who had invested in gold mines," Ruth said. "My attorney and I flew out to Spokane to meet with them, and we told them what we wanted. They led us to believe it; (the deal) was good to go. My attorney flew home, and Orville went into his wooing act. He had me out with a realtor looking at property. He then dropped the bomb that they didn't want the deal.

"He apparently wanted me to move the AHRA headquarters to Spokane, and he would just get it for nothing. I finally got out of Spokane, almost missing my plane in Salt Lake City. I finally got home to a ringing phone. I answered and it was my sister informing me that my dad just passed away! I threw the phone on the floor. I couldn't believe her. I should have been home, but I was dealing with Orville. He never intended to buy the company—just to steal it! I really thought we were close to Orville and his family, and Gerald Pritchard and his family, but apparently not when it came to money."

According to George Eisenhart, who also had interest in the AHRA, he was outside Jim Tice's bedroom door and clearly recalled Pritchard say the following to Tice as he lay on his deathbed:

"Jim, you want me to take over, don't you? You want me to take over. Tell these guys."

Although he was conscious, Tice didn't respond. Pritchard, like Moe, didn't want to buy Tice out, he just wanted to take over as president. Ruth felt that they both (Moe and Pritchard) cared for Jim but really treated her poorly. All the while, there was another race to prepare for.

1984 Winter Nationals

The 1984 Winter Nationals at Tucson was the last AHRA race run under the ownership of Ruth Tice. Both participation and attendance numbers were down at the season opener. I guess that's what happens when your sponsor, Coors (in this instance), sponsors two major events on the same weekend within 50 miles of each other. Some great racing was witnessed by those who chose to attend the winter meet, and they definitely got their money's worth.

There was no quit in Don Garlits. Burning the candle at both ends, he won the AHRA and the NHRA events in 1984. (Photo Courtesy Geno Gastemuse/Stephen Justice)

By 1984, veteran driver Mike Dunn was wheeling the Hawaiian Punch entry of Roland Leong. The best Dunn could do with the Dodge Daytona in the abbreviated 1984 season was a runner-up at US-30. (Photo Courtesy Mike Sopko Sr.)

Top Fuel

Don Garlits came back to Tucson to win his fifth Winter Nationals in a row. By no means was it an easy feat. Garlits ran a 5.83 ET at 244.56 mph for top speed before facing Gene Snow in the final. Snow had run a 5.80 in the semifinals for low ET. In the final, Snow handed the win and the $7,500 that went with it to Garlits when he got out of shape and couldn't recover.

Funny Car

Don Prudhomme ran low ET and top speed of the meet with a 6.15 at 232.55 mph and earned his third event victory in a row. Prudhomme soloed in the final with a 6.56 ET when opponent Henry Harrison broke. Semifinal round losers were Mike Dunn in the *Hawaiian Punch* and Bryan Raines in John Lindsay's *Impulse*.

Pro Stock

Ed Carmichael hauled his beautiful Carmichael & Clark 1984 Camaro from Tennessee to take Pro Stock honors in the six-car field. In the final, Carmichael defeated Benny Flowers driving the ex–Yuill brothers 1981 Camaro, now campaigned by Dopson & Flowers.

Other Action

Chuck Phelps was all smiles taking home BB/FC honors, as was Mark Niver, whose Alcohol Dragster won class with a 7.23 ET at 195 mph. John Linton soloed in Super Comp, Pro Comp was won by Cyril Leon, and Mod Gas went to Lonnie Dull's colorful 1968 Camaro. Harry Larsen took Top Comp, Noel Zweigler used his Chevy-powered Triumph TR3 to win Pro Gas, and Mod Super Stock was won by Lester Goff and his 1965 Chevelle wagon. ET Stock went

The Texas-based team of Dopson & Flowers purchased their Camaro from the Yuill brothers and had their share of success. Benny Flowers drove to a class win at the 1983 Winter Nationals and was runner-up at the 1984 Winter Nationals. (Photo Courtesy Richard Thomas III)

The team of Mickey Winters and driver Chuck Phelps kicked off the year by winning the Winter Nationals. Their* Bad Moon Rising *Firebird was powered by a Keith Black engine. (Photo Courtesy Tim Newmeyer)

to Gene Fiore, whose 302-ci Maverick ran high-13 times to take honors for the second year in a row.

Busted!

On a side note, Tucson track owner Gerald Johns was charged in 1981 with drug smuggling, and he was eventually convicted. It seems that Johns had discovered a more lucrative use for Tucson Raceway, and during quiet evening hours, he had planeloads of dope flown in from south of the border. Johns did hard time for his misdeeds, serving 23 years before being released in 2019. Tucson closed in 1985, after holding the American Drag Racing Association's first winter meet, which was actually run by the Drug Enforcement Agency (DEA).

The AHRA Changes Hands

Although both Gerald Pritchard and Orville Moe desired to take over the AHRA, neither one was willing to buy Ruth out. They both figured she should just hand it over to them and they would run it for her, but that's not what she needed or wanted. Then, a new suitor entered the scene.

Flying west from Florida for the winter meet was Mike Grey, CEO of Terminal Van Lines, who was traveling with his friend Don Garlits. Grey's racing involvement included campaigning a successful Fuel Bike that was driven in 1980 by Bo O'Brochta and in 1981 by Sam Wills. Additionally, Grey was known for his development work on fuel systems and blowers for Fuel Bikes. He traveled west with Garlits, figuring that his knowledge of fuel systems and blowers may be of some value.

While in Tucson, Garlits introduced Grey to Ruth Tice. Garlits had filled in Grey on the current situation with the AHRA and informed him that Ruth was looking to sell. Although Grey knew nothing of running a sanctioning body, he was intrigued enough that he called his right-hand man, Dick Wade, back in St. Petersburg to see if they could afford to buy the troubled AHRA. The answer was a resounding yes.

Shortly after, Grey initiated discussions with Ruth before flying into Kansas City to visit her. An agreement to purchase was made, and by the end of March, the deal was done.

"I can never say a bad word about Mike Grey," Ruth said. "He lived up to his contract and kept his word on everything."

Several track owners ("regional vice presidents," as they were now called) felt blindsided by the sale and refused to deal with Grey. Orville Moe, the AHRA's 1983 track operator of the year, took the move the hardest. Moe had convinced himself and anyone who would listen that he'd be running the AHRA in 1984. The turn of events put the AHRA schedule in danger of collapse. As it stood, seven series events and a dozen or so point meets

WARNING

RACERS—SPONSORS—FANS

BEWARE!

Through rumors, flyers or other means, you have probably heard of an attempt to form a new organization with a somewhat familiar sounding name. Regardless of the similarity between this American Drag Racing Association and the American Hot Rod Association in name, service mark (shield), race dates/names/sites, let it be known that the AHRA has no connection with the ADRA, and will not recognize its races, its points or its memberships.

Things got ugly quick after Jim Tice passed, with the AHRA dividing into factions. Nobody won, and in the end, everybody lost.

were scheduled to be run.

Led by Moe, several tracks that were scheduled to hold events turned on Ruth and Mike Grey, jumping ship to form the American Drag Racing Association (ADRA).

"Owners felt betrayed by Ruth," said Charles Harmon Jr., operator of Kansas City International Raceway. "We didn't know Grey and he wasn't impressive to us, so we went our own way."

The official announcement of the formation of the ADRA was made in May at the Spring Nationals.

Former Modified racer Jim Ehlen stepped up to Pro Stock with the purchase of Lee Hunter's Mercury. The Willie Rells–chassis car was tough. (Photo Courtesy Mike Sopko Sr.)

Four to Go

With just three tracks aligned with the AHRA capable of hosting a national event (St. Louis; US-30 in Gary, Indiana; and the new track in Eunice, Louisiana), Mike Grey's AHRA was in trouble. Little did he realize just how much.

Tulsa

Gerald Pritchard's Tulsa International Raceway, home of the Spring Nationals since 1977, saw its final spring meet run from May 3 to 6. Leading up to the race, Mike Grey fronted Pritchard in the neighborhood of $250,000 to upgrade track conditions. Obviously, Grey wasn't aware that this would be his only race at Tulsa.

To help ensure the event was a success, Grey brought his own crew, as well as a 40-foot truck stocked full of equipment, including safety gear, track blowers, dryers, and traction compound.

John Force and his new Coca-Cola sponsor saw a few runner-up finishes in 1984. (Photo Courtesy Bob Snyder)

During a pre-race press conference, the formation of the ADRA was announced, and with members of both factions present, things got pretty tense. The race had a good turnout of cars and fans, and surprisingly, outside of rain that forced the event to be run over a 10-day period, the whole deal went pretty smoothly. With lines drawn between the two associations, the race was run as both an AHRA and an ADRA series event. Both bodies counted points and recognized any new class records. The pro category winners were Don Garlits, Ron Correnti, and Jerry Haas.

St. Louis

The St. Louis race, which was June 14 to 17, went well, excluding a few oil downs Saturday that pushed qualifying to 3:30 a.m. The AHRA had a policy that stated Saturday's session was mandatory, otherwise you wouldn't get paid.

In the Top Fuel final, low qualifier (5.78) Gene Snow defeated Frank Bradley. In Funny Car, Don Prudhomme defeated John Force with a 6.11 ET, and in Pro Stock, Darrell Alderman ran a 7.81 ET to defeat low qualifier (7.80) Jerry Haas, who was driving the Camaro of Gary Duckworth.

Gary, Indiana

Mike Grey's third race was held at US-30 near Gary, Indiana, from July 6 to 8. Prior to the event, the facility was given some attention: a general cleanup and makeover brought it up par.

After a successful run in Alcohol Funny Car, Bill "Captain Crazy" Dunlap stepped up to AA/FC in 1984. With Gary Southern at the wheel, the Keith Black–powered Ford Tempo was always in contention. (Photo Courtesy Mike Sopko Sr.)

I doubt that drag racing has ever seen a more successful pairing of brothers than Bill and Larry Mitchell. Between the two, they won seven world titles. This is Bill and his automatic Camaro. (Photo Courtesy Bill Mitchell)

By 1984, "Animal" Jim Feurer was running a big-inch Kaase Boss under the Mercury's fiberglass hood. Nitrous was later added, making the car one wild outlaw Pro Stock. (Photo Courtesy Mike Sopko Sr.)

The racing was good and saw Frank Bradley defeat Don Garlits in the Top Fuel final with a 5.60 ET. Frank Hawley won Funny Car, and Pro Stock went to the second-generation Camaro of Barry Shirley. The 1984 season was the end of the line for US-30. After 27 years, it succumbed to noise complaints from encroaching neighbors.

Kansas City

The 1984 Summer Nationals were run at Kansas City International Raceway, as it had been since 1979. Jim Tice brought the AHRA to town as a promise to track operator Chuck Harmon. Harmon wore many hats, and one was concessionaire, which he operated with a close friend. This friend was convinced by Tice to invest his savings into the AHRA. Long story short, the savings was invested by Tice and lost. The man, who happened to be Italian with reported mob connections, entertained the thought of having Tice "taken care of." To cool the situation, Harmon repaid his friend in full, and as thanks, Tice repaid him by bringing in the Summer Nationals.

The 1984 Summer Nationals fell on the weekend of August 2 to 5. According to track operator, Charles Harmon Jr., this race was also run as both an AHRA and an ADRA event.

"It was easy enough to do, as the ADRA mimicked the AHRA in rules and class structure," Harmon said.

All points earned in AHRA competition were honored by the ADRA.

Keith Washburn, the track announcer, said, "We ran the race as both an AHRA and ADRA event because we really didn't know what was going on."

Washburn vividly recalled Ruth Tice being at the race.

"The tension was very thick, and those on the 'other' side weren't making Ruth feel all that welcome," Washburn said.

Category winners included Garlits, who went home with Top Fuel honors after defeating Dick LaHaie's 5.80 ET with a 5.76. In Funny Car, Don Prudhomme defeated John Force with a 5.99 ET to a 6.00. Pro Stock went to Jerry Yeoman, who took Rod Urish with a 7.76 ET to an 8.34. Lee Young took Alcohol Dragster, Richard Smith won BB/FC, perennial winner Walt Niesen won Pro Comp, Scott Johnson won Top Comp, and Gene Carter won Pro Gas. Rick Ducusin won Mod Gas, Jim Ruble won Mod Super Stock, Super Street honors went home with John Rewoldt, and Doug Frisbie won ET Stock.

1984 World Finals: The End of the Line

In October 1982, Louis Doucet and a dozen investors bought the site of the old Linzay Downs horse track located in Eunice, Louisiana. They went to work converting the site into a drag racing facility. Doucet filed papers incorporating Acadiana International Raceway Park on February 3, 1984.

In May 1984, before the strip had even been paved, it was announced that the AHRA World Finals would be held at the track from September 28 to 30. With plans for a 1985 season, Mike Grey obviously had no idea going into the race that this would be the end of the line.

Top Fuel

Heading into the world finals, it was a three-way tie between Don Garlits, Gene Snow, and Frank Bradley for the points championship. Bradley made it a two-way tie when he chose to stay home in California as opposed to making the cross-country trek.

Fresh off of a win at the NHRA U.S. Nationals, Garlits in his resurrected *Swamp Rat 26* grabbed the number-one qualifying spot by laying down a 5.54 ET at 247.25 mph. Lagging behind was Dick LaHaie with a 5.80, followed by Snow's 5.82, and Chris Karamesines's 5.84. These were the heavy hitters in the eight-car field.

It seems only fitting that the final Top Fuel round of AHRA's final race boiled down to the two old foes: Don Garlits and Chris Karamesines. A person couldn't ask for a more appropriate final matchup. Garlits found his way by defeating Bill Mullins in the first round then beating Snow in what was the quickest side-by-side race in AHRA history: a 5.567 ET at a record 257.14 mph to Snow's 5.662 at 248.61. The Greek had an easier go of it, as both of his opponents, George Talon and Dick LaHaie, faded with mechanical ills.

In the final, it was Karamesines out first, opening up with a car length on Garlits. However, the revitalized Garlits could never be counted out. Although the Greek laid down his best effort of the weekend, a 5.71 ET at 243.24 mph, it just wasn't enough. Garlits came around him to take the win with a 5.56 at 256.41. He closed the season having earned his 10th AHRA world title.

Funny Car

Funny Car was run without its two points leaders, as West Coast residents Mike Dunn and Don Prudhomme chose to stay home. This left second-place contenders John Force and Doc Halladay with high hopes of being the last men standing in the eight-car field. Force qualified number-one with a 5.80 ET at 248.61 mph, ahead of Mark Oswald in the Candies & Hughes Pontiac, Tom McEwen, and Jim White.

Force singled in round one, while Halladay lost to McEwen. Oswald then defeated a fouling Gary Southern, which was followed by White defeating Jim Robbins

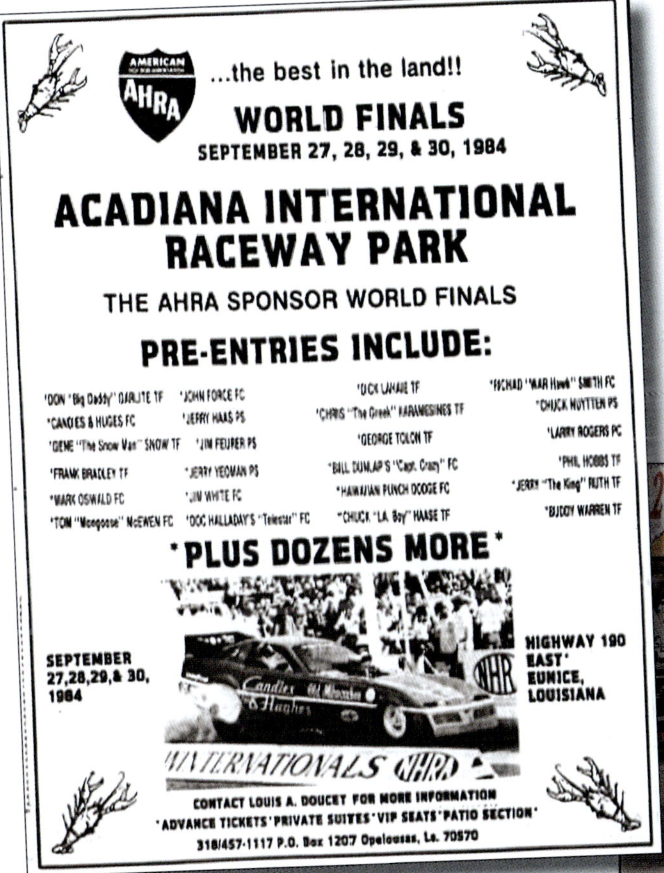

Little did anyone know that this was the final go-round for the AHRA. One would think that they could have used an AHRA photo for the advertisement.

What a storied career the Greek has had. It was only fitting that he and Garlits met in the final round of the final AHRA race. (Photo Courtesy Grant Bittner)

with a 6.14 ET at 238.09 mph.

In the semifinals, Halladay found himself back in after McEwen, discovering a broken block, chose to load up his Corvette and go home as opposed to installing his backup mill. Halladay and his *Telstar* faced Force, and it would have been a good one, if Halladay hadn't lit the red light. Meanwhile, Force launched his Camaro into the air, came down hard, and crossed the centerline. In the other semifinal round, White went up in smoke as Oswald went on for the win.

Force locked up his first world title with his semifinal win but still had to face Oswald in the final. The Candies & Hughes Pontiac was handed the win when Force, again, took off for the sky. Oswald's winning time was 5.72 at 257.87 mph.

Pro Stock

Leading the eight-car Pro Stock field was Gary Duckworth, who, in place of hired gun Ronnie Sox, hopped behind the wheel of his Camaro. He grabbed the number-one qualifying spot and set a new class record with a 7.57 ET at 182.92 mph. Behind him were Pro Stock rookie Jerry Yeoman and his Don Ness Camaro with a 7.63 as well as Ed Machacek, whose Camaro recorded a 7.79. Points champ Jerry Haas, who had given up his nitrous small-block for a 615-ci Reher-Morrison-Shepherd-powered Camaro held the final spot with an off-pace 8.08 ET. Yeoman suffered trying to dial in his combination, and his Camaro fell in the first round of eliminations to Jim Buzzard. Other first-round losers included Benny Flowers in his new Haas-built Camaro, Barry Shirley, and Eddie Conrad, who failed to show.

Doc Halladay and his Telstar *were always in contention and never taken lightly. A Plymouth Arrow shell hid a Pat Foster, Jim Hume (H&H Race Cars) chassis and Keith Black engine. (Photo Courtesy Mike Spoko Sr.)*

In October 1982, Jerry Haas shocked the world of drag racing at Bret Kepner's Outlaw Pro Stock World Championship in St. Louis when his small-block, nitrous-equipped Chevy broke into the 7s. Haas ran a qualifying time of 7.97 at 170 mph. (Photo Courtesy Michael Ball/David Ball)

In the semifinals, Buzzard lost out to Yeoman's 7.67 ET at 179.64 mph. Duckworth then reset his own record when he ran a 7.53 ET at 183.29 mph while defeating Machacek's 7.73 at 174.41.

In the final, odds-on favorite Duckworth was out late against Yeoman and just couldn't make up the distance. Yeoman led all the way and took the win with a 7.61 ET at 177.86 mph to a quicker and faster 7.57 at 183.29 mph.

Other Action

In BB/FC, Chuck Phelps took the championship while Lanny Bell won his first and only Grand-Am race, defeating Fred Leslie in the final with a 7.26 ET at 178.57 mph. Pro Comp honors went to Al DaPazzo, who was trailing Ron Dudley by 200 points heading into the World Finals. Dudley failed to qualify, and DaPazzo won the event by defeating Bill Mullins with a record-setting 6.30 ET at 215.31 mph.

In Super Comp, Walt Niesen took honors with a 7.90 ET. Scott Johnson went home with the Top Comp win and the championship. Pro Gas belonged to Ed Theiss, while Mod Gas went to Greg McKinney and his Firebird. Rusty Butterworth took Super Street and the world title. His wife, Anita, won the ET Street championship while Caulane Belfour won the event. In the always-overlooked Bike Eliminator, Craig Manuel took home the gold.

The Aftermath

Fans did not come out to the World Finals in the droves that were anticipated. Making the bad situation worse, within days of completion of the race, checks issued on a track account began to bounce.

"Mike Grey covered some of the debt, but the track

owner (Doucet) was liable for the majority of the expenses," historian Bret Kepner said. "Grey was so disenchanted [that] he dumped the whole mess only a few weeks later."

After 30 years of racing, innovation, and controversy, the AHRA was done.

So Goes the ADRA

The ADRA, which was formed in 1984 by disgruntled AHRA track owners, lasted through 1986. It held events at Tucson Dragway, Alamo Dragway, Tulsa International Raceway, Kansas City International Raceway, Ozark Raceway, Dragway 42, Spokane, and Carlsbad Raceway before folding.

Although this photo was taken in 1985, Walt Niesen used the same ride to win the AHRA Super Comp (7.90 index) world title in 1984. A 520-ci Donovan and 3-speed transmission propelled Walt to his fifth world title. (Photo Courtesy Grant Bittner)

Epilogue

(Not So) Fast-Forward

Spokane's Orville Moe resurrected the AHRA name after the ADRA folded. He ran his annual AHRA World Finals (sometimes referred to as the World Finals Hot Rod Association). There were no series events to support it. Moe's World Finals came to an end in 2005.

In 2006, he was ousted from his position as operator of Spokane Raceway Park. The original investors, all 500 of them, sued Moe, stating that they had been swindled after seeing no return on their $2-million investment, while according to court papers, Moe became a multimillionaire.

Born Again

In 2008, Panama City, Florida, deputy sheriff Rod Saint, an old drag racer at heart, sought out the AHRA name and trademarked it. Saint had big plans to restore the name to its former glory, but circumstances (some beyond his control) ended that dream.

In 2017, Saint sold the AHRA to retired navy man Dallas Brown. Brown has a vision and is attempting to get the AHRA back to its roots by championing the little guy. He's focused on all three facets of sportsmen racing: Bracket, Index, and Heads-Up—and it seems to be working. His back-to-basics format seems to be resonating with fans, and, as of this writing, a number of tracks are flying the AHRA banner.

The AHRA is a name steeped in drag racing history. Only time will tell where the new AHRA goes and whether it will prosper like the old AHRA once did. In the meantime, drag racing thrives and the memories live on.

The roots of drag racing are its door cars, and Dallas Brown's new AHRA makes them the focal point. Here, a pair of Camaros launch like the Pro Stocks of old. (Photo Courtesy Dallas Brown)

AHRA Points Champions 1960–1984

1960–1969	
Year	**Winner**
1960	Bob Nickelson
1961	Competition Division: Zane Shubert
1961	Street Division: Don Biggers
1962	Competition Division: Pusch & Crews (John Pusch, Bob Crews)
1962	Street Division: Mike Donnelly
1963	Overall Points Champ: Don Elliot & Ron Martin
1964	Overall Points Champ: Chris Karamesines
1965	Overall Points Champ: Paul Sutherland
1966	Overall Points Champ: Jerry Butler
1966	Competition Division: Chris Karamesines
1966	Street Division: Bill Hielscher
1967	Overall Points Champ: Bill Hielscher
1967	Competition Division: Bennie Osborn
1967	Street Division: Bill Hielscher
1968	Top Fuel: Bennie Osborn
1968	Jr. Fuel: Rex Cox
1968	Top Gas: Don Cain
1968	Funny Car: Terry Hedrick
1968	Comp: Ron Bolz
1968	Super Stock: Herb McCandless
1968	Street: Gary Belt
1968	Top Stock: Jerry Velk
1968	Middle Stock: Ted Reed
1968	Little Stock: Robert Shaw
1969	Top Fuel: Leroy Goldstein
1969	Jr. Fuel: Adams & Enriquez
1969	Funny Car: Dick Harrell
1969	Top Gas: Mark Pieri
1969	Comp: Delmar Hines
1969	Super Stock: Gary Kimball
1969	Street: Dave Atkins/Bill Heilscher
1969	Top Stock: Bob Coble
1969	Mr. Stock: George Eberst

Pro Category Point Champions, 1970–1984

Top Fuel Champions	
Year	**Winner**
1970	John Wiebe
1971	Don Garlits
1972	Don Garlits
1973	Don Garlits
1974	Don Garlits
1975	John Wiebe
1976	John Wiebe
1977	Jeb Allen
1978	Don Garlits
1979	Don Garlits
1980	Don Garlits
1981	Shirley Muldowney
1982	Don Garlits
1983	Don Garlits
1984	Don Garlits

Funny Car Champions	
Year	**Winner**
1970	Gene Snow
1971	Gene Snow
1972	Leroy Goldstein
1973	Don Schumacher
1974	Don Prudhomme
1975	Tom McEwen
1976	Tom Hoover
1977	Tom Hoover
1978	Gene Snow
1979	Tom McEwen
1980	Don Prudhomme
1981	Don Prudhomme
1982	Don Prudhomme
1983	Tom McEwen
1984	John Force

Super Stock/Pro Stock Champions	
Year	**Winner**
1970	Sox & Martin
1971	Jim Hayter
1972	Don Nicholson
1973	Dick Landy
1974	Larry Huff
1975	Ken Dondero
1976	Ken Dondero
1977	Larry Lombardo
1978	Shelby Jester
1979	*Bobby Marriott/Lee Shepherd
1980	Shelby Jester
1981	Jerry Haas
1982	Tom Chelbana
1983	Chuck Aronson
1984	Jerry Haas

* No champion clearly defined

Sportsman Category Point Champions, 1970–1984

Year	Winner
1970	GT-1: Kimball Bros-Hill
1970	GT-2: Hielscher-Jones
1970	GT-3: Hiner-Miller
1970	Competition: Hahn-Turner
1970	Street: Hielscher-Atkins
1970	Top Stock: Tom Akin
1971	GT-1: Tomlinson-Topletz
1971	GT-2: Gary Kimball
1971	Competition: Joe Williamson
1971	Street: Joe Williams
1971	Top Stock: Allen Patterson
1972	GT-1: Tomlison-Topletz
1972	GT-2: Scott Shafiroff
1972	Competition: Don Toia
1972	Street: Joe Rundle
1972	Super Stock: John Greenwood
1972	Stock: Dennis Kucera
1973	Competition: Walt Niesen
1973	Street: Pete Peery
1973	Super Stock: Allen Patterson
1973	Stock: Glenn Pittman
1974	Pro Comp: Dale Armstrong
1974	Modified: Walt Niesen
1974	Street: Whatley Bros.
1974	Super Stock: Gary Grame (Marlat & Grame)
1974	Stock: Glenn Erlandson
1975	Pro Comp: Wayne Stoeckel
1975	Modified: Walt Niesen
1975	Street: Ed Ponder
1975	Super Stock: Billy Ray

1975	Stock: Glenn Erlandson
1976	Pro Comp: Dion Stewart
1976	Top Comp: Mike McCloskey
1976	Modified Street: Jim Ruble
1976	Super Street: Bill Mitchell
1976	Super Stock: Larry Mitchell
1976	Stock: Dave Workman
1977	Pro Comp Dragster: Richard Ogg
1977	Pro Comp F/C: Mike Savage
1977	Top Comp: Mike McCloskey
1977	Modified Street: Donnie Anderson
1977	Super Street: Jim Williams
1977	Super Stock: Noel Zweigler
1977	Stock: Don Spencer
1978	Pro Comp Dragster: Brian Raymer
1978	Pro Comp F/C: Simon Menzies
1978	Top Comp: Terry Green
1978	Modified Street: Larry Smith
1978	Super Street: Richard Wegner
1978	Super Stock: Roy Kempe
1978	Stock: Bob Bowe
1979	Pro Comp Dragster: Porter Donn
1979	Pro Comp F/C: Mike Savage
1979	Top Comp: Joe Williams
1979	Modified Street: Roy Kempe
1979	Super Street: Barry Shirley
1979	Super Stock: Larry Mitchell
1979	Stock: Rick Ducusin
1980	Pro Comp Dragster: Porter Donn
1980	Pro Comp F/C: Richard Day
1980	Top Comp: Larry Smith
1980	Modified Street: Bill Mitchell
1980	Super Street: Wayne Smith
1980	Super Stock: Billy Ray
1980	Stock: Rick Ducusin
1981	Pro Comp Dragster: Jerry Goddard
1981	Pro Comp F/C: Chuck Beal
1981	Top Comp: Walt Niesen
1981	Pro Gas (9.90 index): Ed Bottoms
1981	Modified Street: Stan Leerkamp
1981	Super Street: Al Young
1981	Super Stock: Delmer and Tony Wood
1981	Stock: Rusty Butterworth
1982	Pro Comp Dragster: Porter Donn
1982	Pro Comp F/C: Chuck Beal
1982	Top Comp: John Polk
1982	Pro Gas (9.90 index): Bill Fetter
1982	Modified Gas (10.90 index): Ruble & White

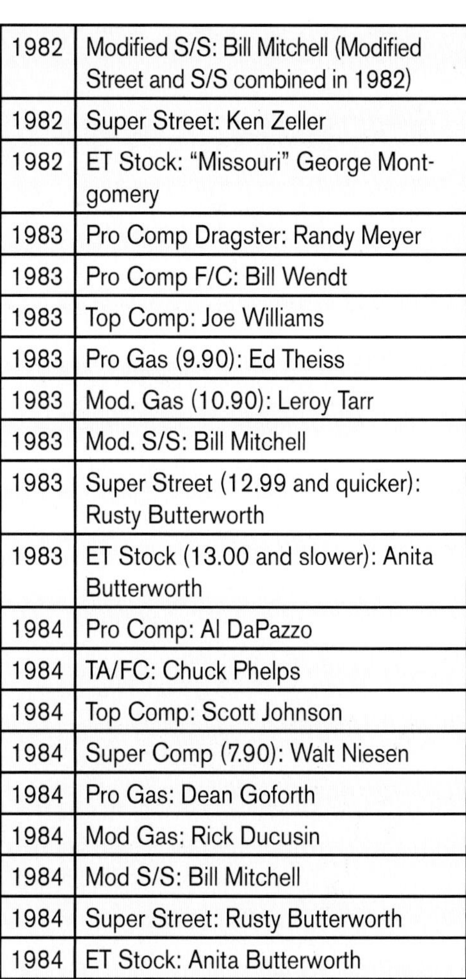

1982	Modified S/S: Bill Mitchell (Modified Street and S/S combined in 1982)
1982	Super Street: Ken Zeller
1982	ET Stock: "Missouri" George Montgomery
1983	Pro Comp Dragster: Randy Meyer
1983	Pro Comp F/C: Bill Wendt
1983	Top Comp: Joe Williams
1983	Pro Gas (9.90): Ed Theiss
1983	Mod. Gas (10.90): Leroy Tarr
1983	Mod. S/S: Bill Mitchell
1983	Super Street (12.99 and quicker): Rusty Butterworth
1983	ET Stock (13.00 and slower): Anita Butterworth
1984	Pro Comp: Al DaPazzo
1984	TA/FC: Chuck Phelps
1984	Top Comp: Scott Johnson
1984	Super Comp (7.90): Walt Niesen
1984	Pro Gas: Dean Goforth
1984	Mod Gas: Rick Ducusin
1984	Mod S/S: Bill Mitchell
1984	Super Street: Rusty Butterworth
1984	ET Stock: Anita Butterworth

(Photo Courtesy J.R. Bloom)

Additional books that may interest you...

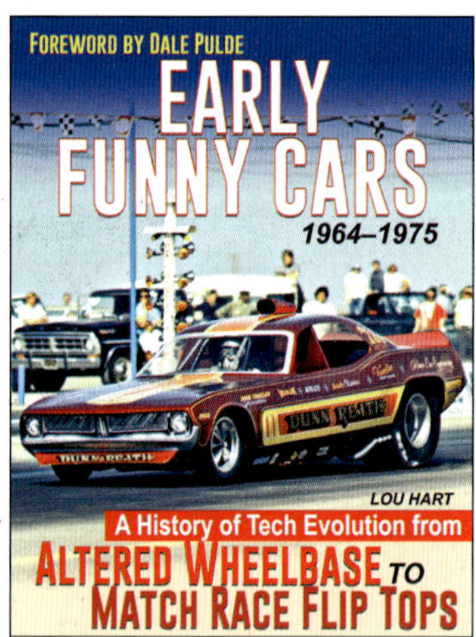

EARLY FUNNY CARS: A History of Tech Evolution from Altered Wheelbase to Match Race Flip Tops 1964–1975 *by Lou Hart*
Blast through the evolving early years of Funny Car drag racing when doorslammers morphed into flip-top rail monsters. The era features historic mounts from Arnie "the Farmer" Beswick, Al "the Flying Dutchman" Vanderwoude, Don "the Snake" Prudhomme, and many more! 8.5 x 11", 192 pgs, 452 photos, Sftbd. ISBN 97816132569858 Part # CT683

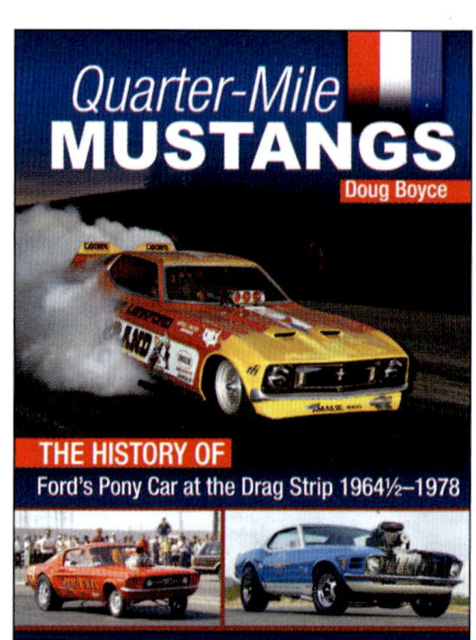

QUARTER-MILE MUSTANGS: The History of Ford's Pony Car at the Drag Strip 1964½–1978
by Doug Boyce The most in-depth coverage of Mustangs on the quarter mile is brought forward by drag racing historian Doug Boyce. He highlights the many successes of pioneers, such as "Dyno" Don Nicholson, Les Ritchey, Phil Bonner, Hubert Platt, Al Joniec, and the many names that followed. 8.5 x 11", 144 pgs, 352 photos, Sftbd. ISBN 9781613255988 Part # CT680

DRAG RACING IN THE 1960s: The Evolution in Race Car Technology
by Doug Boyce
In this book, veteran author Doug Boyce takes you on a ride through the entire decade from a technological point of view rather than a results-based one. 8.5 x 11", 176 pgs, 350 photos, Sftbd. ISBN 9781613255827 Part # CT674

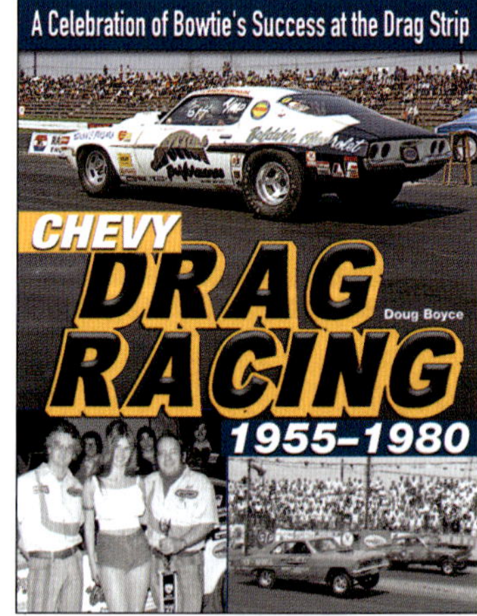

CHEVY DRAG RACING 1955–1980: A Celebration of Bowtie's Success at the Drag Strip *by Doug Boyce*
Accomplished racing author Doug Boyce takes a celebratory look at Chevy's years of drag racing success, with a focus on the first 25 years (1955 through 1980). 8.5 x 11", 176 pgs, 313 photos, Sftbd. ISBN 9781613254998 Part # CT659

www.cartechbooks.com or 1-800-551-4754